MW01008425

The City of Ugarit

at Tell Ras Shamra

The City of Ugarit
at Tell Ras Shamra

Marguerite Yon

Winona Lake, Indiana
Eisenbrauns
2006

Printed in Singapore.

www.eisenbrauns.com

Library of Congress Cataloging-in-Publication Data

Yon, Marguerite.
[Cité d'Ougarit sur le tell de Ras Shamra. English]
The city of Ugarit at Tell Ras Shamra / Marguerite Yon.
p. cm.
Includes bibliographical references and index.
ISBN-13 : 978-1-57506-029-3 (hardback : alk. paper)
1. Ugarit (Extinct city) 2. Excavations (Archaeology)—Syria.
I. Title.
DS99.U35Y6613 2006
939′.43—dc22
2006003735

The paper used in this publication meets the minimum requirements of the American National Standard for Information Sciences—Permanence of Paper for Printed Library Materials, ANSI Z39.48-1984. ♾™

Contents

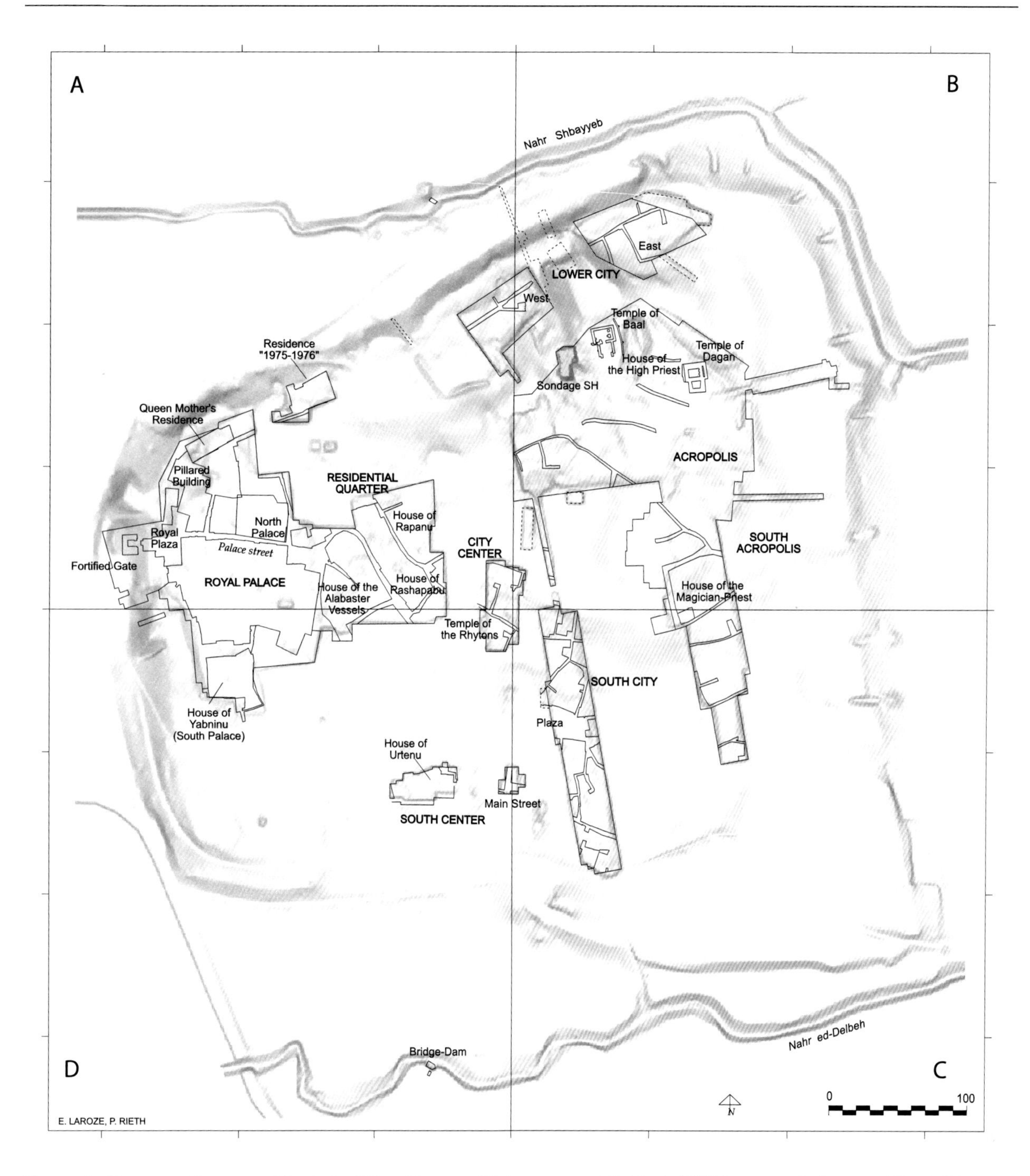

Figure 1. Topographic map of the tell of Ras Shamra (E. Laroze and P. Rieth 2003): excavated areas. The tell is partitioned into four quadrants—A, B, C, and D—and divided into 10-meter squares with the squares in each quadrant numbered sequentially from the center of the tell (point 0).

Figure 2. Jabal al-Aqra / Mount Saphon, north of the kingdom of Ugarit as seen from the tell of Ras Shamra, 1984.

Preface

Prof.-Dr. Sultan Muhesen
Director General of Antiquities and Museums

The coast of Syria has been inhabited since Early Paleolithic times. In the Neolithic period, farming villages were established along the coast. Ras Shamra was one of those early farming settlements in this region. The tell was occupied continuously from the end of the 8th millennium until the end of the 2nd millennium B.C.E. But it was during the Late Bronze Age, in the latter half of the 2nd millennium, that the site experienced its heyday, and the kingdom of Ugarit was born. The archaeological excavations on the tell, continuing now for more than half a century, have shown that Ugarit was the most important Canaanite kingdom of the Late Bronze Age.

Because of the city's strategic location and its natural resources, it managed to play a major role in the political, economic, and cultural affairs of the region. Its role was not merely that of a port city; it was a crossroads for the surrounding regions because of strategic policies that enabled it to influence culture and commerce extending from Mesopotamia to Egypt. Although it was also influenced by neighboring nations, Ugaritic civilization clearly possessed a distinctive Syrian character. It also managed to survive regional conflicts involving the great powers of its time, the Hittites, Assyrians, and Egyptians, and this too contributed to ensuring its diplomatic fame.

Among the key discoveries unearthed at the site are the palace, temples, tombs, fortifications, and houses, along with many precious objects in metal, ceramic, and ivory, not to mention the rich archives of tablets and the world's first abecedaries, all of which have greatly enriched our knowledge of the region's history and culture.

But Ugarit has yet to yield all its secrets, and new discoveries come to light with each new campaign. The search is no longer limited to artifacts and objects to place in museums. The focus has shifted to application of scientific and interdisciplinary methods for the study of the kingdom's geographical, economic, and cultural heritage.

Although a considerable number of scholarly publications have appeared on the subject of Ugarit, this book is a rare contribution, guaranteed to make this archaeological knowledge about the ancient Near East available to the wider public. Its author, Marguerite Yon, merits our heartfelt thanks.

Photo Anwar Abd el-Ghafur.

Figure 3: Aerial view of the tell from the south, 1991.

Foreword

We owe our deepest gratitude to the Syrian authorities, who have annually made it possible for the mission that I have directed since 1978 to pursue historical investigation that has importance for a large region of the ancient Near East—a region that figures prominently in the origins of Western civilization. I would first like to extend my thanks to Dr. A. Abou Assaf, Director General of Antiquities and Museums until June 1993, and Prof.-Dr. S. Muhesen, who took his place thereafter; Dr. A. Bounni, Director of the Division of Excavations in Syria; those in charge of antiquities in the Latakia Province, Mr. W. Mellah until 1992 and Mrs. N. Khaskiyeh thereafter. Last, I would like to thank Mr. G. Saadé, one of the foremost experts in Ugarit's history, for his valuable, unfailing help.

The excavation campaigns are regularly subsidized by the Board of Cultural Relations for the French Ministry of Foreign Affairs (Commission for Excavations), and over the years we have continually benefited from the support of those in charge: Mr. P. Guillemin, Mrs. M.-P. de Cossé-Brissac, Mr. Y. Saint-Geours, and Mr. M. Jolivet. Applications for our research and publishing activities are conducted with the assistance of CNRS research teams: at the Maison de l'Orient, Lyon, the Institut-F. Courby (University of Lyon), which is in charge of the French mission; and at the Collège de France, Paris, the Institut d'Études Sémitiques, where the mission's epigraphic programs are administered. In Damascus, the Institut Français d'Archéologie du Proche-Orient has always extended a hearty welcome to the mission.

Research programs have always been conducted in close collaboration with the various mission members, and the present publication is no exception. It benefited from fruitful contributions, on site and in France, from those in charge of the various programs: P. Bordreuil (epigraphy), Y. Calvet (archaeology), and A. Caubet (museums). I would also like to stress the role of O. Callot, mission architect, in the preparation of this book (drawings).

* * * * *

This volume clearly owes much to the work of our predecessors and especially the founder of the mission, Claude Schaeffer, who was present on the site for the last time in 1979, on the occasion of the Latakia colloquium that marked the fiftieth anniversary of its discovery. We are also particularly endebted to Mrs. O. Schaeffer, who gave us access to some of her husband's work files after his death in 1981, and who continues to show her interest in a mission that was truly hers for many years. Allow me, finally, to call to mind J.-C. Courtois, who vanished from our midst in 1991, and to whom Ugaritic research owes so very much. Finally, I extend my thanks to H. de Contenson and J. Margueron, who directed the mission before me, and A. Bounni and J. Lagarce, who are responsible for the excavations at the nearby site of Ras Ibn Hani.

During the period of more than 15 years since our team began its work, a wide variety of studies have been undertaken on the tell itself, using the documentation accumulated by our predecessors. Many of these studies have been published. In addition to a good many articles appearing in French and foreign journals, the mission has since 1983 published 11 volumes in the Ras Shamra–Ougarit (RSO) series (Editions ERC-ADPF). This book presents the results of these investigations or the current state (in

Figure 4. The last visit of C. Schaeffer to the tell in 1979 at the beginning of the excavation season conducted by the new "mission" team (photo: A. Caubet).

1994) of studies still underway, and I would like to thank all those on our team who have contributed to deepening our knowledge concerning the site and its history: A. Caubet, J. Gachet, P. Lombard, J. Mallet, V. Matoïan, J.-Y. Monchambert, M. Pic, J.-Y. Breuil, and C. Castel, the archaeologists responsible over the years for the various digs; Y. Calvet and B. Geyer, for their research on environment and hydrology; J. Margueron and O. Callot, who are preparing the publication of the Royal Palace; J.-F. Salles and S. Marchegay for their work on funerary architecture; the following epigraphers, who were quite eager to take part in the fieldwork: P. Bordreuil, D. Pardee, and F. Briquel (Ugaritologists), and also D. Arnaud, B. André-Salvini, S. Lackenbacher-Teixidor, and F. Malbran-Labat (Assyriologists); P. Desfarges, M. Renisio, and L. Volay, architects who have followed the progress of the excavations; B. Arzens and T. Monloup, who handle mission archives; and J. Chevalier, J.-P. Lange, J.-P. Boulanger, and V. Bernard, who have been responsible for the drawings of the objects.

The French version of this volume was first published in the IFAPO Guides Collection, Editions ERC. Finally, I am grateful to J. Eisenbraun for publishing this English version, to G. Walker and B. Schmidt for the translation, and to A. Caubet and D. Pardee, who agreed to review and correct the English text.

Lyon, May 1996

Unless otherwise specified, all the plans, diagrams, and restorations in this book were done by O. Callot; many of these are hithereto unpublished drawings based on the latest architectural analyses. The photos come from the mission's archives, and for recent years I would like to thank, in particular, A. Caubet, V. Matoïan, and Y. Calvet.

Brief Update (2005) for the Publication of the English Edition

M. Yon served as director of the Mission de Ras Shamra from 1978 to 1998. In 1999, the official status of the excavations changed from French to Franco-Syrian. Yves Calvet succeeded Yon as the French director and Bassam Jamous was named as his Syrian counterpart. When the latter became Director of Antiquities in 2005, he was replaced on the Mission de Ras Shamra by Jamal Haïdar. In 2002, Michel al-Maqdissi was named Director of the Department of Excavations in the Direction Générale des Antiquités et des Musées and thereby became the chief Syrian official to whom the directors of the Mission de Ras Shamra report.

The activities of the Mission de Ras Shamra continue, as in preceding years, to focus on two primary areas—excavation and preparing the excavated material, from both past and present digs, for publication.

On the tell itself, the excavation of the House of Urtenu (pp. 87–88) was brought to completion in 2002 and plans for its publication are underway. The area known as "Main Street" (pp. 84–85) was extended to the north during the 2005 season and a building of exceptional extent and quality has begun to emerge. Further excavation of the "Residence '1975–76'" has succeeded in determining its northern boundary. To the south of the tell, the southern pier of the bridge/dam (p. 90) spanning the Nahr el-Delbeh has been uncovered.

Renewed study of former excavations has made significant progress in the architectural analysis of the "Residential Quarter" (pp. 64–77), the "East Terrace" (p. 122), the "North Palace" (pp. 60–63), and of some 250 built tombs. The "Royal Palace" (pp. 36–45) has become the object of a program that brings together archaeologists, architects, and epigraphers for the purpose of analyzing the phases of the palace and the small objects discovered therein during excavations that began in 1939, just before World War II, and were not completed until the late 1950s. This study is three-pronged, bringing together data from a new analysis of the remains as preserved on the tell, of the objects preserved in various museums, and of the archives of the Mission de Ras Shamra. Renewed analysis of excavation archives has also led to a better understanding of the site of Minet el-Beida (p. 9); new light was shed on this site in 1997 when a tomb was discovered which appears not to have been pillaged in antiquity (see p. 14).

Another series of studies has been pursued based on the analysis of the archives of the Mission de Ras Shamra and on objects preserved in the museums of Aleppo, Damascus, Lattakia, Saint-Germain-en-Laye, and the Louvre. These sources of information, including unpublished documents, have contributed in various ways to the publication of various types of data in the series Ras Shamra–Ougarit: the ritual texts (vol. XII: D. Pardee), Mycenaean pottery (vol. XIII: M. Yon, V. Karageorghis, N. Hirschfeld), reports on research conducted during the years 1985–1995 (vol. XIV, edited by M. Yon and D. Arnaud), Syrian pottery (vol. XV: J.-Y. Monchambert), and the ivories (vol. XVI: J. Gachet). Studies, already completed or in progress, of the tombs, of the objects of faience and other glass-like materials, of various materials (wood, stone, and metal), of the systems of weights and measures, and of Ugaritic society as defined by the texts, will eventually be published.

Several international meetings have taken place where those involved could present their research and where contrasting viewpoints on the meaning of this research could emerge: Lyon in November of 2001, in October of 2004, and in December of 2005; Lyon and Paris in November of 2004; Sherbrooke, Ontario, in July of 2005. The proceedings of each of these conferences will eventually be published.

Finally, a major exhibition of artifacts representing the culture of Ugarit was on view at the Musée des Beaux-Arts in Lyon from October of 2004 through January of 2005. It bore the title *At the Origins of the Alphabet: The Kingdom of Ugarit*. Presentations of the artifacts, 341 in number, and their cultural context were provided in the accompanying catalogue, which was authored by the members of the Mission de Ras Shamra and edited by Y. Calvet and G. Galliano.

Below, updates have been inserted, particularly of a bibliographical nature, within and/or at the end of each chapter.

M. Y., December 2005

Introduction

About 12 kilometers north of Latakia, less than a kilometer from the Mediterranean coast of Syria, lies the tell of Ras Shamra, which has been the site of archaeological investigations for more than 60 years. The area is covered with the remains of the ancient city of Ugarit, capital of the Canaanite kingdom of the same name that flourished in the 2nd millennium B.C.E.

The excavations have so far unearthed only a small portion of these vestiges, including impressive architectural constructions, numerous artifacts, and tablets with cuneiform inscriptions (both alphabetic and syllabic), which have brought to light the final chapters of the city's history at the end of the Late Bronze Age, from the 14th century B.C.E. to the beginning of the 12th century B.C.E. Yet the tell was at that time already the site of 6,000 years of uninterrupted occupation, starting with the farming settlements in the Neolithic Period in the 8th millennium B.C.E.

This extremely long period of occupation makes of Ras Shamra a reference point for the early history of the Near East and the eastern Mediterranean world; hence the importance of pursuing research on the tell.

The Discovery

In 1929, the accidental discovery of a tomb near the coast by a peasant led to initial excavations, which were carried out by René Dussaud and Claude Schaeffer at Minet el-Beida Bay. These brought to light settlements dating to the Late Bronze Age of the latter half of the 2nd millennium B.C.E.

It appeared to the excavators that the port settlement must have been connected to a more important site. The focus then shifted to a tell 800 meters inland, known at the time as Ras esh-Shamra, translated by G. Saadé as "fennil hill" (*Ougarit*, 1979, 36). Because it was transcribed in the first report as Ras Shamra, this form of the name has continued in use in archaeological publications and has passed into current toponymy. The research conducted on the site that year immediately revealed documents of exceptional interest, in particular, clay tablets written in a hitherto unknown cuneiform script used to represent an unknown language.

In the following years, the excavations were extended, and the texts were deciphered. An entire city with palaces, temples, houses, and streets came to light. The unknown script turned out to be alphabetic in nature, and the language, dubbed Ugaritic after the ancient name of the city, proved to be a new West Semitic language related to Amorite, Canaanite, and Arabic. Among the Ugaritic texts, was an exceptional group of mythological texts with El, Baal, and Anat as the principal deities.

History of Excavations

The excavations at Ras Shamra were conducted by C. Schaeffer through 1939, interrupted by the war, and then were resumed in 1948. They were taken over by H. de Contenson (1972–73), followed by J. Margueron (1975–76), and then myself since 1978 (see pp. 5–6 above [2005]).

In the general environs of Ras Shamra, two associated sites have been located and excavated: Minet el-Beida, which was mentioned previously, and Ras Ibn Hani (*Fig. 11*).

As an annex to the nearby capital, the port of Minet el-Beida was excavated by C. Schaeffer from 1929 to 1935. It is ancient *Mahadu*, which the texts indicate was the main port of Ugarit. Excavations have uncovered an urban settlement beginning in the Late Bronze Age, the organization of which can be better understood by comparing it with the organization of the city as revealed on the tell of Ras Shamra. The early digs revealed streets lined with houses containing richly furnished tombs (nos. **25**, **33**, **47**), places of worship, storehouses attesting to export and import trade (nos. **30–31**), and so on. A modern military port is now located there, making access to the archaeological site of Minet el-Beida impossible.

In the 1970s, tourist development projects accidentally brought to light the existence of a Ugaritic settlement on the cape of Ras Ibn Hani (now facing the Meridien Hotel). This settlement was closely connected to the nearby capital, for it was founded by the king of Ugarit in the 13th century B.C.E. The place was occupied again during the Hellenistic Period, when it was protected by a defensive fortress. Salvage excavations conducted on the site in 1977 gave way to a long-term mission under the joint Syrian-French direction of A. Bounni and J. Lagarce. Fortifications, magnificent houses belonging to prominent people (e.g., the so-called North Palace), and tombs have been discovered at the site.

On the tell of Ras Shamra proper, which had already been the subject of half a century of archaeological studies, we began in 1978 a new program of excavation and thematic studies with a multidisciplinary team of specialists. The new focus was on studying texts, architecture, city planning, and artistic techniques, employing so-called archaeometric methods. This program is still ongoing.

Sixty years of research at this site have brought to light the urban quarters of a capital city, temples, the remnants of a fortification, an immense royal palace, and many private homes with textual archives—in Akkadian and Ugaritic, but also in several other languages (Hittite, Hurrian, Egyptian, and Cypro-Minoan)—along with a wide variety of archaeological artifacts, some of outstanding quality, but virtually all of significance.

These objects are held in Syrian museums located in Damascus, Aleppo, Latakia, and Tartus, and in the Louvre Museum in Paris.

Note: A selection of 66 objects that illustrate the monuments or excavated zones, as well as the character of the Ugaritic culture, are presented in chapter 3. The reader will find references to them in the text (nos. **1–66**).

Chapter 1

Geography and History

The Site and Setting

Note: The geographical names in italics correspond to the ancient names that appear in the tablets from Late Bronze Age Ugarit or in later Greek and Latin texts.

The transcription of the various cuneiform scripts is sometimes difficult for the layperson, and even scholars do not entirely agree on a system. We have therefore adopted a simplified system of transcribing proper nouns in Semitic languages without resorting to the use of diacritic signs.

The Territory of the Kingdom (Fig. 6)

The boundaries of the kingdom as they are known from Late Bronze Age written documents underwent changes in the course of its history. The kingdom of Ugarit basically occupied the northern part of the Levantine coast, covering approximately the same area as that of the current Mohafazat of Latakia, that is, a surface of about 2,000 square kilometers.

The massif of Bayer and Bassit constituted its northern limit. There rises Mount Saphon, the dwelling of Baal, the storm god. It is called Sapanu in Ugaritic, Hazzi in the Hittite and Akkadian texts, later Κάσιος in Greek, Casius in Latin, and today Jabal al-Aqra. In clear weather its summit, 1,780 meters high, can be seen on the northern horizon (*Fig. 2*).

The kingdom stretched south to the territory of *Siyannu*, whose name is also preserved in the name Nahr es-Sinn, a river south of Jablah. To the east, it was separated from the inland regions by the Alawi mountain range (Jabal al-Ansariyeh), 1,567 meters at its peak. To the south, this chain approaches the sea, thereby narrowing the coastal plain at Nahr es-Sinn and marking the boundary of the territory.

The valley of the *Rahbanu* (modern Nahr al-Kabir), the only permanent river of any importance, is situated between the northern massif of Bassit and Jabal al-Ansariyeh. This valley opens the way to the northeast toward inland Syria and the Euphrates.

The Area around the Capital (Fig. 11)

The capital, located near the sea on the tell of Ras Shamra, was the site of six millennia of virtually uninterrupted occupation, beginning in the Neolithic Period (8th millennium B.C.E.). It is surrounded by a large, fertile, and fairly well-irrigated plain, separating the sea from the Bahluliyeh plateau and the Jabal al-Ansariyeh mountain range. Less than a kilometer from the tell and visible from the temple quarter on the acropolis, was the excellent port of Mahadu—Minet el-Beida, the Greek Λευκὸς Λιμήν, where the maritime activities of the capital were concentrated.

a. The coast and the harbor of Minet el-Beida, 1936.
Aerial view by the French *Armée du Levant*.

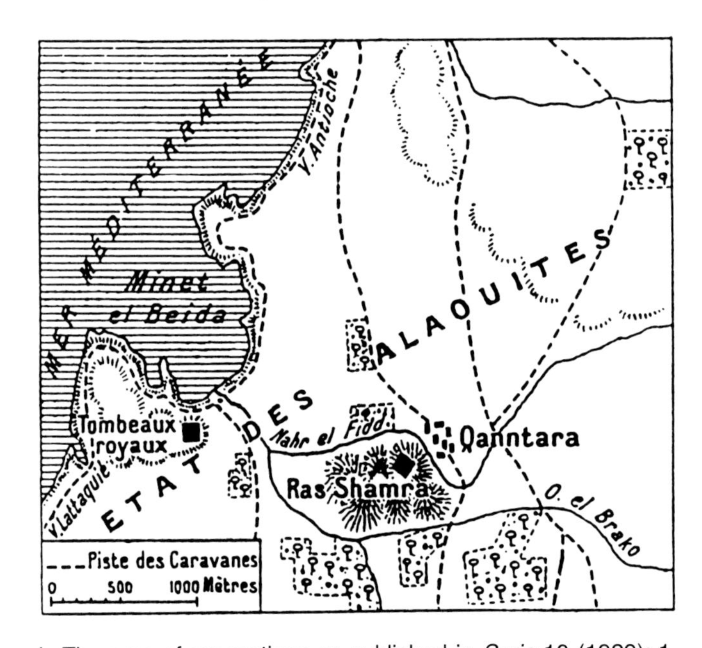

b. The area of excavations as published in *Syria* 10 (1929): 1.

Figure 5. Excavations at Minet el-Beida.

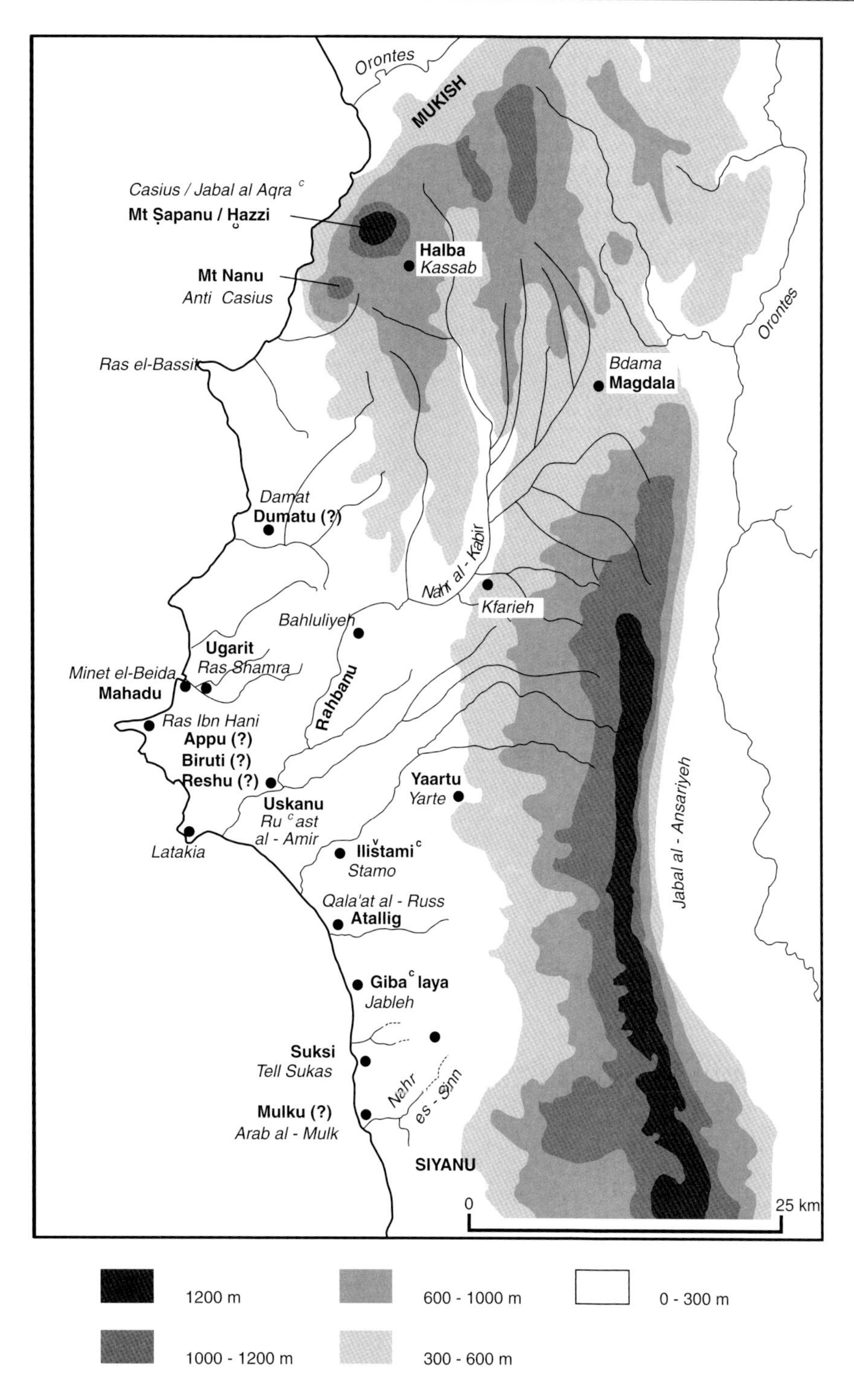

Figure 6. The kingdom of Ugarit in its geographical and historical environment; toponymns are cited, for the most part, according to their Late Bronze Age forms.

Five kilometers south, on the promontory known as Ras Ibn Hani, which constituted an excellent lookout post for the Ugaritians, an installation was built during the city's period of expansion and prosperity at the beginning of the 13th century B.C.E. The ancient name of the site is still unclear (perhaps *Appu*, *Biruti*, or *Reshu*?).

Climate

The presence of mountainous areas along with the proximity of the sea provide favorable conditions for agriculture in the region surrounding the tell. The mountain chain to the east protects the plain from the dry winds of the Syrian Desert steppe, while retaining the rain coming from the sea. Temperatures are fairly mild (an average of 11° centigrade in winter and 27° in summer), and there is an average rainfall of more than 800 millimeters during the long rainy period extending over seven to eight months from fall to spring.

Hydrography

Two small streams run along the north and south sides of the tell; the Nahr Shbayyeb to the north, and the Nahr ed-Delbeh to the south (the latter was referred to as the "Ouadi el-Brako" in the first report, written in 1929, *Fig. 5b*). They meet to the west of the tell to form the Nahr al-Fidd (or rather the Nahr al-Fayd, according to G. Saadé, *Ougarit*, 1979, p. 36), which runs into the bay of Minet el-Beida. For several months during the summer, these streams are dry, but the fairly shallow water table feeds several springs that flow at the foot of the tell, and the many wells discovered throughout the city once tapped this source. A well-devised system of dams retained the water, thereby maintaining the level in the wells and the springs during at least part of the dry season.

Natural resources

The Mediterranean climate provided favorable conditions for cultivating the three traditional crops of ancient times—grapes, cereals, and olives (*Fig. 7a*). Arboreal cultivation (almond and pistachio trees) and small livestock husbandry were practiced in the coastal areas, where there are now groves of citrus fruit (*Fig. 3*). The hills and mountains, which were also sites of husbandry, were at the time covered with forests of cedars, pines, cypress, and oak trees, and so forth—an environment somewhat like what is found today in the north of the kingdom (the forest on the road to Kassab) but that has been destroyed everywhere else and is therefore difficult to imagine.

Local mineral, agricultural, and forest resources played a part in commercial maritime exchange with countries near and far (as far as Egypt and the Aegean world) in providing for the needs of the inhabitants and in the development of construction techniques and architecture. Textual evidence corroborates archaeological finds in this respect. The presence of numerous oil presses on the tell, for example, bears out the importance of this agricultural industry.

Insofar as architectural construction is concerned, the region provided the necessary raw materials in the form of stone, earth, wood, and reeds. Building stone was obtained from quarries such as those in the village of Mqateh (called "Qanntara" in the first report of 1929; see *Fig. 5b*), a few hundred meters north of the tell, and at Minet el-Helu on the coast (*Fig. 7b*).

The walls were reinforced with timber from the nearby mountains and hills, and the flat mud roofs were sustained by wooden beams and reeds (the latter grew in abundance on the banks of nearby streams). The bitumen coating on walls (e.g., the North Palace) came from deposits at Kfarieh, 30 kilometers northeast in the Nahr al-Kabir Valley.

a. Fields of wheat and olive trees, 1992.

b. The coast with the stone quarries of Minet el-Helu between Minet el-Beida and Ibn Hani, 1989.

Figure 7. The landscape of the region of Ugarit.

The development of Ras Shamra certainly owed much to geographical factors: on the one hand, to climatic conditions favorable to agricultural activities; and on the other, to its location on the Mediterranean coast, with an excellent port that made commerce possible with countries accessible by the sea (e.g., Egypt, the Levantine coast, Cyprus, the Anatolian coast, and the Greek world, etc.). Caravan travel on the road following the valley of Nahr al-Kabir put the kingdom in contact with northern and inland Syria, the Hittite world, Mesopotamia, and the Mitannian Kingdom.

Selected Bibliography

1940, Weulersse (J.), *Le pays des Alaouites*, Tours.
1979, Saadé (G.), *Ougarit, Métropole cananéenne*, Beirut.
1995, Calvet (Y.) and Geyer (B.), "Environnement et ressources en eau dans la région d'Ougarit," in *RSO* XI, Paris, pp. 169–82.

Minet el-Beida

1929, 1931, 1932, 1933, 1935, Schaeffer (C.), "Rapports . . . ," *Syria* 10, 1929, 285–94; 12, 1931, 1–4; 13, 1932, 1–14; 14, 1933, 93–108; 16, 1935, 168–71.
1994, Yon (M.), "Minet el-Beida," in *Reallexicon für Assyriologie* 8.3/4, Berlin–New York, pp. 213–15.
1995, Saadé (G.), "Le port d'Ougarit," in *RSO* XI, pp. 141–54.

Ras Ibn Hani

1987, Bounni (A.), Lagarce (E. and J.) and Saliby (N.), *Ras Ibn Hani: Achéologie et Histoire*, Damascus.
1995, Lagarce (J. and E.), "Ras Ibn Hani," in *RSO* XI, pp. 141–54.

[2005] A thirteenth-century burial chamber was discovered at Minet el-Beida in 1997 and excavated for the Department of Antiquities by J. Haïdar in 1998. It appears to have been unpillaged, and the burials and funerary offerings were discovered intact, including various pottery forms (remarkable for the small percentage of Mycenaean imports) and bronze weapons and tools (the latter in exceptional numbers and state of preservation). See S. Marchegay in *Aux origines de l'alphabet* (Lyon, 2004), pp. 246–55 (nos. 273–302).

Figure 7bis. Bronze omphalos bowl from Tomb 1008 at Minet el-Beida, discovered in 1998 (Latakia M2148, diameter 17.3 cm); Marchegay, in *Aux origines de l'alphabet, Lyon*, 2004: no. 290.

Publications of Excavations of the Mission (see p. 25)

Minet el-Beida

1997, Yon (M.), "Ougarit et le port de Mahadou–Minet el-Beida," in *Res Maritimae*, ed. S. Swiny, R. Hohfelder, and L. Swiny, Atlanta, pp. 357–69.
2001, Marchegay (S.), "Un plan des fouilles 1929–1935 à Minet el-Beida le port d'Ougarit," in *RSO* XIV, pp. 11–40.

Ras Ibn Hani

1998, Bounni (A.) and Lagarce (E. and J.), *Ras Ibn Hani I: Le Palais Nord du Bronze Récent*, BAH, Beirut.

Prehistory and Protohistory: 8th–2nd Millennia B.C.E.

"Ugaritic" designates the period for which we have references to Ugarit in the texts from the tell of Ras Shamra, that is to say, the last phase of its existence. Apart from perhaps one isolated mention at Ebla in the 3rd millennium B.C.E. (ca. 2400), these references mainly come from the 2nd millennium B.C.E. (the Middle Bronze Age and especially the Late Bronze Age). References to this name have been found at Mari on the Euphrates in the 18th century B.C.E., and later at Alalakh, at the Hittite capital of Boghazkoy, at El-Amarna in Egypt (14th century B.C.E.), and at Ugarit itself in the texts that date from the early 14th to the early 12th century B.C.E., just before the final disappearance of the kingdom.

We know relatively little about the earliest periods of the site, from Neolithic times to the beginning of the Late Bronze Age. On the other hand, the texts that have been consistently found on the tell over the last 60 years, and in particular the archives that were kept in the Royal Palace from ca. 1370 B.C.E. onward, provide us with much information concerning the last period of the history of Ugarit.

Deep soundings, especially the one designated "Sondage SH" on the western slope of the acropolis (see p. 104), provide evidence that the first human settlement dates to the 8th millennium B.C.E. During this phase of the **Neolithic** Period, which was a time of sedentarization in Syria and Palestine, a group of farmers (as well as hunters and fishermen) settled at Ras Shamra (*Level V C*).

By 7000, new techniques had appeared in agriculture (e.g., the breeding of domestic animals), in architecture (houses with a quadrangular plan, made of stone; *Fig.* 8), and in the production of wares: minerals were used to produce "white ware" in plaster, as in other contemporary sites, and notably, fired "ceramics"; we can trace improvement in the manufacture of the latter throughout the following millennium. *Level V B* (7000–6500 B.C.E.) and *Level V A* (6500–6000 B.C.E.; *Fig.* 8) have equivalents in other sites on the coast of the Levant and in inland Syria; this points to the development of a civilization with common features throughout a large part of the Near East.

Although the site of Ras Shamra developed considerably during the Neolithic Period, its inhabited area diminished during the **Chalcolithic** Period (*Level IV*). Apparently, the transition between the two periods coincided with significant sociocultural disturbances and with the arrival of new ethnic groups from the east, which caused profound cultural upheaval.

This level reveals characteristics similar to the so-called "Halaf" civilization that prospered in northern Mesopotamia and Syria, particularly decorated ceramics of excellent quality. At this stage, from about 5250 to 4300 B.C.E., the architecture becomes more diversified (*Fig.* 9), the artisans become specialized (in ceramics, for instance), and there is an increase in the importance of breeding small livestock such as sheep and goats.

The period from the end of the 6th millennium B.C.E. through the 5th and 4th (*Levels III C and B*) was apparently a less prosperous time for the inhabitants of Ras Shamra. Still characterized by links with Mesopotamia, this age corresponds to the period that is called "Ubaid." A significant feature of this age was the first use of copper.

The final phase of Level III (*Level III A*) corresponds to the **Early Bronze Age**. Beginning in about 3000 B.C.E., the site exhibits notable development, apparently gradually, without an abrupt break from Level III B. The settlement begins to take on a truly urban character, complete with narrow streets and a rampart. The use of unbaked clay bricks in the architecture (Early Bronze Age I) gives way to the increasing use of stone, especially in defensive constructions. The flint industry still prevailed but there were also metal tools made from copper and bronze. The wide variety of ceramics attests to exchange with regions such as Cilicia, northern Syria, Palestine, and eventually with inland Syria (Amuq, Orontes, etc.).

In Early Bronze Age III, Ras Shamra experienced the same rapid development in metallurgy as other regions. Bronze was used mainly to produce weapons such as spear-heads and daggers, as well as tools (flat axes, needles, etc.) and jewelry (pins, etc.).

What may be the first reference to Ugarit *(Ug-ga-ra-at*^{ki}*)* appears in a list of place-names (ca. 2400 B.C.E.) discovered in Ebla, in inland western Syria. But some scholars have questioned the identification of the name with the coastal city of Ugarit.

Around 2200 B.C.E., as in many other places in the Levant, the tell was apparently abandoned for at least one century, perhaps two, during the transitional period that also marked the end of the Old Kingdom in Egypt and the collapse of the Akkadian Empire in Mesopotamia.

A new settlement on the site began around 2000 B.C.E., in the **Middle Bronze Age**, with the arrival of nomadic groups such as the Amorites from inland Syria, who gradually became sedentary in Syria. Some of the people who settled on the acropolis of Ugarit were apparently experts in metallurgy; the excavator called them "*torque*-bearers" because of the round metal necklaces (*torque*) found in their graves as well as on silver figurines. In addition to these pieces of jewelry, their weapons (triangular daggers, socketed spears, fenestrated axes) are typical, and the discovery of molds demonstrates that these items were manufactured locally.

Although there are large collective graves dating to this first phase of the Middle Bronze Age, there is no evidence of architecture from this period (due perhaps to the accident of excavation; or perhaps only nomads were present at this time). It is with the second and third phases of the Middle Bronze Age (ca. 1900 to 1650 B.C.E.) that the site underwent spectacular urban development, in which traditions from coastal Syria merge with contributions from the newcomers. Little by little, the city covered the whole area of the tell and came to be protected by a strong rampart, the glacis of which can still be seen in several spots.

Certain monuments have been attributed to this phase. According to the excavator, the two temples on the acropolis and the "Hurrian Temple" (in the Royal Zone northwest of the tell) may have been built at the end of the Middle Bronze Age, although it is also possible that they were constructed at the beginning of the Late Bronze Age. In any case, they were in use throughout the following period and until the end of the Late Bronze Age, in the early 12th century B.C.E.

On the other hand, a sounding in 1994 showed that the building known as the "North Palace," the construction of which was first dated to the end of the Middle Bronze Age, was in fact built during the Late Bronze Age I (ca. 1600 B.C.E.). It was abandoned during the construction of the Royal Palace in the Late Bronze Age.

Excavations have unearthed a large number of objects dating to the Middle Bronze Age. One of the most striking characteristics of the period is the presence of Egyptian objects. Many of these bear hieroglyphic inscriptions: a bead inscribed with the name of Pharaoh Sesostris I (1970–1936 B.C.E.); funerary figurines bearing the name of an unknown person; statues of more notable figures, sometimes mutilated, as in the case of the statue of Chnoumet, daughter of Pharaoh Amenemhet II and wife of Sesostris II (no. 12), and the sphinx from the Temple of Baal. These apparently delib-

Figure 8. Level V A (Neolithic), in the *Sondage SH*, west of the acropolis, as viewed from the north, 1972.

Figure 9. Level IV (Chalcolithic), in the *Sondage SH* (west of the acropolis), as seen from the northeast, 1972.

erate mutilations have given rise to several interpretations. They may have been mutilated in a demonstration of hostility during a time of international conflict. It is also possible that they were spoils of war from the period of Hyksos domination in Egypt. At any rate, what is important is the extensive scope of Egyptian relations with the kingdoms of the Levantine coast at the time. There are theories that the political rule of the 12th Dynasty extended to Ugarit but, without additional information, they remain mere hypotheses. Furthermore, references to Ugarit at the time in texts from Mari on the Euphrates attest to ongoing relations between the coastal kingdom and Upper Mesopotamia. Mention is made of the desire of the king of Ugarit to see the Mari palace and of a visit to Ugarit by the king of Mari. The economic archives refer to the city specifically in the context of tin trade.

As is the case for other sites of the Levant, little is known about Ugarit at the end of the Middle Bronze Age (ca. 1650 B.C.E.) or the first phase of the **Late Bronze Age** (15th century B.C.E.) down through the Amarna period. All that can be said is that Ugarit went through troubled times and experienced a decline that might even have led to the abandonment of the city but not to its total destruction, because the temples on the acropolis clearly survived until the end of Ugarit in the early 12th century. In any case, the city retained its name throughout the 2nd millennium.

With the 14th century B.C.E., the best documented age in the history of Ugarit begins and continues during most of the Late Bronze Age (*Level 1*). Furthermore, the structures that appeared beneath the picks of the excavators and that can now be seen on the tell also date, for the most part, to this period.

The Kingdom and Its Written Documents 14th–12th Centuries B.C.E.

Following all of the above-mentioned years of obscurity (about which we have much less information because we have not yet excavated the corresponding archaeological levels, nor have we discovered the Middle Bronze Age city or its texts), the history of Ugarit abruptly comes to light in the Late Bronze Age (*Level 1*), thanks to the discovery of written documents that have shaken the foundations of our historical knowledge. This period, during which writing played an ever-larger role, was characterized at Ugarit by the development of an alphabetic cuneiform script (unknown to linguists before these excavations).

The Late Bronze Age was the period when urban development reached new heights, the kingdom prospered more than ever, and the power of the monarchy assumed growing importance. We are able to track the increase of power from the 15th to the 12th centuries B.C.E. by means of the texts found at Ugarit and abroad (e.g., the El-Amarna archives in Egypt) and impressions of seals on official documents that have enabled us to establish the royal succession.

The history of the kingdom is closely bound up with the history of the powers that surrounded it and in turn exerted their influence: Mitanni, Egypt, and Hatti; as well as neighboring kingdoms with which Ugarit had friendly or hostile relations, depending on the circumstances in the periods: Mukish, Carchemish, Amurru, Siyannu, Kadesh;

or the kingdoms on the coast farther to the south, such as Byblos, Beirut, Tyre, and Sidon.

Power was in the hands of the king, whose prerogatives increased until, by the end of the Late Bronze Age, the Royal Palace had become the center of decision-making and wealth.

The king embodied Baal's image on earth and represented him. He is sometimes depicted as a powerful sovereign and warrior in a chariot on a hunt (for instance, on a gold bowl from the Temple of Baal; no. 57), or in priestly garments enjoying the privileged protection of a god (as on the "Stele of Baal with Thunderbolt," see no. 18; see also no. 41).

In the texts discovered on the site, at least eight names of kings are mentioned, beginning in the 14th century B.C.E. It appears that the kings used dynastic cylinder seals, one of which perhaps dates several centuries earlier to an ancestor named Yaqaru, of whom we otherwise have little knowledge.

A list of the succession of kings covering two centuries, from Ammistamru I to Ammurapi, the last king at the beginning of the 12th century B.C.E. (see table, p. 24), has been established on the basis

Figure 10. The site of Ugarit: Palace Street, looking east, 1989.

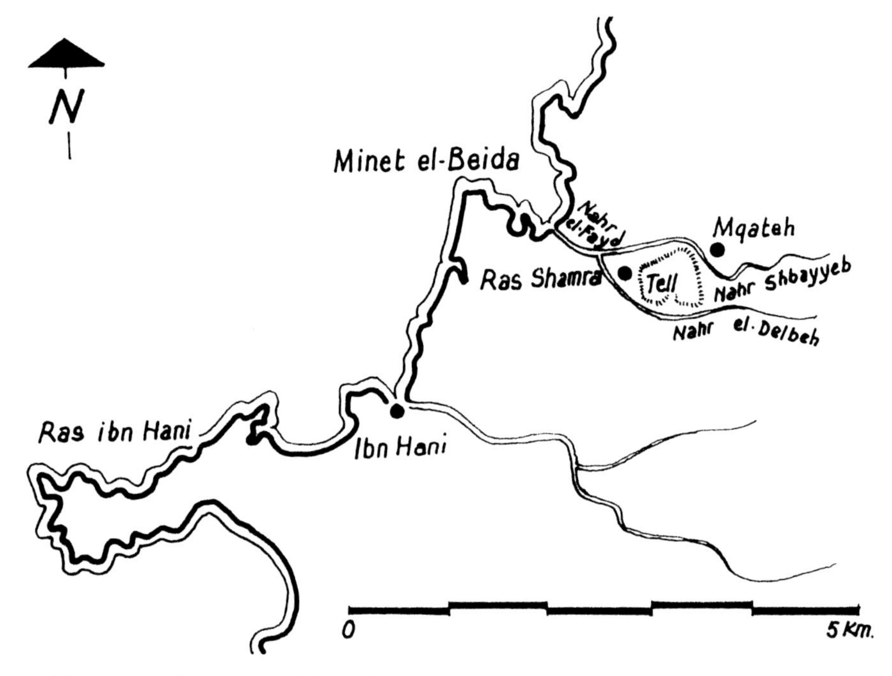

Figure 11. The region of Ras Shamra. The capital on the tell of Ras Shamra, the port of Minet el-Beida, and the settlement of Ras Ibn Hani.

of synchronisms with 18th- and 19th-Dynasty Egypt and with Mesopotamian history. But the discoveries made in 1994 in the "House of Urtenu" have brought to light new facts concerning the royal lineage. These recent finds are currently in the process of being deciphered and analyzed.

From about 1400 to 1350 B.C.E., Ugarit was under Egyptian rule. Around 1360 B.C.E., a fire destroyed part of the Royal Palace, and earlier archives must have disappeared during the reconstruction work, because the royal archives as we know them start with the reign of Niqmaddu II in the mid-14th century B.C.E. The El-Amarna documents and a few references in the archives of Niqmaddu II seem to indicate that his father, Ammistamru I, was in a subordinate position to Amenophis III (whose cartouche was found at Ugarit; no. 10). The fact that the Egyptians did not rule directly, however, is borne out by a treaty between King Niqmaddu II and the king of Amurru around 1350 B.C.E., which imposed an Amorite protectorate of sorts on Ugarit. However, the city was still within the Egyptian sphere of influence.

Sometime after 1350, Suppiluliuma, the king of Hatti, undertook an expedition against Mitanni and its Syrian vassals. When Mitanni succumbed to Hittite control, Ugarit, Amurru, and Kadesh fell within the Hittite sphere of influence. Following a period of clashes with the lands of Nuhasse and Carchemish, Hittite domination stabilized during the reign of the Ugaritic king Niqmepa (1332–1260 B.C.E.; cf. no. 11).

By the end of the 14th century, the king of Carchemish clearly played an important role as the administrator of Hittite political affairs in Syria. In quite a few cases, he was sent on delegations by the

Great King of Hatti, whose control over the region was firmly established by settling conflicts between Ugarit and neighboring countries such as Siyannu to the south and Mukish to the north.

During the reign of the Ugaritic king Ammistamru II (mid-13th century), the rivalries and alliances between Ugarit and Amurru took the form of extremely complex matrimonial arrangements, episodes of which have been preserved in the royal correspondence (see no. 7). The role played by the kings of Hatti and Carchemish in these alliances demonstrates the implications for international politics. Many texts also mention legal and commercial agreements aimed at settling trade disputes or at guaranteeing the safe passage of caravans. The presence of Hittite officials at Ugarit is certain, although Ugarit continued to maintain commercial relations with Egypt and areas under Egyptian control (such as Palestine), particularly after the Hittite-Egyptian treaty in 1270 B.C.E. between the Hittite king Hattusilis III and Ramses II.

It is clear that the wealth of Ugarit, which came principally from a flourishing economy (maritime trade in particular), was concentrated in the hands of the royalty, especially in the second half of the 13th century. Be that as it may, the military capacity of the kingdom continued to decline. For this reason, around 1230 B.C.E., King Ibiranu tried to avoid involvement in the Hittite sovereign's war effort. The texts seem to indicate that in the late 13th century B.C.E. the kings of Ugarit preferred making financial contributions over sending troops to Hatti. Although the kingdom was economically prosperous, it was weak militarily.

The End of a Civilization
ca. 1190/1185 B.C.E.

The end of the kingdom of Ugarit is considered to be approximately 1200 B.C.E., during the time of Kings Niqmadu III and Ammurapi. Attacks by the "Sea Peoples" were causing increased concern in the coastal lands, as well as for the Hittite and Egyptian rulers, as revealed in their correspondence.

The arrival of these new invaders created an upheaval in the Near East at the turn of the 12th century B.C.E. The "Sea Peoples," thus designated by the Egyptians who saw them arriving by boat, were probably groups of invaders from the northwest who attacked in several waves over a period of years. They can be traced throughout the eastern Mediterranean area, on the coasts of Anatolia and the Levant, and in Cyprus. The Sea Peoples have been identified as the Sikila, the Peleset-Philistines, and the Sherden, mentioned on the Medinet-Habu monument erected by Ramses III after he defeated them in 1182 B.C.E. Biblical texts refer to the Philistines, descendants of the Peleset, who had settled on the coast of Palestine and gave it their name.

In all likelihood the Sea Peoples played a decisive role in the destruction of Ugarit, as well as other sites. At Ugarit itself, one text mentions the Sikila, "who live on boats" and whose movements were to be watched. Several letters refer to the fact that King Ammurapi was concerned with the danger from the sea and asked advice of a neighboring king. The Sea Peoples are held responsible for much of the destruction and upheaval that have been noted by archaeologists in Anatolia and in northern Syria in the fairly short period that spans the end of the 13th century B.C.E. and the first few decades of the 12th. In the case of Ugarit, the kingdom and its culture simply collapsed under this pressure, never to be revived.

The capital, which the last King Ammurapi probably left badly defended (the fortifications seem to have been neglected), was seized, set ablaze, and abandoned. The political and administrative structures linked to the royal power did not survive the capital, and the government and civilization disappeared.

Based on the texts, some of which were discovered during the seasons between 1986 and 1994 in the "House of Urtenu" on the southern part of the city, we can set the time of this event around 1190–1185 B.C.E. The houses were abandoned by their inhabitants, then pillaged and burned.

Thereafter, no other urban settlement was ever located on the site. There is evidence of isolated occupation and a few farming installations on certain portions of the tell during Persian, Hellenistic, and Roman times, but these farms did not involve the kind of collective organization that characterizes city life.

Thus, the miraculous development that had lasted some 6,000 years, when a Neolithic village had become first a city and then the capital of a kingdom that left its mark on the history of its day, came to an end.

Figure 12. Aerial view of excavations, 1939, as viewed from the north.

C. Schaeffer, *Ugaritica* IV, p. 6, fig. 3.

The photograph was taken prior to the planting of the groves that today surround the tell. 2, 4: "Lower city, east and west"; 6, 7: temples of Baal and Dagan; 12: road to Latakia; 16–17: the Royal Palace before the excavations of 1939; 19: path to Minet el-Beida.

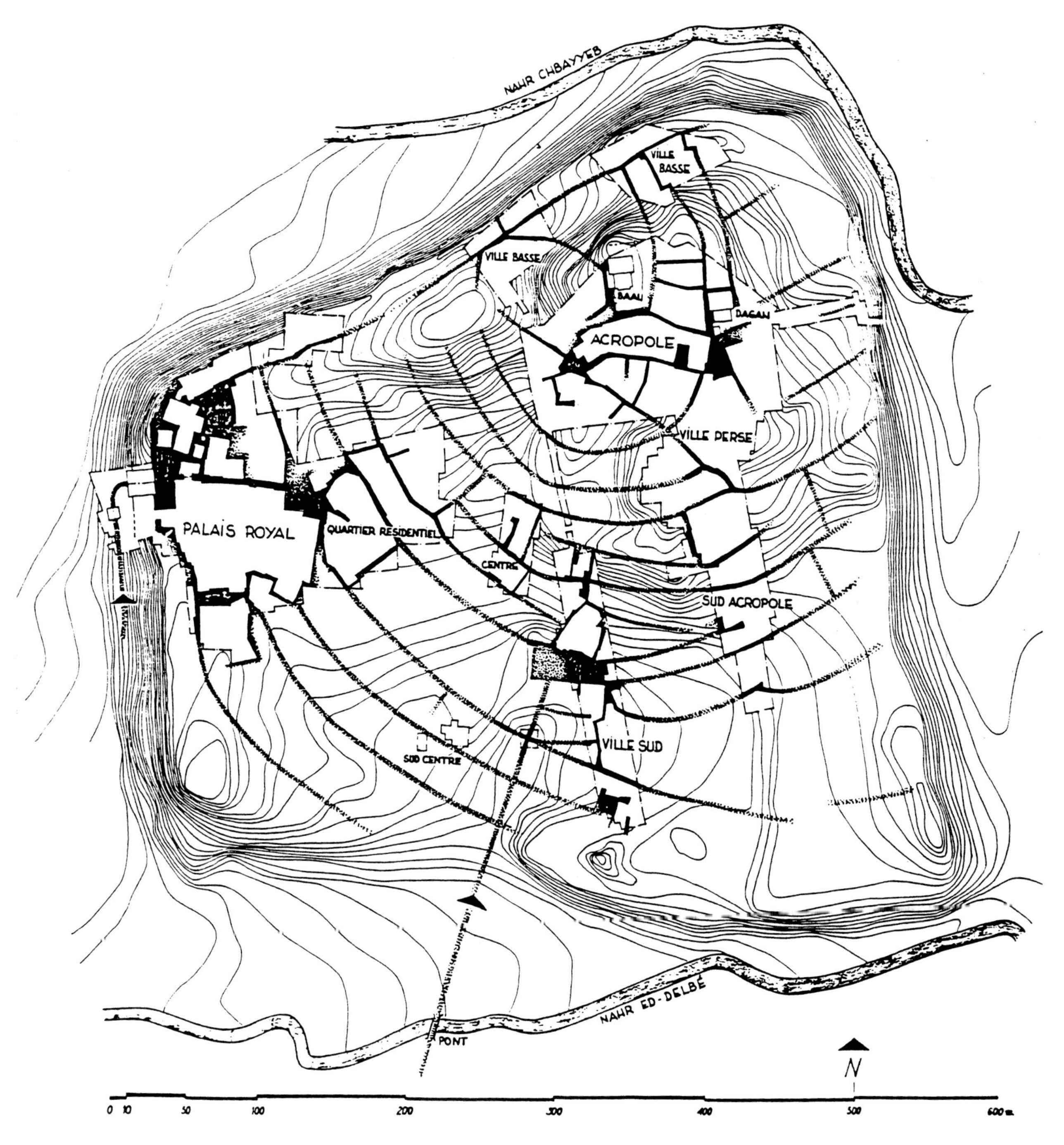

Figure 13. Theoretical restoration of thoroughfares in the final phase of the city (based on streets excavated through 1992).

CHRONOLOGICAL TABLE

Approximate dates B.C.E.	*Life on the Ras Shamra tell*	*Level*	*Period*
Ca. 7500	First settlements; farming	V C	Pre-pottery Neolithic
Ca. 7000	Pastoralism; ceramics; stone architecture (rectangular rooms)	V B	Pottery Neolithic
Ca. 6000	Differentiated architecture; specialized crafts	V A	"Halaf" Chalcolithic
4th millennium	Appearance of copper	III C III B	"Ubaid"
Ca. 3000	City-type agglomeration, rampart; copper metallurgy	IIIA	Early Bronze Age
Ca. 2200	Abandonment		
Beginning of 2nd millennium	Arrival of Amorite population; urban development: temples (?), rampart)	II	Middle Bronze Age
Ca. 1650	Abandonment? temporary decline?		
Ca. 1600	New urban period	I	Late Bronze Age
14th–13th centuries: ? – ca. 1370 ca. 1370–1340/35 ca. 1340/35–1332 ca. 1332–1260 ca. 1260–1230 ca. 1230–1210 ca. 1210–1200 ca. 1200–1190/85	Kings of Ugarit (from texts): Ammistamru I Niqmaddu II Arhalbu Niqmepa Ammistamru II Ibiranu Niqmaddu III Ammurapi		
Ca. 1190/85	Destruction and abandonment, under attacks by the "Sea Peoples" (?)		
5th–4th centuries	Small settlement on the tell		Persian period
1st century	A few traces of occupation		Roman period

We offer here the most up-to-date results available, based on the calibration of radiocarbon dating (C^{14}) for the ancient Near East. Thus, with the results of the chronology established, the date for the first installation attested on the site of Ras Shamra must be raised by 1,000 years (see, for example, J. Cauvin, *Naissance des divinités: Naissance de l'agriculture* [Paris: CNRS, 1994]).

Selected Bibliography

Publications of Excavations of the Mission

1939–1978, under the direction of C. F.-A. Schaeffer, *Ugaritica* I–VII, Paris.
1983–1995, under the direction of M. Yon, *Ras Shamra–Ougarit* (= *RSO*) I–XI, Paris; others in progress.

The texts of the Royal Palace have appeared in the series *Palais Royal d'Ougarit* (= *PRU*) II à VI, Paris, 1957 to 1970.

The excavation reports have appeared regularly in the journal *Syria* since 1929 ; some preliminary reports have also appeared in *AAAS* and *CRAIBL*.

General Studies

1979, *SDB*: Courtois (J.-C.), "Ras Shamra," in *Supplément au Dictionnaire de la Bible*, cols. 1124–1362, Paris.
1979, Saadé (G.),*Ougarit, métropole cananéenne*, Beirut.
1987, *Le Monde de la Bible*, special issue "Ougarit," no. 48, Paris.
1992, Klengel (H.), *Syria, 3000 to 300* B.C., Berlin (English edition).
1992, Yon (M.), "Ugarit Excavations," in *Anchor Bible Dictionary* 6, pp. 695–706, New York-London.

Prehistory: Contenson (H. de), 1992, *Préhistoire d'Ougarit, RSO* VIII, Paris.
The End of Ugarit: Yon (M.), Sznycer (M.), and Bordreuil (P.), eds., 1995, *RSO* XI, Paris.
Persian Period: Stucky (R.), 1981, *Leukos Limen*, Paris.

[2005] A new list of divinized kings of Ugarit discovered in 1994 in the House of Urtenu (see p. 20) and published in preliminary form in 1999 (RS 94.2518, in syllabic script, with three duplicates) provides new data on the dynastic line. The list is complete but consists only of a list of names, and its absolute chronology is thus open to debate. According to its editor (Arnaud 1999), the kings named reigned from the 18th century through the 12th; for an alternative view of the relationship between this list and the previously attested list in alphabetic script (RS 24.257), see Pardee 2002, pp. 195–210.

1999, Arnaud (D.), "Prolégomènes à la rédaction d'une histoire d'Ougarit, II: Les borderaux de rois divinisés," *Studi Micenei ed Egeo-Anatolici* 41/2, pp. 155–73.
2002, Pardee (D.), *Ritual and Cult at Ugarit*.Writings from the Ancient World 10; Atlanta: Society of Biblical Literature.
2004, Roche (C.), in *Aux origines de l'alphabet: Catalogue Lyon 2004*, no. 47, pp. 162–64.

Figure 13bis. List of divinized kings, RS 94.2518. Tablet in syllabic script from the House of Urtenu.

[2005]

Publications of Excavations of the Mission

2000, *RSO* XII, D. Pardee, *Les Textes rituels*.
2000, *RSO* XIII, M. Yon, V. Karageorghis, N. Hirschfeld, *Céramiques mycéniennes*, 2000.
2001, *RSO* XIV, M. Yon, D. Arnaud dir., *Études Ougaritiques 1: Travaux 1985–1995*, 2001.
2004, *RSO* XV, J.-Y. Monchambert, *La céramique d'Ougarit, Campagnes de fouilles 1975 et 1976*.
In press, *RSO* XVI, J. Gachet, *Les ivoires d'Ougarit et l'art des ivoiriers du Levant*.

General Studies

1999, *Handbook of Ugaritic Studies*, ed. W. G. E. Watson and N. Wyatt, Leiden-Boston-Cologne.
2004, *Aux origines de l'alphabet. Le royaume d'Ougarit: Catalogue Exposition Lyon 2004–2005*, ed. Y. Calvet and G. Galliano, Paris-Lyon.
In press, *Actes du Colloque Lyon 2001*, ed. Y. Calvet, Lyon.

Chapter 2

Description of the Tell

Tour of the Tell

A tour of the tell begins today on the western side, near the modern village of Ras Shamra, opposite the remains of the fortified entrance, with its large tower and postern gate. A modern stairway leads to the caretaker's house (*Fig.* 15:20) built on the vast heap of rubble from the excavations of the 1950s. Visitors descend on the other side to a small, paved plaza, called the Royal Plaza, where the official entrance to the Royal Palace was located. The tour then follows a meandering route eastward through the city.

The various areas of the city bear the names that the excavators gave to them as they were discovered (often as a function of the interpretation that was attributed to them) and as they are found in the excavation reports. Apart from a few rare exceptions, these French names have been retained for the sake of convention, and the English terms given here are only an approximate translation of the conventional French names (see Index).

Note: There are enormous gaps in the current state of our knowledge concerning the sites and monuments described in this chapter and, hence, in the interpretations that we can offer. Some of the earliest excavated areas, in a highly damaged state today, were merely mentioned in short preliminary reports with very few details; some excavation archives were lost during World War II. On the other hand, since 1978, certain sectors have been the focus of extremely detailed architectural analyses, which are already published or are in preparation. Our descriptions and interpretations reflect the state of affairs in 1994; hence the uneven treatment of the data.

The topographical landmarks (*Fig. 1*) have been established on the basis of a grid, with the north–south and east–west axes intersecting at the center of the tell.

City Planning

The various quarters of the city and the monuments that appear today on the tell were those in use in the final phase, in the Late Bronze Age. Exceptions include a few buildings that were already destroyed at the time, such as the North Palace.

Only about one-sixth of the surface of the tell has been excavated, and for this reason we cannot yet determine the overall configuration of the city or the distribution of its quarters. This would be true even if we were to limit our consideration to the final phase of its occupation (13th to the beginning of the 12th century).

We can identify a few specific zones by their characteristics, such as the Royal Zone comprising the Royal Palace and the other related buildings located to the north (*Fig. 15*), the acropolis with its temples, the Library of the High Priest, and the urban residential quarters, especially those located on the southern slope of the tell.

The various areas excavated over a period of more than 50 years have revealed densely populated quarters to the east of the Royal Zone, below the acropolis, with narrow streets (generally 1 to 2.5 meters wide) around blocks of houses where the residents of Ugarit lived. To the north lies what is called the East and West Lower City; to the east of the Royal Palace is the "Residential Quarter"; and on the pleasantly situated slope on the southern side of the tell are the excavation zones known as the "City Center," "South Central Area," "South City," and "South Acropolis." These districts, covering several hectares, bear witness to a thriving city with a variety of structures.

Our recent research on the city planning and domestic architecture have focused on building techniques and the organization of dwellings, especially in the areas of the South City (excavated in 1960) and the City Center (1978–90 seasons). Corresponding reports have been published in *RSO*, volumes I, III, and X.

Even though the architectural remains reveal only the floor plans, we can determine the original height of some of the houses on the basis of these

Figure 14. A typical housing quarter: the "City Center," looking south, in 1979.

plans, the structure of the walls, and the presence of stairways. Often, several stone steps of the first flight of a stairway have been preserved (*Fig. 48*).

The houses, situated in blocks that constituted the architectural unit of Ugaritic urban organization, are varied in shape and size. In the two zones recently studied in detail (i.e., the South City and the City Center), the houses range in size between 80 and 800 square meters. Large, luxurious homes stand beside more modest homes, and these often adjoin nonresidential buildings, such as temples or shops.

The houses are so varied in shape and size, that it is impossible to determine a typical layout scheme. On the other hand, we can note some characteristic features, even though no individual home contains all of these features. Among these are the frequent presence of an entrance vestibule that leads to a courtyard and provides access to a stairway, the frequent presence of a well, drainage pits under the stairway for the toilets and on the street curb for rainwater, silos dug into floors, small courtyards that allow light and air to reach the ground floor, and one upper story or two, very dark ground floors (some of which include windowless rooms for storage), the division of a house into two distinct parts connected to each other on the inside and provided with separate entrances on the street, with one of the parts housing the family's cult tomb, and living quarters upstairs with terraces for the household's everyday activities.

We can reconstruct the setting of everyday life, handicrafts, and family activities on the basis of stone, ceramic, ivory, and metal objects found in the houses and tombs (nos. **25**, **27–29**, **33–34**, **43–44**, **53–55**, etc.). It should not be forgotten, however, that what we see of this everyday setting is partial, because many objects were made of perishable materials such as wood, straw, leather, and cloth and thus have not survived.

Together, the above factors yield an overall picture of a densely inhabited city where private citizens found refuge at the ends of narrow streets. The city had no regular layout, because it was the outgrowth of many centuries of continual reconstruction on the same spot.

Selected Bibliography

1979, Courtois (J.-C.), "L'architecture domestique à Ugarit au Bronze Récent," *Ugarit-Forschungen* 11, pp. 105–34.

1985, Yon (M.), "La ville d'Ougarit au XIIIe s. av. J.-C.," *CRAIBL*, pp. 705–21.

1992, Yon (M.), "Ugarit: The urban habitat. The present state of the archaeological picture," *BASOR* 286, pp. 19–34.

1994, Callot (O.), *RSO* X, *La tranchée "Ville sud,"* Paris.

1995, Callot (O.) and Yon (M.), "Urbanisme et architecture," in *RSO* XI, pp. 155–68.

[2005]

1997, Yon (M.) and Callot (O.), "L'habitat à Ougarit à la fin du Bronze Récent," in *La Maison dans la Syrie antique: Colloque Damas 1992*, ed. C. Castel and F. Villeneuve, Beirut, pp. 15–28.

2001, Mallet (J.) and Matoïan (V.), "Une maison au sud du 'Temple aux rhytons'," in *RSO* XIV, pp. 83–190.

Figure 15. Schematic plan of the northwest part of the tell: Royal Zone and fortified Gate.

The Royal Fortress and the City Ramparts

At the beginning of the 2nd millennium B.C.E., the Middle Bronze Age city must have been surrounded by a rampart, and in all likelihood these defensive barriers were maintained throughout at least part of the Late Bronze Age. The only part of the rampart that is well known today is the small portion of the fortification that protected the Royal Palace on the western side of the city (*Fig.* 15:1–3, 16, 17, 18).

The excavations conducted here by C. Schaeffer in 1938–39 were interrupted by the war, resumed in 1948, and then developed more fully beginning in 1950.

In spite of the monumental appearance of the large square tower, which survived to a height of several meters, and the stone glacis, and in spite of the excellent state of conservation of the postern gate (*Fig.* 16), the evolution of the entrance system is not easy to understand. It apparently underwent modifications in various phases of the Late Bronze Age.

Near the modern stairway leading to the tell from the modern village of Ras Shamra stands a square tower 14 meters wide (*Fig.* 15:1, 16, 17) with thick walls made of carved stone blocks. The tower, which protrudes from the rampart, might have been built at the end of the Middle Bronze Age or at the very beginning of the Late Bronze Age. It remained in use throughout the first part of the Late Bronze Age (16–15th centuries).

Along with major construction work on the Royal Palace in the 15th and 14th centuries B.C.E., the fortifications to the west of the Palace were also transformed. The fortified complex (*Figs.* 16, 17, 18*a*) includes the square tower (*Fig.* 18*a*:1) and a strongly-angled glacis abutting it. Leading up to the entrance of the tower from the plain was a long ramp that ran parallel to the glacis from the north and turned into the tower. This tower, through which the passage turned at a right angle, contained the doorway that led to the eastern side of the Royal Plaza in front of the palace (*Fig.* 15:4). Immediately to the south of the tower, a corbeled, vaulted postern gate (*Fig.* 18*a*:2) was cut into the glacis and led to a stepped underground corridor, turning at a right angle within the wall. This postern thus served as a secondary passageway behind the tower.

Still later (possibly in the 13th century B.C.E.), it appears that the defensive system was once again radically transformed (*Fig.* 18*b*): the postern gate was blocked and the old tower destroyed. The access ramp was now situated on the south, and the foot of the access to the ramp was probably protected by a square tower (*Fig.* 18*b*:4), only a few vestiges of which remain. This new entrance ramp ran in front of the postern gate and turned at a right angle before reaching a monumental doorway (*Fig.* 18*b*:3). This doorway was set on the ruins of the old tower and led to the Royal Plaza (*Fig.* 15:3–4). Inside this entranceway was an elaborate gate system consisting of a central passage between symmetrical recesses. The entrance was closed on the Royal Plaza side to the east by hinged doors, and one door-socket is still visible in the stone doorsill.

The postern gate (*Figs.* 15:2, 16; 18*a*:2) has been completely cleared so that the quality of its design and construction is now fully exposed; it is the most spectacular monument at Ras Shamra today. But one should keep in mind that this was not how it looked during the last phase of the city's history.

It is not clear whether the city was still protected by a fortification wall at the very end of the city's existence in the early 12th century B.C.E. In

Figure 16. Excavation of the gate and its fortification in 1939, looking north.

Figure 17. Fortification of the Royal Zone, looking southeast, 1992:
the tower, the glacis, and the postern gate (to the right). In the background is the Royal Palace.

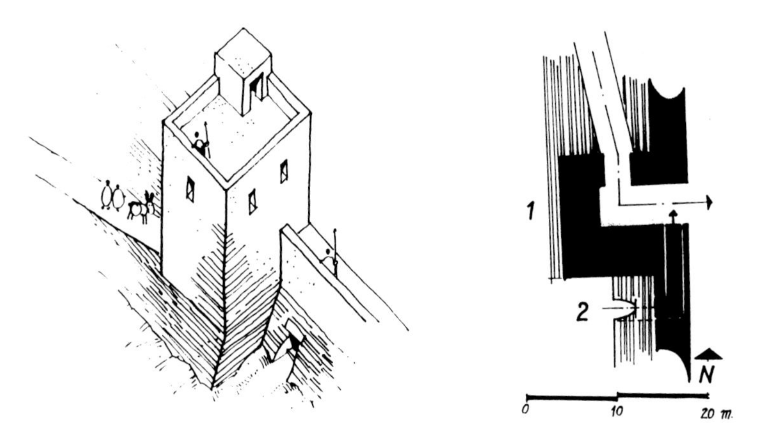

a. The 15th–14th-century complex: ramp approaching from the north along with (1) tower and (2) postern gate.

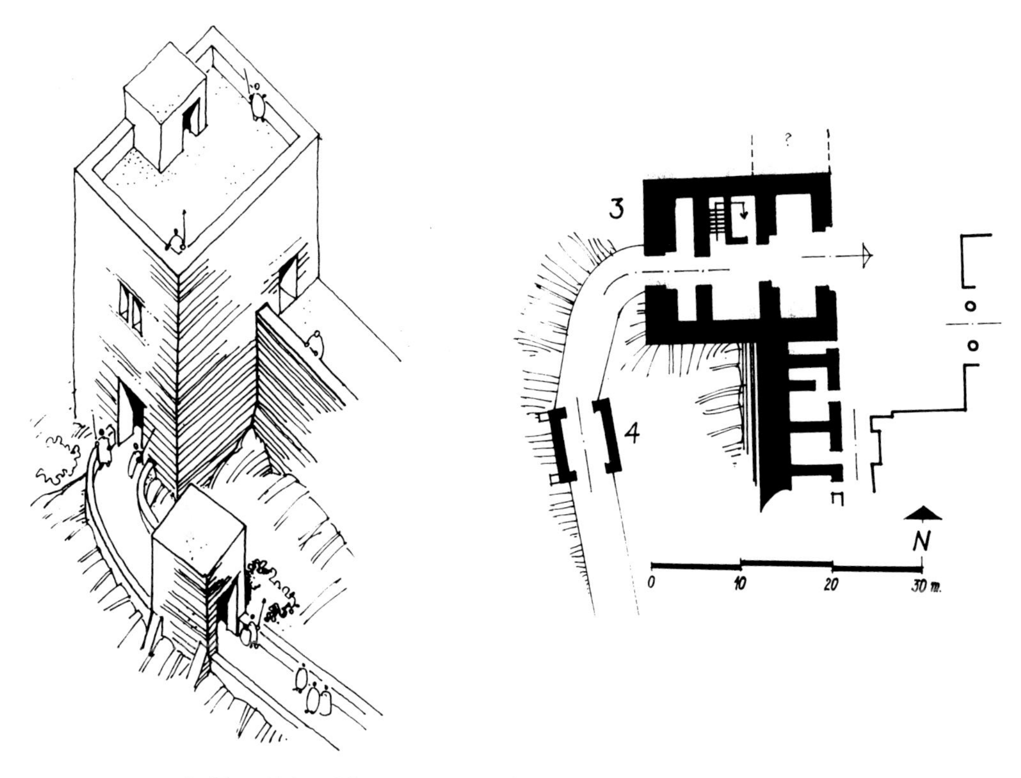

b. The 13th–12th-century complex: new small exterior tower (4);
ramp approaching from the south (and walling up the postern gate) and new expanded gate entrance (3).

Figure 18. Proposed restorations of the fortified entrance system of the Royal Zone during the Late Bronze Age.

answer to a letter in which the last king of Ugarit, Ammurapi, expressed his concern regarding the danger of attacks from the sea and asked for help and advice, a royal corrrespondent advised him to "protect the cities with defensive walls," as though the city was then open and facing a serious threat.

Selected Bibliography

1939, Schaeffer (C.), "Les fouilles de Ras Shamra–Ugarit: 10e et 11e campagnes (1938–1939)," *Syria* 20, pp. 288–92.

1951, Schaeffer (C.), "Reprise des recherches archéologiques à Ras Shamra–Ugarit," *Syria* 28, pp. 1–9.

1984, Lagarce (J.), "Remarques sur des ouvrages de soutènement et de défense à Ras Shamra et à Ras Ibn Hani," *Syria* 61, pp. 153–79.

1986, Callot (O.), "La région nord du Palais Royal d'Ougarit," *CRAIBL*, 1986, pp. 735–55.

The Royal Zone

To the west of the city proper, a considerable area, more than 10,000 square meters, was reserved for palace activities and carefully set apart from the rest of the city (*Figs.* 15, 19). For convenience of reference, this area will be referred to as the Royal Zone. The Palace itself was protected by a fortress to the west and cut off from the rest of the community by a security system of two doors: one was positioned across the Palace Street (*Fig.* 20b; cf. p. 37) and the other on the rampart side to the southwest of the area that hereafter will be designated the Royal Plaza (*Fig.* 20d).

As we will see below, the royal quarter also included annexes located to the north of the Royal Plaza (*Fig.* 25): the building designated an "Arsenal" in the early reports (*Fig.* 20c), which was actually a Guardpost; the so-called "Hurrian" temple, which might have been the royal temple; and the paved "Pillared Building," which was probably used in connection with ceremonies held in the neighboring temple. The royal quarter had its own system of water drainage, complete with a massive main sewer.

The large fortified gate (see above, p. 31) led to a fairly large plaza (the Royal Plaza), from which access was gained to the interior of the Royal Zone. There were benches all around the walls of this plaza, and some elements of the pavement have survived. A very large, nearly circular paving stone, 2 meters in diameter and 25 centimeters thick, has also been found here. Now set against the south wall of the plaza, the function of this stone in antiquity is difficult to determine. It appears too large to have served as a cover for a drainage pit.

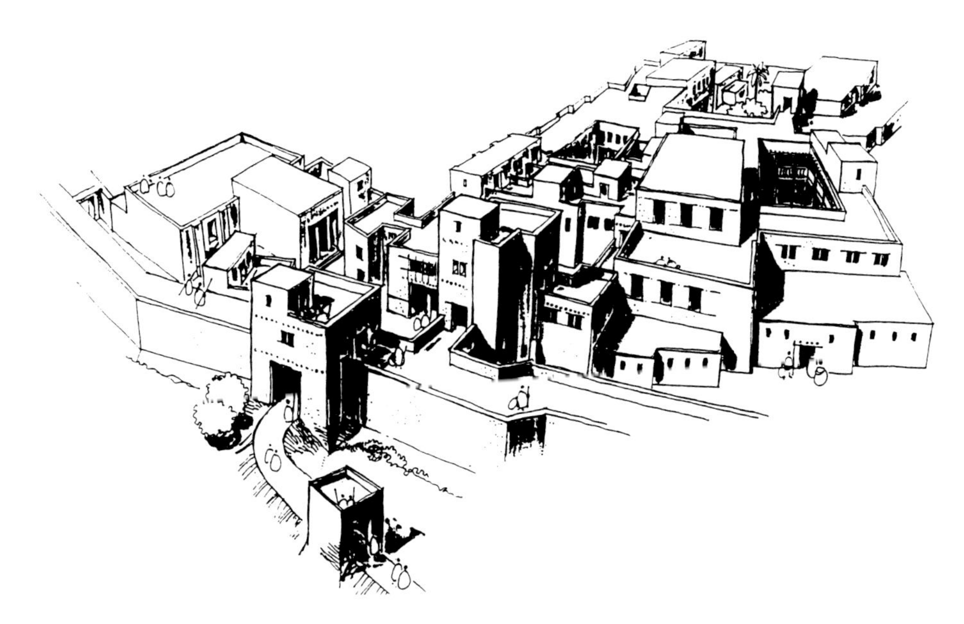

Figure 19. Axonometric view of the fortified entrance, the Royal Palace, and its northern annexes in the final phase of the city, looking northeast, 1994.

The Royal Palace

The "Royal Palace," the initial exploration of which began immediately before World War II, was extensively excavated afterward, between 1950 and 1955. A large plan of the remains uncovered, along with a report of the excavations, was published in 1962 in *Ugaritica* IV, but a thorough architectural analysis has only just begun. In the coming years, this analysis should lead to important advances in our understanding of the functions of the various spaces and the succession of phases in the construction and evolution of the complex. The plan that is presented here (*Fig.* 20) incorporates modifications that are based on recent observations and on studies that are currently underway.

Built in several stages between the 15th and 13th centuries B.C.E., the Royal Palace covered nearly 7,000 square meters. The admiration that it sparked in its day is exemplified by a reference to it in a letter written by the king of Byblos to Pharaoh Amenophis III that was found at El-Amarna.

The palace ruins are still spectacular, in spite of damage caused by a fire that destroyed it and despite three subsequent millennia of stone pillaging and erosion (*Figs.* 10, 21). The stone walls in certain spots have survived to a height of one story, and there are some traces of the plaster with which inner walls were covered (for instance, at the entrance to room 12, along with traces of wooden beams and even red paint that covered the plaster).

It is not always easy to interpret the ruins of the palace because it has undergone so many changes. These include partial destruction by fire (traces of which can be seen on the walls), in particular the fire around 1370/60 B.C.E. that "destroyed half of the Palace of Ugarit," according to a letter from the king of Tyre in the El-Amarna archives. Other factors include probable damage from the earthquake ca. 1250 and subsequent reconstructions, before it was pillaged, burned, and abandoned in the early 12th century B.C.E.

As the administrative center of the kingdom and home to the royal family, the palace yielded extensive archives of clay tablets, mainly written in Akkadian (using a syllabic cuneiform script) and Ugaritic (in an alphabetic cuneiform script). These have provided us with a great deal of information about the management of the affairs of the kingdom, its economic life, events affecting domestic politics, foreign diplomacy, and relations with the major powers of the day (the Hittite overlords and Egyptian pharaohs) and with the small neighboring kingdoms in Syria and along what later became the Phoenician coast.

Access

The palace was built near the rampart that protected it to the west. It was isolated and protected from the city to the east by a continuous wall with few entrances. The most spectacular part of the enclosure is to the north, running along "Palace Street," which led into the city. Adjacent to the street ran a 90-meter-long wall, nearly 4 meters high, with a facade of high architectural quality (*Figs.* 10, 24). The large, embossed ashlars were carefully fitted together and reinforced horizontally and vertically with wooden beams.

The elegant official entrance (*Fig.* 20; cf. *Fig.* 15:4) from the "Royal Plaza" to the northwest of the building is located inside the Royal Zone. To the southwest, there is a discreet passage (*Fig.* 20:84), 1.5 meters wide, that leads directly into what appears to be a public road linking the palace to the city along the rampart (excavations on this side have not yet been completed).

There may have been another entrance to the Palace near its southeast corner for delivery of wheat or oil, which was stored in the jars found in the storerooms (*Fig.* 20:90). However, we can only hypothesize because the wall bordering the street is

Figure 20. Plan of the Royal Palace and its passageways according to research through 1994. [2005]: Courtyards I–VI of the palace have been renumbered as follows: **128** (I), **139** (II), **148** (III), **152** (IV), **153** (V), **132** (VI).

not well preserved. The eastern boundary does not usually appear in the plans currently available. The excavations were not complete here, but our on-site inspections since then show that the foundation of the wall has survived.

The excavator thought that there was an opening protected by a Guardpost to the northeast (*Fig.* 20:53, near the *Northeast Archives*), and a doorway appears in the plan that was published in 1968. But it is not yet clear whether this northeastern doorway was present in all periods (research is underway).

Spatial Organization

Nearly one hundred separate loci on the level of the ground floor have been identified by the excavator as "rooms" (numbered from 1 to 90) and open "courtyards" (I–VI). But the research that is now being conducted on these spaces leads us to believe that this distinction between roofed rooms and open courtyards should in certain cases be modified.

An assessment of the overall area reveals the existence of at least one upper story, perhaps more, because there are at least 12 stairways. The private royal apartments must have been situated upstairs, and, judging from how the tablets were dispersed in the rubble (see below: the Palace Archives), so were a good number of scribal offices and archives.

The layout and the nature of the archaeological documents and archives found in various parts of the palace point to a division of space, with areas reserved for royal use (the Throne Room: *Fig. 20:71*) and administrative purposes, private areas, as well as space reserved for the funerary cult that was observed by the royal family (*Fig. 20:28*).

Itinerary and Description

There are several ways of proceeding through the Royal Palace. What follows is one possible itinerary through most of the building (*Fig. 20*).

Entrance and Western Sector

The official entrance (a) is located to the northwest. From the Royal Plaza (cf. *Fig. 15:4*), one enters the building through a majestic paved porch (*Fig. 20a*), which is supported by two columns, the stone bases of which have survived (the wooden columns themselves have disappeared). There are benches along the walls that were used by visitors who came for a royal audience; a well is located in the southeastern corner.

The entrance porch leads to a small vestibule with a central pillar (1). To the left, a door gives access to a group of small rooms (2–5) that may have served as cloakrooms. This is where the so-called *West Archives* were located, although the tablets found there actually fell from the upper story.

To the right of the vestibule (1) is a large stone-paved open space (Courtyard I). This courtyard, 16 meters by 14 meters, is equipped with a well and a large stone trough that is now broken. All that have survived are the base and one side, which is set against the wall. Behind this is a small, paved washroom (10) with a drainage system.

At the far end of Courtyard I, another porch with two columns (72) leads directly into the "Throne Room" (71), a space covering 10 meters square. A door situated in the center of one wall of the large courtyard provided access to the reception area reserved for royalty. From the apartments on the upper story, the king could reach the Throne Room and the other reception spaces (in particular "Hall VI") by means of a stairway.

To the west of this official area and the large paved courtyard (I) are constructions that must have been part of the defense system linked to the rampart (cf. *Fig. 19*). The walls are thick enough to sustain the tower above the rampart, and there is a stairway leading to the upper floors. Room 6 must have served as a guard-room. One can still see the small triangular openings that were cut into the stones of the wall, enabling the guards to observe and hear what was happening in the plaza.

Some administrative texts were found in the small room to the west of the Throne Room (73), the so-called *Annex Office of Archives*. As happened elsewhere in the Palace, the tablets no doubt fell from the upper floor when the building was destroyed.

From the northwest entrance vestibule, one can also proceed to the central parts of the palace, either by heading toward room 13 at the northeast corner of Courtyard I, or by heading east from the porch in front of the "Throne Room" (from 72 to 20). At the far end of the Throne Room itself, a narrow passage (76) leads to the royal apartments on the second floor by means of a stairway (85) which, as we have seen, was reserved for the king's official appearances.

This passage also gave the king access to the large room (known as "Courtyard VI") located on the eastern side of the Throne Room, which visitors could enter through the door on the eastern side of the porch with two columns (72). Recent research leads us to believe that this large space (VI) was in fact a room with a roof and may have been a banquet hall. To the south of the room, there was a sort of raised dais (78) where the king must have sat, near a small vestibule (77) that

Figure 21. The Royal Palace from the northwest, 1994. At right is the entrance from the "Royal Plaza."

would have been reserved for his use, for it leads to the Throne Room and to a stairway to the upstairs apartments. In the southeast corner is a kind of small annex (perhaps a cloakroom or a guardroom), with an opening to a long, narrow room equipped with a system of water pipes (67).

The so-called *Central Archives* were found dispersed in the area of Hall VI and Courtyard IV. They clearly fell here when the upper floor fell.

Southern Sector

There is a passage leading from the southeastern corner of Hall VI to the so-called "Courtyard V" (it is not clear if this space was really an open courtyard: research in progress). It contains a large shallow pool (8 m × 6 m; 0.38 m deep), the bottom of which was sealed in its final phase with plaster containing small gravel inclusions. The pool is positioned slightly to the east of the center, leaving room on the west for a well and a stone trough.

Three steps in the southwestern corner led down into the pool (these were hidden in the final phase). An 18-meter-long channel, passing under the wall and the street, was used to bring water from a building outside the palace walls (to the southeast; *Figs. 15:12; 20e*), where it was drawn from a well. A drainage channel in the northwest corner was linked to the main sewer to the west.

At the southwestern corner of the pool, the excavator thought he had identified an oven, designated in early reports as the "tablets oven" (see description of *South Archives* below for more details about this designation).

To the south of the courtyard is a wing of the building that has no direct egress to the outside. To the west, through room 84, is a door leading to the street along the rampart. The stairwells (69 and 80; the first flight of stone steps has survived) bear witness to the importance of the upstairs rooms. It is possible that this courtyard (or at least a part) was roofed, and the floor above (or at least a gallery upstairs) connected the southern wing of the building to the rest of the palace. Excavations uncovered many tablets in this area. Those that were found, scattered by their fall in the southern rooms and the southern part of the courtyard, are known as the *South Archives*. The tablets found in the ruins to the west of the courtyard are referred to as the *Southwest Archives*.

Central Sector

From the northeast corner of "Courtyard V," one can gain access to the northern area through a passage (62) and then across room 63 into an open room (64) with two columns that leads to Courtyard IV. The archives that were found in the southeast of this courtyard are known as the *Central Archives*.

A visitor would continue north from room 64 through rooms 34 and 35, each with stairwells that lead to the upstairs apartments; this may well have been the first part of the building that was constructed (highly altered in the 13th century B.C.E.). This brings us to Courtyard II.

Flanking this large courtyard to the east is a large, two-columned portico (38), the basalt bases of which have survived (in the final phase, they were hidden by renovations to the portico). This courtyard is equipped with a small square trough made of dressed flagstones. When it was discovered, it was filled with ashes from the fire that had destroyed the Palace, and this led the excavator to mistakenly designate it an oven, when in fact it must have contained water.

Courtyard II, which provides access to the palace's burial area, may have been the site of related ceremonies, for it leads on the north to room 28, where there are two large stone burial vaults, now very damaged. These royal tombs were pillaged in antiquity, and at the time of excavation they were unfortunately found with neither the remains of the deceased nor funerary offerings.

Figure 22. The Royal Palace: "Courtyard V" with basin, looking east, 1979.

Figure 23. The Royal Palace: garden of Courtyard III as seen from near pavilion 86, looking southwest, 1990. At the center: sounding of 1954.

Eastern Sector and Garden

Heading back south through Courtyard II, one can reach the eastern sector of the Palace (see *Fig. 24*), centered around a garden, the so-called Courtyard III (soundings were conducted in the middle of the courtyard in 1954–55 in order to examine earlier levels).

The highly damaged wall to the east marks the eastern boundary of the Palace. One is tempted to propose that there was an opening in it that would have made it possible to bring in provisions from the city to storerooms 89 and 90.

This "courtyard" actually comprised two parts. The first was a garden in the center surrounded by a circulation area leading to several buildings. The garden proper (that is to say, the part that must have been planted with trees and flowers) is surrounded by a stone wall that was perhaps 1.8 meters to 2 meters high. At any rate, it was high enough to ensure that the garden was secluded and hidden from sight. There are two doors in the garden wall, one to the north, the other to the south. In the northeastern corner is a small pavilion (86) with two columns in the front wall. Opening directly

Figure 24. The Royal Palace, looking northeast, 1990. On the right, an entrance to Palace Street between the Royal Palace and the North Palace; in the foreground is the "Oven House."

onto the garden and equipped with a well and a large stone trough, the pavilion must have been a cool, refreshing spot. One could walk through the corridor (87) behind the pavilion without disturbing those inside.

At the northwestern corner of Courtyard III, a small construction (44) butts against the strong walls of the buildings behind it. Among the remains of luxurious furniture found here were various high-quality objects made from elephant ivory, including decorative elements set into the wooden top of a round pedestal table, the head of a young male sculpted in the round (no. **22**), and a bed panel decorated in relief (no. **21**).

The southwestern side of the courtyard was bounded by a group of small rooms (58–61) that probably had a practical purpose and may have included a stairway leading directly from the garden to the royal apartments. To the southeast are large storerooms (89–90), one of which was found filled with jars.

Along the north side of Courtyard III is a complex of constructions that evoke an enjoyable life of leisure and festivities. There is a large room (45) with two columns, open along most of its southern side to the northern alley around the garden. Deep enough to provide shelter from the summer sun, the room would have benefited from natural lighting in the winter, when the sun is lower in the sky. In the final phase of the Palace's history, the opening was made narrower by the construction of walls between the columns and the side walls, thus darkening the room considerably. Room 45 leads to a group of rooms to the north that give access to Courtyard II and, by means of stairway 53, to the upper floor. Room 57 leads to another group of small rooms (54–56) where tablets were discovered (mainly administrative documents)—the so-called *East Archives*.

Today, the ruins include a passage in room 53 that leads to the outside and beyond, to Palace Street. Nevertheless, this part of the building was the object of so many alterations that we do not yet know whether such a passage existed during all periods of the Palace's existence.

Palace Archives

As we have already mentioned in the Palace tour above, archives of clay tablets with cuneiform script were discovered in several areas of the Palace. As is the case in other parts of the city, the way in which the tablets were found scattered indicates that they were stored in rooms upstairs but fell when the building was destroyed. These archives, named after the sites where they were found in the Palace, vary somewhat in form and content.

The West Archives

Found near the northwest entrance (rooms 2–5), these tablets are mainly administrative documents written in Ugaritic: lists of personnel (salaries), villages (taxes), and lists of trades. The most famous abecedary (no. **2a**) discovered at Ugarit was found near the base of the north column in the entrance porch. There are also letters in Akkadian and ritual texts in Hurrian.

The Annex Office of Archives

Some 20-odd texts were found in room 73, located to the west of the Throne Room and apparently totally cut off from the rest of the palace. The nature of the documents is quite disparate (letters, legal decisions, a mythological text, several texts concerning wine). These tablets are considered the remnant of an archive that had been moved elsewhere and was stored in an annex; they probably fell from the floor above, as well.

The Central Archives

The tablets in these archives were discovered in Courtyard IV, in the large room designated

Courtyard VI, and in several neighboring rooms, as well as on the remains of the walls. This dispersion supports the theory that the archives were kept on the floor above and fell when the roof collapsed. They are mostly Akkadian documents (no. **7**)—legal texts (contracts between individuals, deeds of sale, royal arbitrations, etc.) and royal letters—but there are also legal texts and letters in Ugaritic.

The Southwest Archives

The documents in the Southwest Archives were primarily found among the ruins in 81, in the nearby stairwell (80), and on the remains of the walls. Once again, this was clearly not their original place, and they must have fallen from the floor above. There is a wide variety of texts: mythological and ritual fragments in Ugaritic: lists of towns, tributes, and trades, two abecedaries, and letters in Akkadian, among others. Also found in room 81 were miniature liver models in ivory (no. **26**).

The South Archives

The documents of the South Archives were found scattered in Courtyard V, in the areas to the south (68, 69), and as far outside the building as the plaza between the Royal Palace and the house known as the South Palace (House of Yabninu). They include an extensive diplomatic correspondence in Akkadian regarding the relations of the kingdom of Ugarit with the Hittite overlord, with the king of Carchemish acting as intermediary, and other diplomatic relations with Syrian kings or high officials. There are a dozen-odd letters, legal documents, and so forth written in Ugaritic.

This is where the question of the so-called "tablets oven" arises. In the reports, the excavator referred to an oven situated in the southwest corner of the pool in Courtyard V, where he discovered tablets, some of which were letters assumed to have been written in the final phase of the kingdom, just before the destruction of the Palace and the city. He suggested that it was an oven used to bake administrative tablets that were kept in the archives. This is an enticing supposition, but it runs into too many undeniable difficulties and does not withstand analysis. To begin with, texts from the same group were found scattered over an extensive area covering the whole southern part of the courtyard itself, stairwell 69, and even outside the Royal Zone on a portion of the plaza separating the Palace from the South Palace. Not all of these sites can be identified as archival rooms.

In all likelihood, these tablets were kept on floors above and became mixed with the other rubble when they fell down with the walls and the ceilings; some of them fell at the spot where the "oven" was and where other, unbaked objects, such as alabaster pieces, also were found. Some of the tablets were hardened by the fire. What is more, the very existence of an oven here at the edge of the pool is questionable. Be that as it may, these considerations do not lessen the significance and the historical relevance of the tablets that were found here, though they can no longer be dated automatically to the very last days of the city.

The East Archives

The texts of the East Archives were found in the northeast section of Garden III in two distinct areas right next to each other but with no direct access between them—namely, in the areas to the northeast of the garden (54–57) and in stairwell 53 and the passage with two columns opposite it.

The texts are primarily in Ugaritic (letters; a mythological text; lists of trades, salaries, agricultural activities, weapons, furniture, etc.). Other documents are in Akkadian (copies of letters written by the king of Ugarit, letters addressed to him, a few legal judgments and accounting documents, etc.). There are also two magic texts in Hurrian, and a bilingual, Akkadian-Hurrian collection of maxims (no. **5**).

Selected Bibliography

1962, Schaeffer (C. F.-A.), 1962, *Ugaritica* IV, Paris, pp. 1–113.
1981, Calvet (Y.), "Installations hydrauliques d'Ugarit," *L'homme et l'eau* I, TMO Lyon, pp. 42–47.
1986, Callot (O.), "La région nord du Palais Royal d'Ougarit," *CRAIBL*, pp. 735–55.
1990, Calvet (Y.), "Les bassins du palais royal," *Syria* 67, pp. 31–42.
1995, Margueron (J.), "Le Palais royal d'Ougarit. Premiers résultats d'une analyse systématique," in *RSO* XI, pp. 183–202.

Publication of the Palace Archives

1957–70, *Palais Royal d'Ugarit*, II–VI, by C. Virolleaud, J. Nougayrol et al., Paris.

[2005] The royal palace, excavated in 1939 and 1948–1956, with secondary work continuing through 1960, but never published in final form, has in recent years become the object of a two-pronged program of research: analysis of the architectural and archaeological remains that are visible today, and a team approach to the study of the small objects (the team includes specialists in the various categories of objects discovered—for example, ceramics, metal, stone, glass and glass-like materials, ivory, bones, weights in various materials, inscriptions in several scripts and languages and the categories of realia named therein).

2001, Gachet (J.) and Pardee (D.), "Les ivoires inscrits du palais royal (fouille 1955)," in *RSO* XIV, pp. 191–230.
2004, Margueron (J.-C.), "Le palais royal d'Ougarit," in *Aux origines de l'alphabet: Catalogue Lyon 2004*, pp. 143–47.
In press, Gachet (J.), *RSO* XVI, *Les ivoires d'Ougarit: L'art des ivoiriers du Levant.*

Palace Annexes, North of the Royal Plaza

The Entrance on Palace Street

On the north side of the Royal Plaza, situated in front of the entrance to the palace, is a doorway leading to Palace Street (*Fig. 25:4*); this is the main entrance to the Palace from the city.

This entrance was well protected. Across the road, just a few meters east of the northwest corner of the Palace is a strong double doorway, with impressive jambs of ashlar stone that can still be seen in the walls on either side of the street (*Fig. 20b;* cf. *Fig. 10*). A sieve-like checkpoint, 3.2 meters long on the inside, was protected by two double doors, 2.75 meters wide on the Royal Plaza side (the stone door sill has survived) and 3 meters wide on the eastern side, leading to the city.

Several steps located on the west side led up from the Royal Plaza to the level of Palace Street. The floor inside the entranceway is level with the street on the city side to the east, despite appearances to the contrary. Because the street has been excavated far below the last level of its use, one receives the false impression that the door-sill stones blocking the passage to the east are steps.

The monumental size of this door and the thickness of its remains can be attributed to the fact that it protected the Royal Zone on the city side. It also may have supported a passage that must have crossed the street above the door, connecting the upper floor of the Palace to the Guardpost on the north side of the street (cf. *Fig. 19*).

The Guardpost (the so-called "Arsenal")

A doorway barred the entrance to Palace Street and also provided a link to the northern wall of the Palace. On the other side of the doorway was a building with an inner stairway (*Fig. 20c; 25:3*), that must have been a guardpost.

The discovery of a document with an inventory of weapons (bows and slings) that had been distributed to soldiers led the excavator to propose that this was the "Military Governor's Residence" and "Arsenal." But it is now clear that the building was simply a guard post protecting the entrance to the city. To anyone approaching the doorway at the end of "Palace Street" from the east, it looked as though the doorway was protected by two bastions, the guard post to the right (wherein a stairway attests to the existence of at least one upper floor), and the northern extension of the Palace wall jutting out to the left.

Behind the guard post (northeast of the Royal Plaza and along the eastern side of the Pillared Building) is an open area (*Fig. 25:5*); its construction implies that it may have had a practical function. All that we can say about this complex, however, is that it was part of the Royal Zone, for the organizational scheme remains unclear to us. The eastern and northern facades have no doors (at least on ground level) and do not directly connect to the city.

The Pillared Building

North of the Royal Plaza is a monumental construction excavated in 1937, which has now been designated the "Pillared Building" (*Fig. 25:2*). It allows no access to the areas situated to the north.

A rectangular building (a), consisting of two porches in a row with columns between them, serves as a monumental entrance from the south. Two parallel accesses, one with a massive stairway, the other in the form of a ramp, lead to a very large hall (b), 29 meters × 10 meters, completely paved, and fitted with a stone trough sunk into the ground (*Fig. 26*). The hall is divided in two. The eastern part served as a vestibule at the top of the stairway, while the larger part to the west constituted the hall proper. Aligned along the main east–west axis are three rectangular stone bases in the hall itself. A fourth is centered in the doorway between the hall and the eastern vestibule; there is also a round

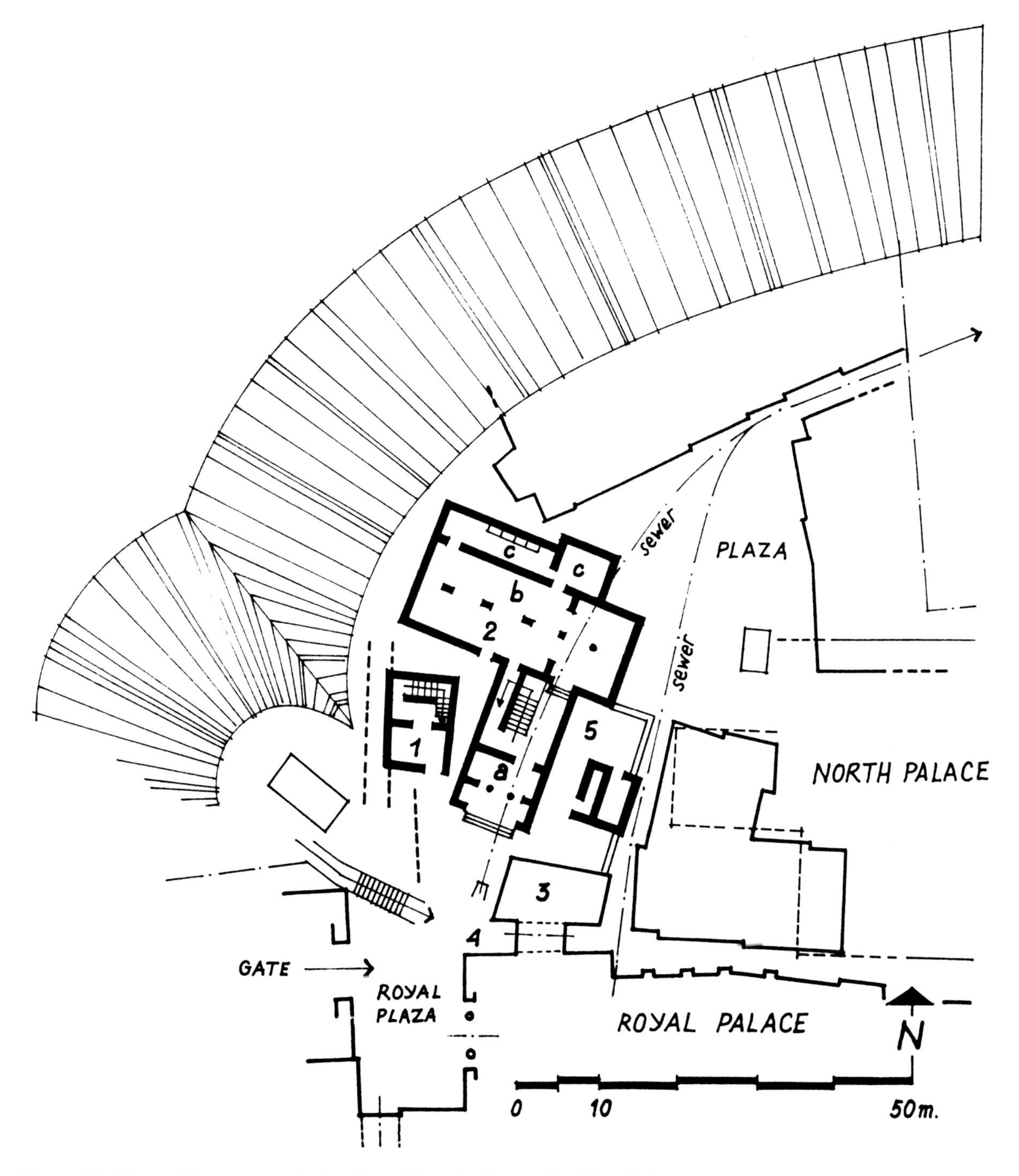

Figure 25. Plan of the annexes in the Royal Zone to the north of the Palace:
1. the "Hurrian Temple," 2. the "Pillared Building," 3. the guard post, 4. chambered doors, 5. open space.

pillar base in the vestibule. These served as bases for the wooden pillars support the roof and probably an upper floor.

Two doorways lead from the hall to rooms on the north (c), which are also paved with stone. One of the rooms is nearly square (5 meters); the other is a sort of corridor, 11 × 3 meters, with four stone troughs lining its northern wall—probably water troughs (rather than mangers).

In the early reports, this building was taken to be the "Stables" (or "Manège Royal" = Riding School) where the king's horses were kept. However, the layout of the entrances, with the monumental portico, stairways, and narrow passageways, and the care with which the large hall was paved render this interpretation unlikely and the designations inappropriate.

This beautiful construction was built in the 13th century B.C.E. and was a functional extension of the Royal Zone, as evidenced by the arrangement of the large entrance and the adjacent temple, both of which open onto the Royal Plaza.

Figure 26. The hall of the "Pillared Building," looking east, 1984.

In all likelihood, this pillared building was used for assemblies and banquets related to the ceremonies held in the temple.

The Palatial or Royal Temple (the So-Called "Hurrian Temple")

Within the angle formed by the large hall and the monumental entrance to the Pillared Building, against the rampart, stands a rectangular edifice (*Fig.* 15:9; 25:1). Its original construction probably dates to the end of the Middle Bronze Age. It was designated the "Hurrian Temple," or the "Temple with the Mitannian axe," in the reports because of the objects that were found in it (see below). The orientation of the complex differs from the Pillared Building, and it is clear that when the latter was built in the 13th century B.C.E., it was constructed in relation to the older temple, which abutted the rampart wall. The remains were already quite damaged at the time of the 1937 excavations, but despite the bad state of the ruins today and the difficulty in analyzing them, the overall layout can be reconstructed as follows.

The building, 12 meters in length from north to south and 8 meters maximum in width, is divided into two rectangular spaces, with an interior doorway in the center. The main entrance on the south side appears to be at the southeast corner instead of being axial, as are the entrances to the temples of Baal and Dagan on the acropolis. The interior doorway offers access from the vestibule to an area with a large stairwell. This is the same temple-tower layout that we will see in the the temples on the acropolis. The stairway would have led to a flat-roof terrace that overlooked the rampart. It is on this terrace that the ceremonies would have been held.

The corridor beneath the stairway yielded numerous lamps and all sorts of miniature vases used for votive offerings. The best-known objects uncovered during excavations (and to which the complex owes its names) are two figurines made of gold- and electrum-plated copper. One is a seated goddess (no. 16), and the other is a standing god. Also found was an exceptional iron axe with a copper and gold handle adorned with a boar (no. 60). C. Schaeffer considered the figurines to be of Hurrian origin and highlighted the affinities of the axe with Mitannian artifacts.

The location of this temple, entirely within the enclosure of the palace area, suggests that it might have served as a royal chapel. Mythological texts from Ugarit often refer to banquets of the gods, and these feasts were closely bound up with festivals and ceremonies held in temples. The need to provide enough space to accommodate the people who attended these events could account for the construction of the Pillared Building adjacent to the temple. Not only is there a long narrow passage along the eastern side of the temple that leads directly to a secondary entrance to the Pillared Building, but the main entrances to both buildings are situated very close to each other on the northern side of the Royal Plaza (*Figs.* 25:1 and 25:2:*a*).

The Main Sewer

The palace area had its own drainage system, instead of the drainage pits used in private homes. A network of pipes carried the water to a large main sewer. One entrance to it was located on the north side of the Royal Plaza (*Fig.* 15:8, 27*a*).

From the Royal Plaza, the main sewer could be reached through an underground passageway now blocked except for a short section at the entrance. The main sewer consisted of a stone-corbeled vault and was constructed in much the same way as the western postern gate and the funerary chambers.

The underground passage, which has been excavated in only a few places, runs north along the edge of the Royal Zone, passing under the guard post and the Pillared Building. In front of the

a. The entrance of the sewer, north of the "Royal Plaza," 1984.

b. The interior of a section of the underground sewer system, in front of the "Queen Mother's Residence," 1986.

Figure 27. The main sewer of the Royal Zone.

"Queen Mother's Residence" (see below), it joins another branch running directly from the Royal Palace under the street. It then turns to the right toward the northwest slope of the tell (*Fig.* 30). Due to the erosion of this edge of the tell, it is difficult to determine exactly where and how it ends. Various pipes carried drainage to the main sewer. The system included pipes from the Palace itself. The sewer also filled with water from the buildings situated along its path, either rain-water spouting from gargoyles to the ground, or water flowing through enclosed channels (see also p. 58).

Selected Bibliography

1986, Callot (O.), "La région nord du Palais Royal d'Ougarit," *CRAIBL*, pp. 735–55.

1989, Calvet (Y.), "La maîtrise de l'eau à Ougarit," *CRAIBL*, pp. 308–26.

The House of Yabninu
(The So-Called "South Palace" or "Small Palace")

The buildings in the southern part of the Royal Palace overlook a sort of plaza (*Fig.* 15:14) to which they have no direct access. Tablets belonging to the *South Archives* (see Royal Palace, p. 36) were found in the northwest part of the plaza.

A large residence is located on the south of the plaza. Excavated in 1955, this residence is generally referred to in earlier excavation reports as the "South Palace" or the "Small Palace." A group of more than 60 tablets was discovered in it. The excavators pointed out a number of interesting artifacts, which were mentioned in the reports, and the texts have been published, but an architectural study has not yet been conducted.

The whole building (*Fig.* 28) is a single architectural unit, surrounded by public roads. Excavation of the southern area has not been completed, but the currently visible part of the house covers more than 1,000 square meters, 35 meters from east to west, 28 meters from north to south along the western facade, and a good deal longer on the eastern facade.

The building was carefully constructed and manifests a fairly regular overall layout, with rectilinear facades on the western and northern sides (except for a stairway jutting out at the northeast corner). Rooms 224–226, a utilitarian complex situated to the southeast, appears to have been added on to the exterior of the building, but the excavation of the southwest area will have to be resumed before we can analyze the complete plan.

The main entrance is on the western side. Based on our current knowledge, we are unable to determine whether there were other entrances, although it is likely. If there were, how many were there, and were there other stairways in addition to the northeastern one (the first flight of this one has survived)? There may have been stairs to the right of entrance 211, and it is likely that there was another stairway to the south near 231. We also would like to determine exactly which areas were enclosed and which were open. The schematic plan published in 1979 (*SDB*, fig. 920) mistakenly designates most of the large areas as courtyards. The plan published here takes into account whenever possible the results of more recent studies of Ugaritic architecture. So far, only the water supply and drainage system in the southeastern part of the building have been analyzed thoroughly.

The main entrance is located nearly in the middle of the west side of the building facing the street that separates the building from the rampart. A large doorway opens onto a large vestibule (211). To the left, an opening leads to a room with a well. In the room in the far northwest corner (214), the excavator thought he had identified a small funerary chamber, but it appears now to be an extremely large drainage pit.

Opposite the main entrance is a slightly off-center doorway leading to a paved courtyard (212), which in turn provides access to the rest of the building. On the north side is a two-columned portico leading to the north rooms where tablets were found. These documents were found scattered over a fairly large area and on top of the ruins of walls. This area included part of the large hall designated 203, and a small room, 204. Some tablets were even recovered outside the building on the plaza to the north. As in the Royal Palace, the dispersion of tablets indicates that they fell from archives situated on the upper story, in the northern part of the residence.

On the eastern side of courtyard 212, the door leading to room 213 was blocked during the final

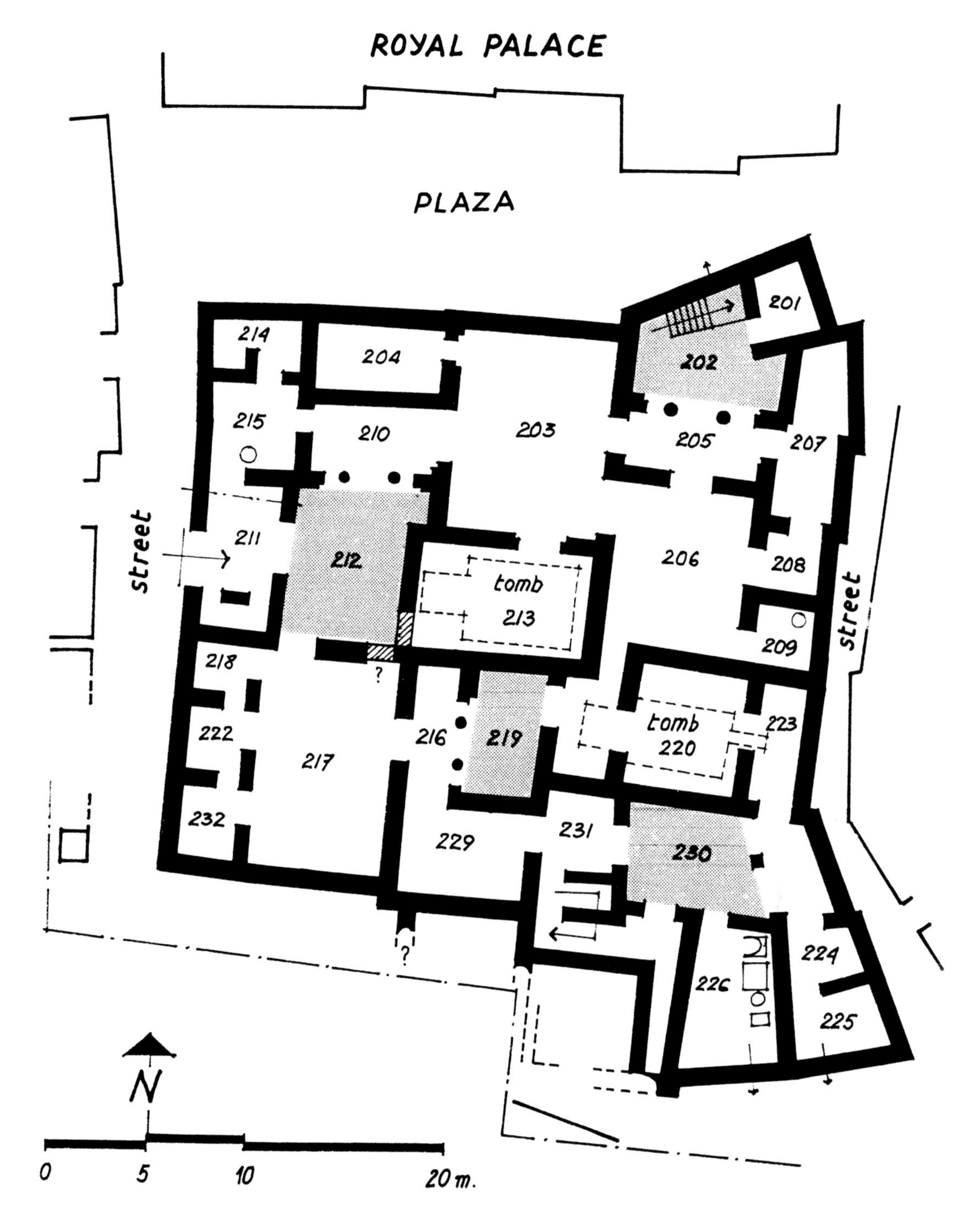

Figure 28. Schematic plan of the House of Yabninu (the so-called "South Palace" or "Small Palace").

years of the city, and it could only be reached from the northern side. In this room, a tomb roofed with corbeled stone was found, making the room one of the largest funerary chambers presently known on the tell. The tomb was looted in antiquity, but the excavator found remains of the rich funerary furnishings, notably alabaster vases including a fragment bearing a cartouche of Pharaoh Ramses II.

An opening on the southern side of the courtyard leads to what was perhaps one of the private areas of the dwelling. The bulk of the southwestern part of the building is occupied by a large hall (217), which opened onto three small rooms with a bath and drain pipes (218, 222, 232). In a nearby courtyard with a two-columned porch (216, 219), a number of vases were found, including locally manufactured storage jars and craters imported from Crete or from the Mycenaean workshops of the Dodecanesus (no. **32**). On the east side of porch 219, a doorway leads to a tomb built under room 220, which is oriented in the same direction as the tomb in room 213.

To the southeast of room 220 is the utilitarian part of the house. This area comprised: a courtyard (230); probably a stairway leading to the first floor (south of 231); and rooms 224–226, which constituted a kitchen area, equipped with an elaborate water supply and drainage system (pipes, wells, stone trough, etc.).

Based on what can be seen today, we can say that this house meets the criteria of typical Ugaritic domestic architecture, though on a larger scale: division between private and professional parts (with the archives kept upstairs), an area for

Figure 29. The House of Yabninu: the southeast section, facing east, 1979.

social activities, utilitarian areas (toilets, storage rooms, kitchens, etc.), family tombs (in this case, two areas were set aside for this purpose, thereby confirming the important place given to family funerary cults). This residence, however, is an example of a quite luxurious residence, reserved for a person of high rank, whose social status is confirmed by the proximity of the house to the Royal Palace.

Texts

Sixty-seven written documents were found in the northern part of the residence itself (203, 204): 60 in Akkadian, 5 in Ugaritic (including an abecedary, no. **2b**), and 2 in Cypro-Minoan. These archives are of great interest and have provided us with what is apparently the name of the last owner of this residence in the final phase of its history, a person named Yabninu who was prominent in the kingdom around 1200 B.C.E.

The documents are primarily economic texts in Akkadian: maritime bills of lading; transactions involving commodities such as grains, oil, milk, fish, animals, wool, tools, and metal ore; lists of foreign residents; and so on.

The texts and archaeological artifacts indicate that Yabninu was in charge of commercial activities with countries linked to Ugarit by sea: Cyprus (tablets in Cypro-Minoan), the Phoenician and Palestinian coast (textual references to Arwad, Byblos, Tyre, Akko, Ashdod, and Ashkelon), Egypt (base of statue inscribed with hieroglyphs), and the Aegean region (Minoan and Mycenaean pottery).

Selected Bibliography

1962, Schaeffer (C.), *Ugaritica* IV, pp. 121–48.
1979, Courtois (J.-C.), in *SDB*, s.v. "Ras Shamra: archéologie," cola. 1234–40.
1981, Calvet (Y.), "Installations hydrauliques d'Ugarit," *L'homme et l'eau* I, Lyon, pp. 40–42.
1990, Courtois (J.-C.), "Yabninu et le palais sud d'Ougarit," *Syria* 67, pp. 103–42.

Publication of the Texts

1965, C. Virolleaud, in *PRU* V.
1970, J. Nougayrol, in *PRU* VI.

The Northwest Area beyond the Royal Zone

Outside the Royal Zone, just on the other side of the doorway that cuts across Palace Street, there is a street on the left that runs in front of the guard-post and leads to the far northwest sector of the tell.

Building (Sanctuary?) with a Rock-Hewn Throne

The complex (*Fig.* 30:1) opposite the palace's north wall, on the corner where the two streets meet, was built during the final phase of the city's history and must have encroached on the south-west corner of the North Palace. Judging from its special architectural features, it is possible that the building housed a place of worship, although this hypothesis cannot be confirmed without further analysis. Remains of sculpted stone blocks were found there, notably a chair or throne with a high back and a piece of worked stone that appears to represent a lion.

The Northwest Plaza

The street proceeds north to an irregularly shaped plaza (*Fig.* 30:4) situated to the east and well below the level of the Pillared Building. This plaza apparently dates to the last phase of the city (mid-13th century B.C.E.?). The architectural remains that can be seen today mainly belong to constructions that date to an earlier phase but that were later buried under the Northwest Plaza, the surface of which was originally much higher than the level reached by excavation.

The branch of the sewer system that approaches from Palace Street runs north along the west side of the Northwest Plaza and joins the branch from the Royal Palace in front of the Queen Mother's Residence. It then turns northeast and continues under the road, parallel to the edge of the tell.

In the middle of the Northwest Plaza, the rectangular construction with four plain walls was in fact sunk into the ground. Its purpose has not been established. The absence of an entrance belies the theory that it was the funerary chamber of a tomb, and although it has features similar to a water pool, there is no evidence of waterproofing, water supply pipes, or cleaning holes.

Finally, note that the excavation of the house on the northeast corner of the plaza (*Fig.* 30:3) has not been completed.

The Queen Mother's Residence

North of the plaza is a large building oriented to the edge of the tell. It was designated the "Queen Mother's Residence" because of a reference in one of the texts found here; it is also sometimes referred to as the "house with lead ingots" because of the large argentiferous lead ingots discovered in the building. Actually, however, the ingots probably belong to an earlier level.

The house, which was excavated in 1938–39, opens to the south, but erosion along the edge of the tell has destroyed the northern part (several doors that open onto the slope of the tell once led to rooms that today have disappeared). The part of the building that can be seen today has a roughly rectangular shape, 35 meters long from east to west and 13 meters wide (more than 400 square meters). The usual features of Ugaritic domestic architecture appear in this complex, but otherwise it contrasts sharply with other common dwellings both in architectural quality and scale.

The complex was excavated well below the level of the last phase of the visible structures. The foundations are now clearly viewable (*Fig.* 31) as are the superimposed thresholds of the various

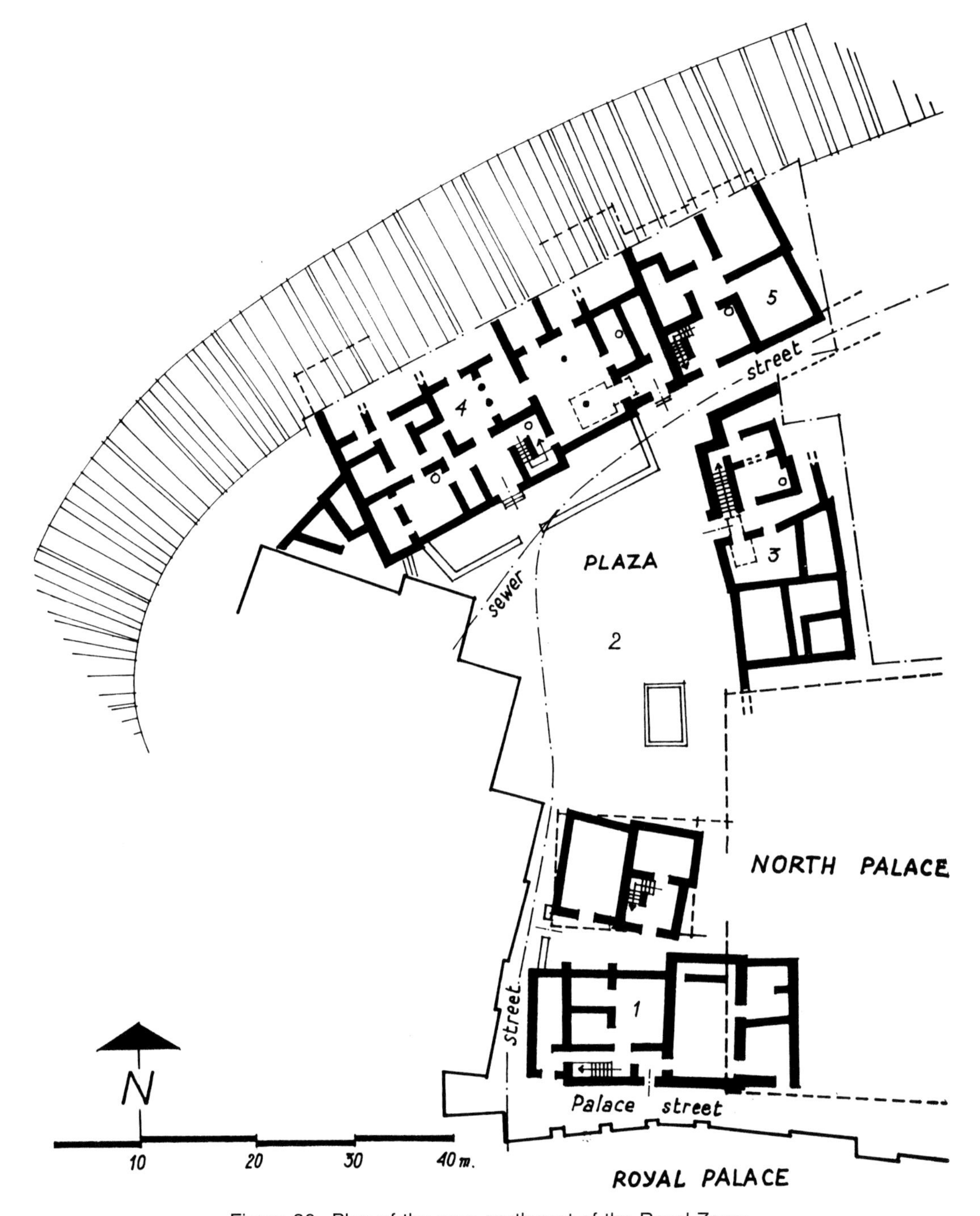

Figure 30. Plan of the area northwest of the Royal Zone:
1. building with rock-hewn throne; 2. Northwest Plaza (13th century); 3. a house to the northeast; 4. the "Queen Mother's Residence"; 5. house adjoining.

Figure 31. Northwest area: southern facade of the "Queen Mother's Residence," 1984.
Note the different levels of thresholds (excavated below ground level) and the channels that join the sewer.

Figure 32. Houses in the northwest section of the tell: 1976 excavations.
a. Residence "1975–1976": portico with column bases; b. house with sink: stone trough filled with tableware.

stages of construction and restoration during the Late Bronze Age. The residence is divided into two communicating parts, each provided with its own entrance from the street to the south.

One enters the western part from the south through a large door (2 meters wide) with a stone sill. A vestibule provides access to the rest of the house. To the right is a stairwell (of which the first flight of stone steps has survived) and the drainage pit of the latrines (as well as a drain pipe).

Opposite the entrance, there is a large courtyard, and to its east, a porch with columns. The courtyard connects with the area in which the tomb was located. The tomb, in accordance with standard Ugaritic configuration, has its own independent entrance from outside leading to the dromos of the tomb. From this area, access is gained to two rooms without windows on the east (perhaps storage rooms), and two doors lead to the north. To the left of the entrance vestibule is a group of rooms around a stone-paved courtyard that also opens onto the north. The living quarters would have been located on the upper floor, which was accessed by the stairway near the main entrance; the living quarters occupied the entire length of the house.

The pipes that pass through the wall at different heights mark the successive levels of the ground floor in various periods. They drained water into the sewer that runs under the street to the south.

Because of the destruction of the northern part (we now have only the slope of the tell), it is impossible to determine the house's shape on the north side, although it is clear from the walls running north–south and from the doors opening onto the void that the complex continued northward.

The House Adjoining the Queen Mother's Residence

In 1972, excavations began on the house to the east of the Queen Mother's Residence that shares a common wall with it (*Fig.* 30:5). Its northern end is also missing. At present, it has a very basic square plan (15 meters), with a small central courtyard, allowing light and air to reach the ground floor. The entrance on the south leads to a large hall with a well and to a stairway situated to the west (of which several stone steps remain). Opposite, a doorway leads to a small, nearly square courtyard (3.2 × 3.5 meters), from which access to the rest of the house is gained.

The Main Sewer (Continued)

The main sewer reappears under the northeast corner of the Pillared Building (see above, p. 46), continues to the edge of the tell, turning east (*Fig.* 27*b*), passes in front of the Queen Mother's Residence (whose drain pipes empty into it), and follows the street that heads northeast between other houses, which have not yet been completely unearthed. Its outer end and its drainage site outside the tell have disappeared because of erosion.

Residence "1975–1976"

Proceeding east along the edge of the tell, one reaches an area excavated in 1975–1976 (cf. *Fig.* 13). The southern part of a large residence was uncovered. The monumental entrance on the south leads to spaces that are difficult to analyze because so much of the dwelling has disappeared with the erosion of the edge of the tell. There is, for instance, a two-columned portico (*Fig.* 32*a*) in the western part of the building that opens onto the void to the north. We can imagine that the entire house covered a surface area of at least 30 square meters.

The remains of this building include elements characteristic of very high-quality architectural work: two double-columned porticoes, courtyards, a stone stairway, and a very fine funerary vault.

House with Sink (Local Tavern?)

To the west of this residence, the 1975–76 excavators began uncovering a house that has not yet been totally exposed. A large stone trough (*Fig.* 32*b*) was found full of tableware, no doubt placed there at the time of the conflict that marked the end of the city and left behind when the inhabitants fled. Could this structure once have served as a tavern?

Selected Bibliography

1938, Schaeffer (C. F.-A.), "Rapport . . . ," *Syria* 19, pp. 313–20, pls. 30, 35.
1977, Margueron (J.), "Rapport . . . ," *Syria* 54, pp. 151–88.
1986, Callot (O.), 1986, "La région nord du Palais Royal d'Ougarit," *CRAIBL*, pp. 735–55.

[2005]

Residence "1975–1976"

In 2002, the excavation of the "Residence 1975–76" was renewed and the northern boundary of the house was discovered at the level of its foundations. An exhaustive analysis of the ceramics unearthed by the original excavation has also appeared.

2002, Monchambert (J.-Y.), "Rapport de chantier," Unpublished archives of the French mission.
2004, Monchambert (J.-Y.), *La céramique d'Ougarit, campagnes de fouille 1975 et 1976*, *RSO* XV, Paris.

The North Palace

Proceeding east on Palace Street, one finds on the left the ruins of the North Palace (*Fig.* 33). This is one of the few structures still visible that was not in use during the last stage of the city's history, except perhaps by squatters. Some parts of the building (the center in particular) are badly preserved and therefore difficult to interpret. On the other hand, there are several massive wall foundations (more than 1.5 meters thick) that are still spectacular. Our knowledge of the building is based on preliminary excavation reports from the 1969–72 seasons. However, the diagrams that were published show only the floor plan and provide no architectural analysis.

The construction seems to be of very high quality. Some sections of the walls have carefully bonded orthostats, and a very hard mortar was used for the floors.

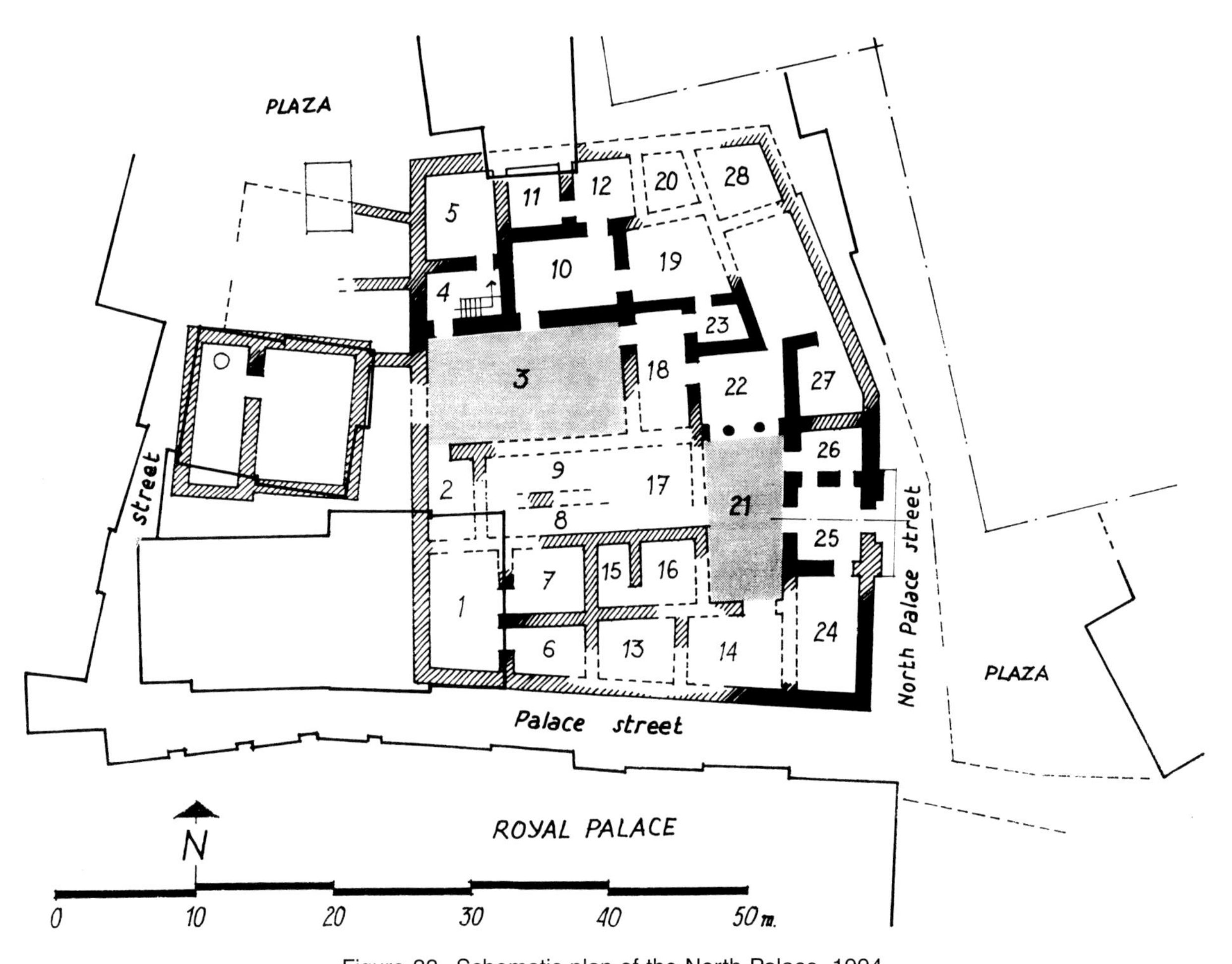

Figure 33. Schematic plan of the North Palace, 1994.

Figure 34. The North Palace. Bitumen-coated orthostats north of Courtyard III, 1992.

Figure 35. The entrance to the North Palace from the east, 1992.

This huge complex must have covered at least 1,500 square meters (although its western limits cannot be determined precisely). It is oriented almost exactly to the points of the compass. The entrance is on the east side, from North Palace Street, while Palace Street runs along its southern side. The northern facade on the edge of the excavations is almost totally destroyed and resists analysis. To the west, it is difficult to distinguish the complex from the later structures that were built on top of it at the end of the Late Bronze Age.

The monumental entrance on North Palace Street is a stairway with two stone steps, one of which is a 3-meter-long monolith (*Fig.* 35). One enters a roofed vestibule (25), which is flanked by two rooms, while straight ahead is a rectangular courtyard (21). The door is located on the longitudinal side of the courtyard, which is 12 meters long. The entrance's monolithic sill bears traces of the double doors that closed it. Extending the longitudinal axis to the north is a 4.7-meter-deep room that opened onto the court (22). The opening was supported by two columns, one base of which has survived. This structural sequence—an entrance vestibule leading to a courtyard extended by an open room with columns perpendicular to the vestibule—is a standard configuration for late Ugaritic palatial architecture. The same layout is found in the House of Yabninu (or South Palace) and in an even more elaborate form in the Royal Palace itself, where the courtyard leads to the throne room. In any case, the example in the North Palace is the oldest yet found on the tell.

Two doorways, on either end at the rear of room 22, provide access to the northern half of the building. This area was probably the private part of the house. Nearby, there is a large courtyard (3), 14.50 × 8.30 meters, with a drainage pit in the center. Its northern wall is lined with orthostats (averaging 1.10 meters high) coated with bitumen. The bitumen may have served as an adhesive for a decorative veneer. Analyses have shown that the bitumen came from a deposit at Kfarieh, in the Nahr el-Kebir Valley, about 30 kilometers away.

The northwest corner of the North Palace has a stairwell (of which several steps have survived) and latrines. Apparently, other facilities such as baths were located in the adjacent room. The rooms in the northeastern part of the complex appear to have had similar utilitarian functions.

Excavation reports mention only one entrance (the monumental entrance on the east) and one stairway (on the northwest, next to the latrines). We would expect a building of this size to be equipped with several secondary entrances, and it is surprising that there is only one small stairway leading to the upper floor (or floors). This is especially true, given the massive thickness of the walls, which were capable of supporting at least one upper story. Equally surprising is the distance between the stairway we know about and the entrance, for in later constructions the two are usually situated in the same vicinity. It is very likely that there in fact were other entrances and stairways that have not been located due to the badly damaged state of the ruins.

The date of construction has long been the subject of debate. At one time, it was thought to be dated to the end of the Middle Bronze Age, but soundings in 1994 beneath the foundations of the southeast corner have demonstrated that it was actually built during Late Bronze I. The relatively abundant, albeit highly fragmentary, ceramics bear witness to the use of the complex in the 16th century. The North Palace was carefully emptied of its contents before being abandoned, perhaps when the king decided to construct the new Royal Palace in the 15th century and, for this reason, very few characteristic objects were discovered in it; nevertheless, the ceramic fragments found in the floors lead us to conclude that the building had fallen out of use by around 1400.

Selected Bibliography

1970, Schaeffer (C. F.-A.), "Rapport . . . ," *Syria* 47, pp. 209–13.

1972, Lagarce (J. et E.), "Chantier du palais aux orthostates (Palais nord)," in H. de Contenson et al., "Rapport . . . ," *Syria* 49, pp.15–25;

1972, Schaeffer (C.), "Note additionnelle sur les fouilles dans le Palais nord d'Ugarit," ibid., pp. 27–29.

1973, H. de Contenson et al., "Rapport . . . 33e campagne," AAAS XXIII, pp. 129–34.

1973, Lagarce (J. and E.), "Le chantier du palais nord," in H. de Contenson et al., "Rapport . . . ," *Syria* 50, pp. 297–308.

1991, Deschesne (O.), Connan (J.), and Dessort (D.), "Les bitumes archéologiques de Ras Shamra," in *RSO* VI, pp. 101–22.

1994, Mallet (J.), "Sondage dans le Palais nord: Rapport de chantier" (unpublished; archives of the French mission).

The "Oven House" and Plaza

Farther east on Palace Street, on the north side, are the remains of a house known as the "Oven House" (*Fig.* 36), excavated in 1973. A 1992 probe beneath the last levels of occupation reached a Middle Bronze level, from which the corpse of a child buried in a jar was unearthed.

In its present state, the building has a somewhat irregular but nearly square shape (12–14 × 10 meters). Three of its sides are detached, while the fourth, to the east, is shared by a block of houses that is still unexcavated. There is an entrance to the south with carved stone door jambs. The entrance leads to a vestibule with access to a variety of rooms on both sides, in which many utilitarian installations and objects were found (ovens, drainage pit, jars, stone vat). The family tomb, situated at the rear and to the right, was pillaged in ancient times.

The building dates to the beginning of the Late Bronze Age and is, along with the North Palace, one of the rare example of construction from this period. It should, however, be kept in mind that it was not visible during the last stage of the city's history. The whole of this zone to the east of the North Palace was transformed in the course of the Late Bronze Age. At the end of this period, when this section was reorganized (ca. 1250 B.C.E.?), the house was demolished and the space was turned into a public area and to provide space for the construction projects around it; it thus became a small "plaza." A building, only a part of which has been unearthed, flanked this plaza on the east.

Selected Bibliography

1974, Contenson (H. de), Courtois (J.-C.), et al., "Rapport . . . ," *Syria* 51, pp. 25–28. Cf. J.-C. Courtois, "L'architecture domestique," *UF* 11, 1979, pp. 106–8, fig. 2.

1992, Mallet (J.), "Sondage dans la Maison aux Fours: Rapport de chantier" (unpublished, archives of the French mission).

The Residential Quarter

Proceeding east toward the center of the tell, Palace Street leads to a large residential area immediately to the east of the Royal Palace and separated from it by only a narrow street (*Fig.* 36). It was excavated between 1953 and 1973, and today its boundaries are hardly distinguishable.

The excavations uncovered public streets and blocks of private "houses," some of which yielded archives of great importance. Due to the nature of the buildings, this zone was sometimes designated the "Residential Quarter" in the reports and sometimes the "Aegean Quarter" because of the discovery of artifacts with connections to Greece and Cyprus (for instance, tablets written in the "Cypro-Minoan" script; e.g., no. 6).

Note: Only a few preliminary reports were published on the excavations in this section. The descriptions that follow are based on these and on our own, on-site observations since 1992, when the study of specific complexes was resumed (although the analyses have not yet been completed). Consequently, many of the conclusions must be considered provisional. We will limit our descriptions of this quarter to a few architectural units ("houses") that have been recognized as such and that we have been able to analyze, and to places that have become well known in specialized literature because of the tablets that were found in them (such as the houses of Rapanu and Rasapabu).

The western side of this residential area (*Fig.* 36) is separated from the Royal Palace by a narrow street. Its northern, eastern, and southern boundaries represent the extent of the excavation and do not reflect the urban structure. The quarter is divided into blocks by two main streets that run more or less northwest to southeast. For the sake of convenience, we have retained the names that the excavators gave them: "Merneptah Street" and "Palace Street" (to which we have added the designation "Eastern section," in order to distinguish it from the part of Palace Street that runs along the north side of the Royal Palace).

In addition to these two streets, the blocks are delimited by streets and dead-end lanes running perpendicular to them. In the current state of excavations, only the first block to the west is entirely delimited by public roads. We know the entire perimeter of a second block in the center, except for a very small portion on the northwest. There is a third block to the east that stretches over a considerable area and well beyond the limits of the excavation to the east and north, but we know neither its shape nor its extent. We can say nothing about the others, the majority of which lie beyond the limits of the excavations.

The remains that can be seen today date to the last phase of construction, and in many cases the structures were remodeled or rebuilt toward the end of the Late Bronze Age (13th century B.C.E.) and then abandoned early in the 12th century. By and large, the buildings are carefully designed and constructed. They are characteristically Ugaritic in architecture, using carved stone blocks for the bases of the walls and door-jambs, combined with carefully fabricated mortar-and-rubble construction.

The Street between the Royal Palace and Block 1

A fairly narrow road, running more or less from north to south, separates the eastern limit of the palace from the rest of the city (alongside the complex known as the "House of the Alabaster Vessels"). The ruins in this area, however, are not preserved well enough for a detailed analysis.

The Eastern Section of Palace Street

The excavator considered the street between Blocks 1 and 2 to be a continuation of Palace

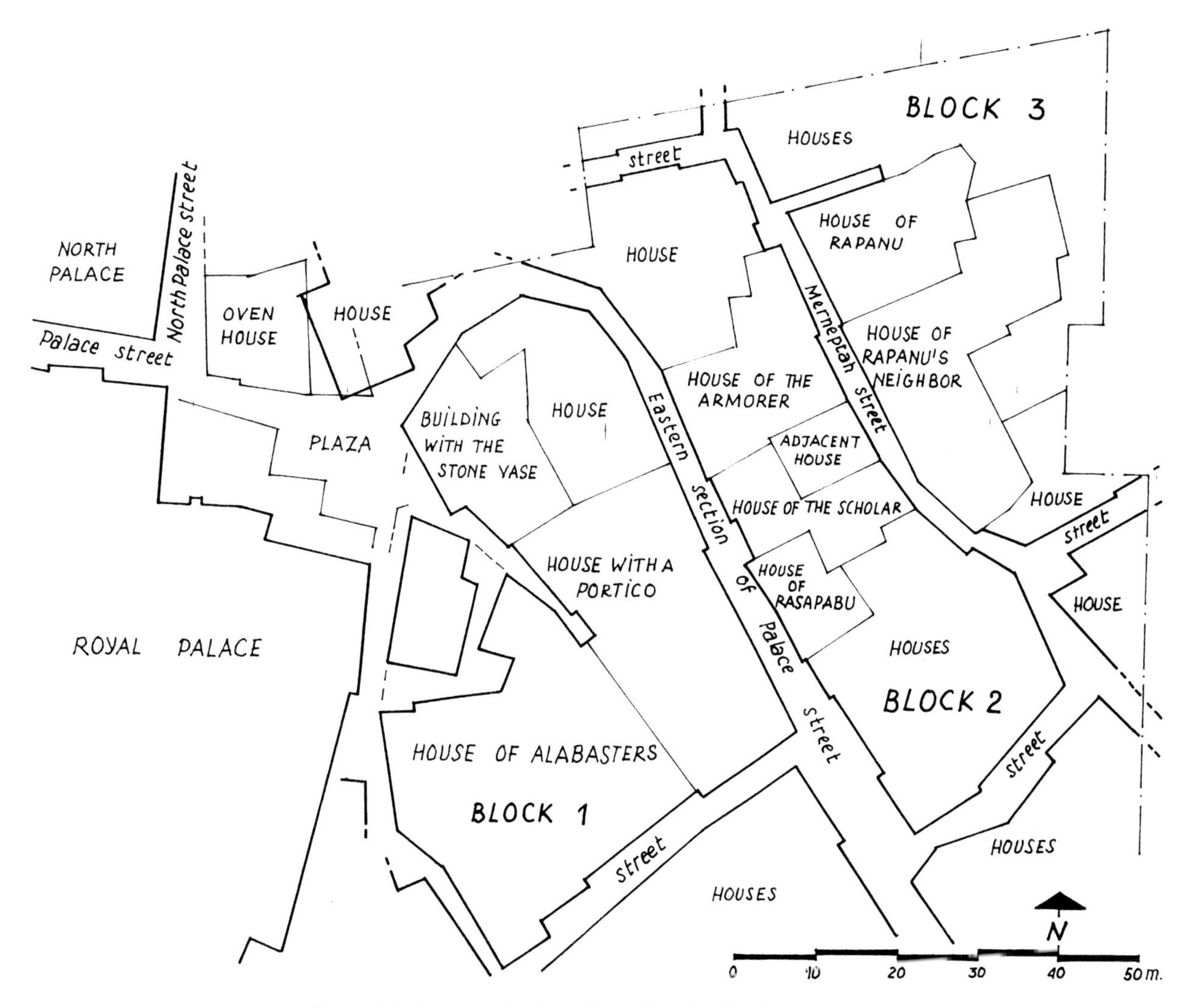

Figure 36. Schematic plan of the Residential Quarter, 1994.
The houses drawn here correspond to the state of the architectural analyses in 1994.

Street. It has been excavated over a length of about 70 meters. The street continues beyond the northeastern corner of the Royal Palace, after which, in the last phase, it widened into a plaza (built over the "Oven House"). It then turns right between two blocks of the residential area and proceeds to the south, where it is intersected by the perpendicular street that runs along the south side of the second block. Its width varies with the structures that flank it: from 2.5 meters in front of the House of the Armorer to 4.3 meters outside the House of the Scholar. It narrows sharply to about 3 meters where the northwestern corner of the House of Rasapabu juts out and then widens again south of the "House with the Portico" into a kind of small, elongated plaza.

Merneptah Street

Merneptah Street has been excavated for 80 meters and is named after the late-13th-century pharaoh whose cartouche was engraved on a sword found in the House of the Armorer (no. **62**). The street is flanked on both sides by houses that we will describe below. The street does not follow a straight line, and its width varies with the buildings that flank it: it is 3.5 meters wide at the northern end of the excavations, and it narrows abruptly to 1.9 meters where the northeastern corner of the House of the Armorer juts out into the street. It averages 2.5 meters wide the rest of the way. At the southern end, it intersects with a street on the east that delimits Block 3 and probably meets up with street 1038 on the east, in the City Center. Farther south, it intersects with the street on the west that marks the southern boundary of Block 2.

Block 1
(west of the easternmost section of Palace Street; Fig. 36)

Southwestern Part:
The House of Alabaster Vessels

To the southwest of the eastern section of Palace Street (*Figs.* 36, 37) stands a large complex with multiple stories, covering 800 square meters). It is located between the street that runs along the eastern edge of the Royal Palace and a dead-end lane coming from the plaza to the north.

This complex was excavated in the early 1970s and is known only from preliminary reports. The excavators considered it a single house and named it the "House of the Alabaster Vessels" because of the 40-odd alabaster vases found in the southwest section. In addition to these vases imported from Egypt, a wide variety of fine furnishings were discovered here. This led to the supposition that, in the last half of the 13th century B.C.E., the owner was a person of high rank whose duties put him in contact with Egypt (perhaps he was a foreign diplomat or Ugaritic merchant).

In all likelihood, here, as elsewhere in the city, the interior was reorganized in the course of time, and the complex seems to have been divided into several distinct houses during its final phase. But despite its apparently disorderly plan, in its original state, this half-block was a single architectural entity built on a series of bench terraces—a construction technique that actually made the entire block into a single architectural unit, despite interior divisions into separate houses.

The plan is roughly triangular (with the summit to the northwest and the base along the street to the south). The complex has several entrances: there are two doors on its 55-meter-long side facing the street to the west; one on the dead-end

Figure 37. Schematic plan of Block 1 (for the proposed demarcation of the houses, see *Fig. 36*). This scheme represents analyses and research as of 1994.

lane to the east (the facade along this street is about 30 m long; the southeast part of the house shares a common wall with the "house with the portico"); and finally, at least one and perhaps two on the street to the south in an area that is largely destroyed.

There are two parts, located on two levels, with nearly a 1.7-meter vertical difference between them. An interior stone stairway in Courtyard U made it possible to move from one part to the other. The section to the south may have been reserved for social activities: in the southeast, reception rooms (?) and a tomb (which had been looted in antiquity); in the southwest, a kitchen and storerooms in which jars were found, along with several Mycenaean rhytons and figurines in bronze and stone (which suggest the existence of a domestic cult). The living quarters were upstairs. Only one stairway has been identified by the excavators; it is located near one of the entrances to the west. But in all likelihood there were others, perhaps in the damaged area along the southern facade. In the final phase, there was an industrial, commercial establishment in the northwest, complete with storerooms and installations for processing olives.

During this phase, some of the doors were blocked, and a series of continuous partition walls (not in line with the rest) seems to have been added to divide the building into two separate houses, each of which may have been further divided into even smaller homes. There would have then been a rectangular part (containing one or two homes) opening onto the street to the south, and a triangular part (with two or three homes) opening onto the dead-end lane to the north and the street on the palace side. The reduction of living space at the beginning of the 12th century B.C.E. is a phenomenon that has been observed in numerous districts (in the City Center, for instance); this phenomenon is consistent with analyses of the economic and fiscal texts and supports the hypothesis that there was an increase in urban population density and a decline in rural population during this period.

Northern Part: The Building with the Large Stone Vase

In the northwest portion of Block 1 (*Figs.* 36, 37) is a small building that has attracted much attention because of the presence of a beautiful stone vase measuring more than a meter high (*Fig.* 38). Its shape is reminiscent of the small round pyxides in ivory that have been found in tombs. This building was excavated in 1966, and the study (unpublished) was resumed in 1992. It is difficult to determine what it was; all that can be said at present is that its layout does not correspond to the plan of a private home.

The entrance, on the plaza to the west, leads to a large rectangular room (1); smaller rooms occupy the northeastern part. The thickness of the walls in Room 1 (0.95 meters) suggests that the building was taller at this spot, and it is possible that, immediately to the left of the entrance, there was a stairway leading to the second floor, and from there to a flat-roof terrace above rooms 3–5. To the south, another area (7–9), divided by a wall, was perhaps related to the other rooms.

Following the curve of the block, there are small "rooms" along of the Eastern section of Palace Street that appear to open onto the street. These rooms may have been shops that formed a kind of bazaar. They were connected by a courtyard to an area that may have been a "house," situated in the eastern part of the block's northern zone. There is a funerary vault in its southern part.

Southeastern Part: House with a Portico

In the southeastern part of the same block (*Figs.* 36, 37), a large house known as the "House with a

Portico" (and sometimes also as the "House with the Porch with columns") stretches over an area of more than 450 square meter. It was excavated in 1953 and 1966. The Eastern section of Palace Street runs along its eastern side. On the west, it opens onto a dead-end lane, and its southwestern part shares a wall with the House of the Alabaster Vessels. Its southern boundary is the street running perpendicular to Palace Street, while its north end is built directly against the other structures.

The house has a nearly rectangular plan. It is made up of two parts that are approximately the same size (one between Palace Street and the dead-end lane; the other adjoining the House of Alabasters). There is one door, 1.75 meters wide, in the center between the two parts (between Room 12 and courtyard 3). The main entrance from Palace Street is located in the southern part of the building and leads to a vestibule (1) and then to a paved courtyard (3), from which access is gained to the two parts of the house. The southern part has very thick walls (up to 1 meter) and a fairly regular plan. To the right of the entrance vestibule (1) is a long narrow space (2), perhaps a stairwell. South of the

Figure 38. Block 1: The Building with the Large Stone Vase, looking southeast, 1994.

courtyard (3) is a sizable room (6) that provides access to a row of large rooms on the west (including a kitchen) and a row of small rooms along the eastern wall.

The other entrance to the house, from the dead-end lane on the west, leads into a vestibule (19), which leads in turn to a space (17) that opens onto the rest of the house. To the northwest is a small recess (18), perhaps a stairwell; to the southeast is the southern part of the house; and straight ahead, through a wide passage with two columns, one of which has a surviving stone base, is the northeast part of the house (20–22). In this area, there are wells, drainage pits, a stone trough, and drainage pipes that pass through the wall and empty into the street. This part of the house had a second story, accessed by two stairways. A group of bronze objects (perhaps hidden) were discovered under the floor in Room 15. No burial vault was found in this house.

Figure 39. Merneptah Street in the Residential Quarter, looking southeast, as viewed in 1996. On the left, the House of Rapanu; on the right, the House of the Armorer.

Block 2
(between the easternmost section of Palace Street and Merneptah Street)

Block 2 (*Fig.* 36) is bounded on the west by Palace Street and on the east by Merneptah Street. Its northern boundary is a small street, about 2.5 meters wide, that runs from west to east, while another (unnamed) street marks its southern limit.

The layout of this block has not yet been studied, but according to the published reports, the excavators identified several "houses," which they designated according to the artifacts found in them. The northern part of the block is occupied by the badly preserved remains of a house, the western side of which has yet to be unearthed. Little is known about the buildings in the south, but they are probably private dwellings. In between are the complexes that merit further attention because of the exceptional objects that were discovered in them: the House of the Armorer, the House of the Scholar and the one contiguous to it, and the House of Rasapabu.

The House of the Armorer

This house, also known as the House of the Coppersmith, occupies the entire width of the block. Excavated in 1953 (unpublished), the house owes its name to the cache of bronze weapons and tools found under the floor of a large room (designated 8 in the report). The most noteworthy find is the sword marked with the cartouche of the Pharaoh Merneptah (no. **62**), which was most likely made at Ugarit (at any rate, it is clearly not of Egyptian manufacture).

The main facade must have been on the western side, judging from the architectural quality of the wall, which is built of ashlar blocks. The door is to the southwest. In accordance with typical Ugaritic house configuration, the entrance vestibule leads to a small courtyard with two wells, and from here one gains access to the rest of the house, including the living quarters on the upper floor, by means of a stairway (six stone steps of which have survived).

There are several entrances to the eastern part of the house from Merneptah Street. The entrance on the southeast accesses a stairwell and leads to a large 7.3 × 6.5 meter room to the north (Room 8; designated a courtyard), where there are two large rectangular stone troughs. To the northeast is the funerary zone, with its own entrance, a well, a stone trough, and a tomb of relatively mediocre quality.

The House of the Scholar and the Adjacent House

Continuing south along Palace Street, one reaches another complex (*Fig.* 36), which adjoins the House of the Armorer and stretches across the entire width of the block. In this case as in many others at Ugarit, the organization of the space was altered during the course of its history. Initially, it may have been a single dwelling, with entrances on the west and on the east, but during the final phase, at least, it was divided into two houses.

The northeast part consists of a small, rectangular house (11 × 8 meters), designated in the report "The House adjacent to the southern edge of the House of the Armorer" and interpreted as an example of the "basic type of domestic architecture."

The rest of the building, known as the House of the Scholar, has an L shape. The excavations yielded tablets that vary greatly in nature and contents, which led to the conclusion that their owner was a scholar. They include magical and medical formulas, encyclopedias, a treatise on the "art of writing," lexicographic texts in Akkadian (i.e., vocabularies, one of which has comments added in the margins). In all likelihood, the tablets found scattered in the southern part of the house, which is next to Rasapabu's, actually came from the same archive and fell from the upper floor, spreading across the ruins of the two neighboring houses.

The House of Rasapabu

Farther south on Palace Street is the House of Rasapabu. The northwest corner of its stone exterior juts out slightly, thereby narrowing the street. It was excavated in 1953 and studied in 1979. The house is relatively small (80 square meters on the ground level), in comparison with the other, larger complexes in this district, but the ashlar-block construction is of a very high architectural quality, and it is a fine example of a well-designed house.

On the ground floor the house is clearly divided into two distinct parts, each with its own entrance from the street; the two sections are linked to each other by an inner passageway near the entrances. The northern part, which was reserved for domestic activities, consists of a paved entrance equipped with an especially elaborate water system (wells and a stone trough that is also accessible from the street), a small courtyard that allowed light and air into the house, and a stairway to the upper floor. The funerary area consists of two rooms in the southern part, and there is a very fine stone tomb.

Among the texts uncovered here—some of great importance—are texts in Ugaritic (including a veterinary treatise on caring for sick horses) and legal and economic texts in Akkadian (including a purchase receipt for wool delivered to Rasapabu). Rasapabu was a high-ranking official, the person who collected taxes on merchandise and was in charge of the market in the port of Ugarit. He was most likely the owner of the house at the end of the 13th century B.C.E.

The Houses at the Southern End of the Block

Other buildings that also seem to exhibit fine domestic architectural design occupy the southern part of Block 2, but because the excavations have not been completed, we cannot yet provide details of their design (research in progress).

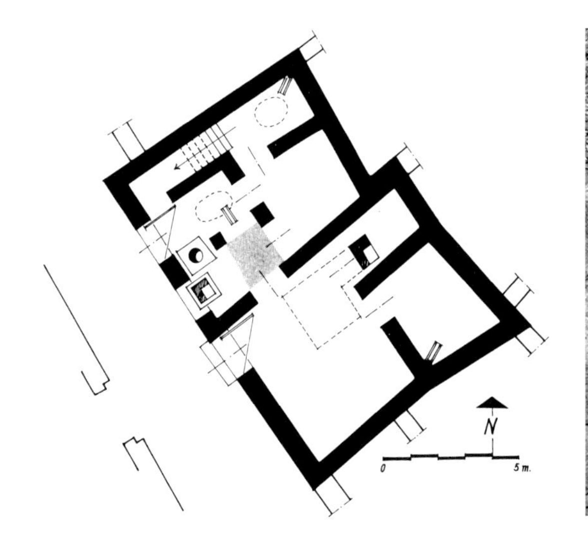

Figure 40. The House of Rasapabu.
a. Schematic plan; b. View from the west, 1979.

Block 3
(east of Merneptah Street)

Situated on the southeastern side of Merneptah Street is a large block (*Fig.* 36), the dimensions of which are unknown because much of it extends beyond the limits of the excavated area. It is the only architectural complex that has been studied to any extent. It has been designated the House of Rapanu (*Fig.* 41) because this name figured in the archives found here.

The Complex Known as the House of Rapanu

This large complex, excavated in 1956 and 1958, has a 40-meter-long facade on Merneptah Street. Our knowledge of it is limited to succinct reports that contain no architectural analysis. For this reason it is difficult to describe its organization or the history of its layout.

The excavators identified 34 different areas on the ground level (courtyards, rooms with various functions, including stairwells and corridors). Stretching to the east of Merneptah Street, its total surface area is around 800 square meters, which greatly exceeds the typical size of a simple house. When it was first built, in the 14th century B.C.E. (?), the complex was intended as two houses, side by side on Merneptah Street, separated by a solid wall.

There is one opening point between the two houses, in the wall between "rooms" 4 and 25, where a well is located. At the time of initial construction, a well with a circular "curbstone" around the upper edge was placed in the opening in the wall so that it could be used by both houses. When the houses were reconstructed in the 13th century B.C.E., the well was enlarged, and two stone edges were added (*Fig.* 42*b*); this enabled each household to draw separately from the same well. The opening in the wall may have been boarded up to provide more privacy.

Because the tablets were mainly found in the northern house, we will be designating it the House of Rapanu and calling the southern part the House of Rapanu's Neighbor.

The House of Rapanu

The ground level of the northern house covers a surface of about 300 square meters. The entrance on the west leads to a vestibule (1), which provides access to the other parts of the house, including the upper level, from the stairway to the left of the entrance. Another entrance on the street leads to a funerary zone via room 3.

One distinctive feature of this house is the presence of two tombs (a third tomb that is now visible actually belongs to an earlier period). The one to the south (6) dates to the construction of the house (in the 14th century B.C.E.?). It was built over an older tomb (early Late Bronze Age) that predates the construction of the house that is visible today and is covered by it. The other tomb (5 and 8) dates to the reconstruction in the 13th century B.C.E.; this very fine, large vault of fine architectural quality (perhaps the best-preserved tomb on the site of Ras Shamra) occupies a choice location in the house.

Although the building itself was neglected in excavation reports, the texts were promptly studied and published in the 1960s. Archives of exceptional interest (more than 200 tablets) were found in the house. The name Rapanu appears in several letters and documents, and he was a high-ranking scribe and adviser to the king who, at the end of the 13th century B.C.E., had access to sensitive

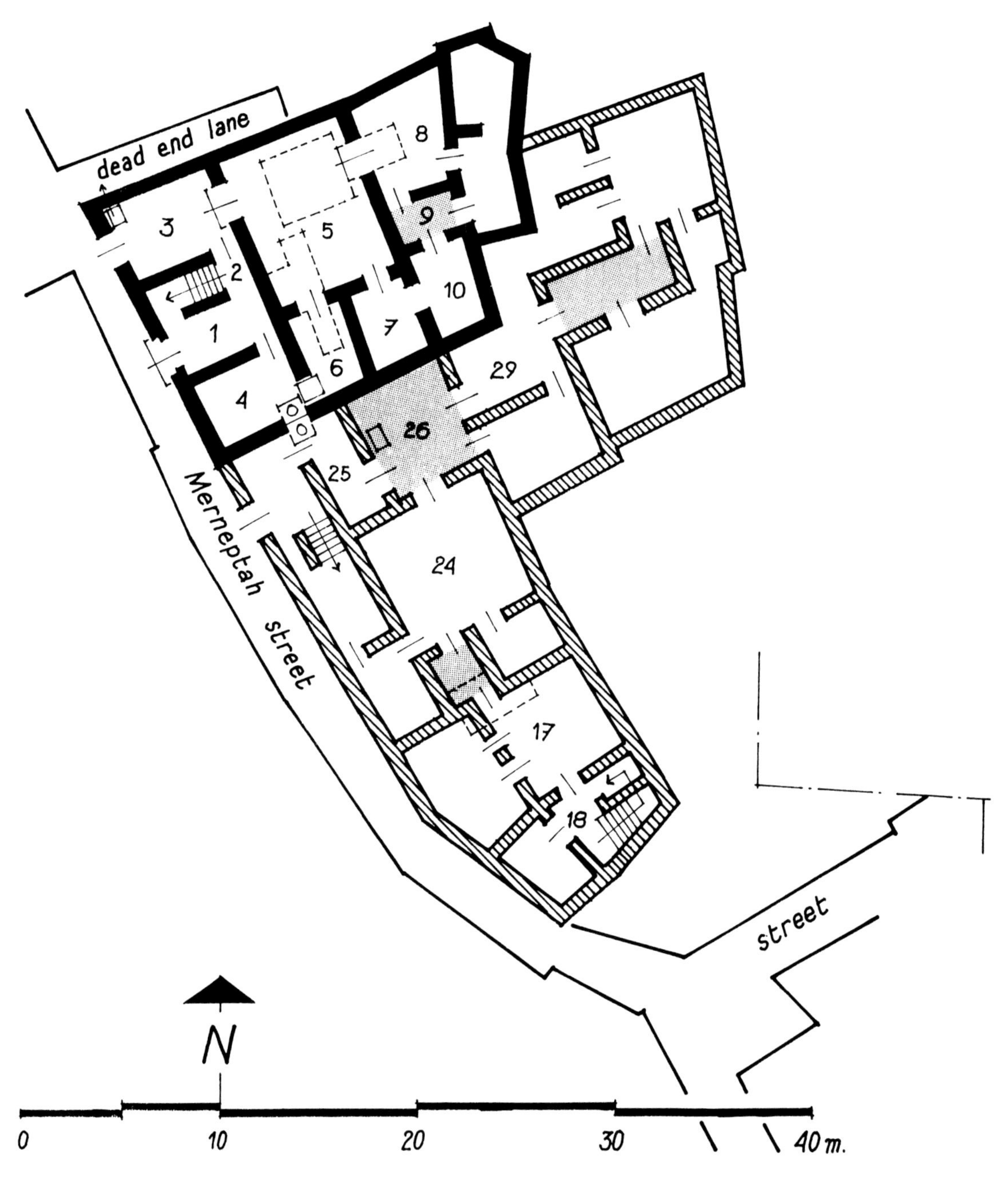

Figure 41. Block 3: Schematic plan of the House of Rapanu and the House of Rapanu's Neighbor. The proposed demarcation of the houses is dependent on recent research or work in progress, but the numbers are the labels used by the excavators.

a. The Houses of Rapanu and his Neighbor as viewed looking west, 1994.

b. A well with a double stone opening between the House of Rapanu (to the left) and the House of his Neighbor, viewed looking east, 1994.

Figure 42. The House of Rapanu in Block 3.

43a. The large built tomb in rooms 5 and 8.

Figure 43. The House of Rapanu, 1994.

affairs of state, although he seems to have maintained older archives as well. The following are some of the many documents of major importance found in his house: correspondence between the king of Ugarit and the king of Alashia (Cyprus) written around 1200 B.C.E., at the time of increasing threat from the "Sea Peoples"; correspondence with the king of Carchemish regarding the abduction of the Hittite king's daughter; correspondence with the Pharaoh concerning an incident with the Canaanites; and a "general's letter" (no. 3) addressed to the king of Ugarit concerning protection of the kingdom's boundaries.

The House of Rapanu's Neighbor

The southern part of the complex under discussion is an L-shaped house with an entrance on the long, western side, on Merneptah Street. Another wing of the house stretches northeast toward the interior of the block. The house's design has the usual features of Ugaritic domestic architecture: entrance with a stairway, tomb, and so on.

We must await the resumption of excavations here before we can report anything about the other buildings in this block, to the north, east, and south.

43b. Stairway of the dromos looking north from inside the funeral chamber.

Selected Bibliography

The "House of the Alabaster Vessels"

1974, Lagarce (J. and E.), dans Contenson (H. de), et al., "Rapport . . . ," *Syria* 51, pp. 5–24 (plan fig. 3) (cf. J.-C. Courtois, *UF* 1979, pp. 117–18, fig. 17).

The "Building with the Stone Vase"

1992, Callot (O.), and Calvet (Y.), "Rapport de chantier 1992" (unpublished, archives of the French mission).

The "House with a Portico"

1967, Schaeffer (C.), *Annuaire du Collège de France* 67, pp. 371–75 (cf. J.-C. Courtois, *UF* 1979, pp. 116–17, fig. 16).

The "House of the Armorer"

1956, Schaeffer (C.), *Ugaritica* III, pp. 169–78 (cf. *Syria* 31, 1954, p. 65 ; J.-C. Courtois, *UF* 1979, pp. 115–16, fig. 14).

The "House of the Scholar" and the "Adjacent House"

1979, cf. Courtois (J.-C.), *UF* 1979, p. 11, fig. 16.

The "House of Rasapabu"

1954 : Schaeffer (C.), "Rapport . . . ," *Syria* 31, p. 64 (cf. J.-C. Courtois, *UF* 1979, pp. 114–15, fig. 13).

1981, Y. Calvet, "Aménagements hydrauliques d'Ugarit," *L'homme et l'eau* I, Lyon, pp. 38–40.

The "House of Rapanu" and the "House of Rapanu's Neighbor"

1961, Schaeffer (C.), *CRAIBL* 1961, pp. 233–34.

1968, Nougayrol (J.), "Les archives de Rap'anu," in *Ugaritica* V, pp. 41–259, 379–433.

1994, Callot (O.) and Calvet (Y.), "Rapport de chantier 1994" (unpublished, archives of the French mission).

[2005] *"The Building with the Stone Vase"*

2001, Callot (O.) and Calvet (Y.), "Le 'bâtiment au vase de pierre' du quartier résidentiel d'Ougarit," in *RSO* XIV, pp. 65–82.

"City Center"

An area located to the east of the Residential Quarter, covering about 30 × 60 meters at the geographical center of the tell, was excavated between 1978 and 1994 (see grid plan, *Fig.* 44). The name "City Center" is simply a conventional topographic name.

Several blocks have been identified. They are delimited by streets that run approximately east to west and intersect other narrow streets and dead-end lanes running perpendicular to them. These streets are a part of the whole city network extending to the west as well as to the east (toward the Residential Quarter and South City Trench; *Fig.* 13).

Stratigraphic evidence and a careful analysis of building techniques and plans in this dwelling area have led to a better understanding of daily life. Among the furnishings found abandoned on the ground floor or in the rubble that fell down when the upper floor collapsed are all kinds of utilitarian objects and personal belongings, such as cosmetic boxes and tools. Many are of only average-quality workmanship (nos. **51**, **54**, **64**), including domestic cult figurines (no. **43**). Judging from these objects, we can characterize this area as a typical residential district. But a cult site adjacent to the houses (see the "Temple of the Rhytons") has also been identified in this zone.

The northern part of the excavation (*Fig.* 13) uncovered a block of buildings. Its western boundary lies outside the excavation area; it is bounded on the east by street 1288 and to the north and south by streets 1038 and 35. Excavations have uncovered 30 meters of streets 1038 and 35, which line up with corresponding streets excavated a considerable distance away, in the South City Trench.

The southern block occupies the area between streets 35 in the north and 186 in the south. It is bounded by the narrow street 109–120 to the east, but its western limit lies outside the excavated area.

Street 1038 is nearly 2.50 meters wide, but street 35 is narrower. The streets running north–south are also narrow: at its widest, 1288 measures 1.2 meters at the top of street, and 109–120 is less than 1 meter wide.

Northern Block

An analysis of the foundations demonstrates the remarkable technical competence of the builders of this section. Constructing buildings several stories high on such a steep slope (14% grade at certain spots) required an enormous amount of preparatory earthwork in order to bench the slopes and and great skill to build on interlocking foundation walls capable of resisting lateral ground thrust.

The northern part of the block is occupied by two houses with entrances to the north (*Figs.* 44, 46). House A to the northwest is a small dwelling (80 square meters) of average architectural quality. It has a simple plan and only slightly differentiated spaces, which we have been able to interpret on the basis of the kind of artifacts found in them (*Fig.* 45; no. **54**). There are two entrances on the street to the north. The entrance on the west leads to a fairly large room that was reserved for domestic activities. A stairway near the entrance (three of the stone steps have survived) led to the upper floor. Windowless storerooms are located at the rear in the south. The other entrance leads to rooms with utilitarian functions (kitchen) and to a small courtyard that let light and air into the house. Private family activities took place on the floors above and on the flat-roof terrace.

House B, in the northeast section, is larger (120 square meters) and of a finer architectural quality.

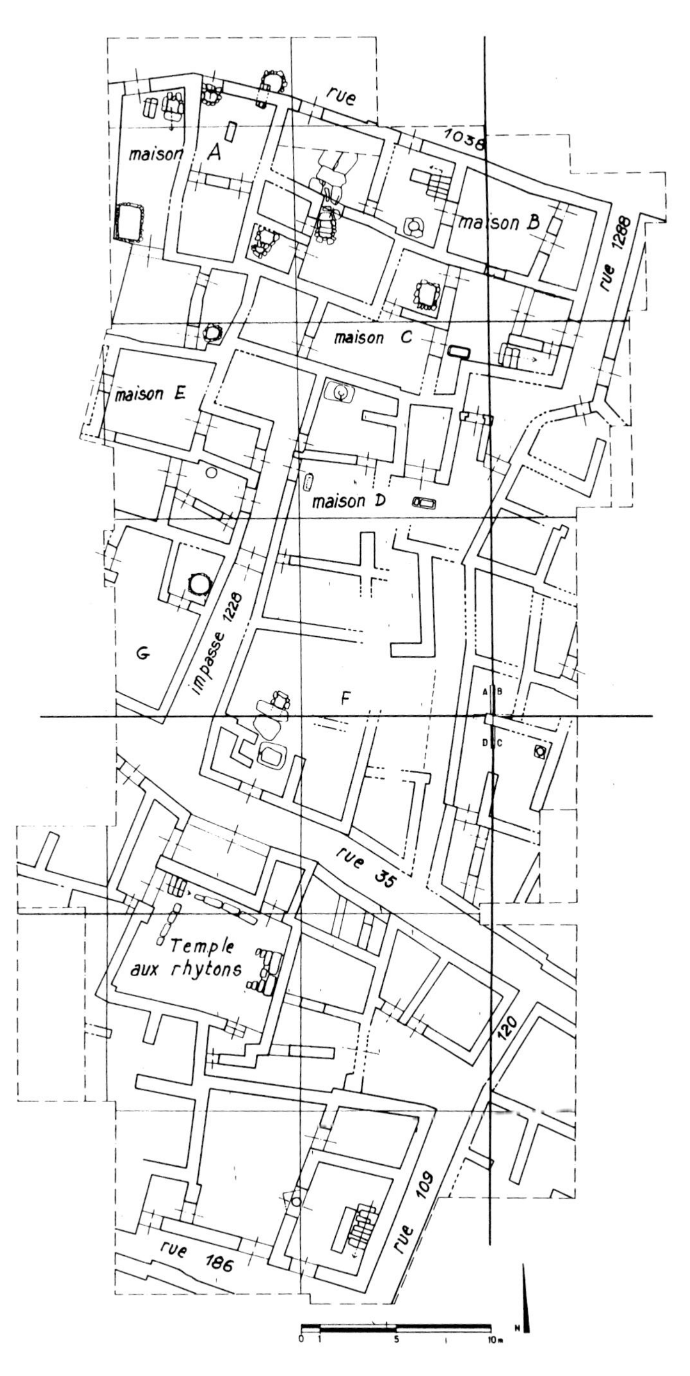

Figure 44. Schematic plan of City Center, 1994
(drawing by L. Volay, after plans by P. Desfarges, M. Renisio, and L. Volay).

Figure 45. City Center: House A with artifacts left on the ground, 1979 (after *RSO* III, p. 128).

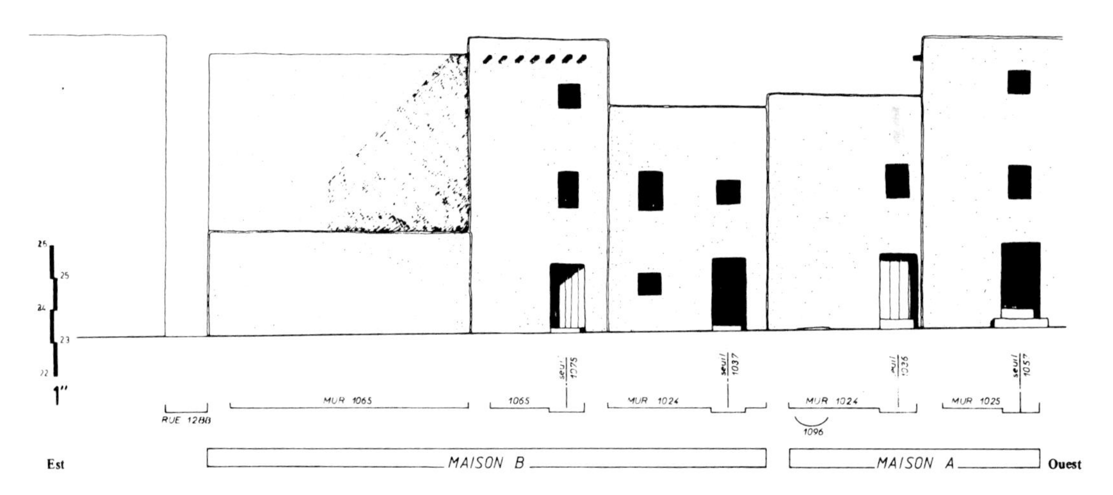

Figure 46. City Center: Reconstruction of Houses A and B on street 1038: the northern facades (drawing by M. Renisio).

Figure 47. The Temple of the Rhytons, looking east, 1990.

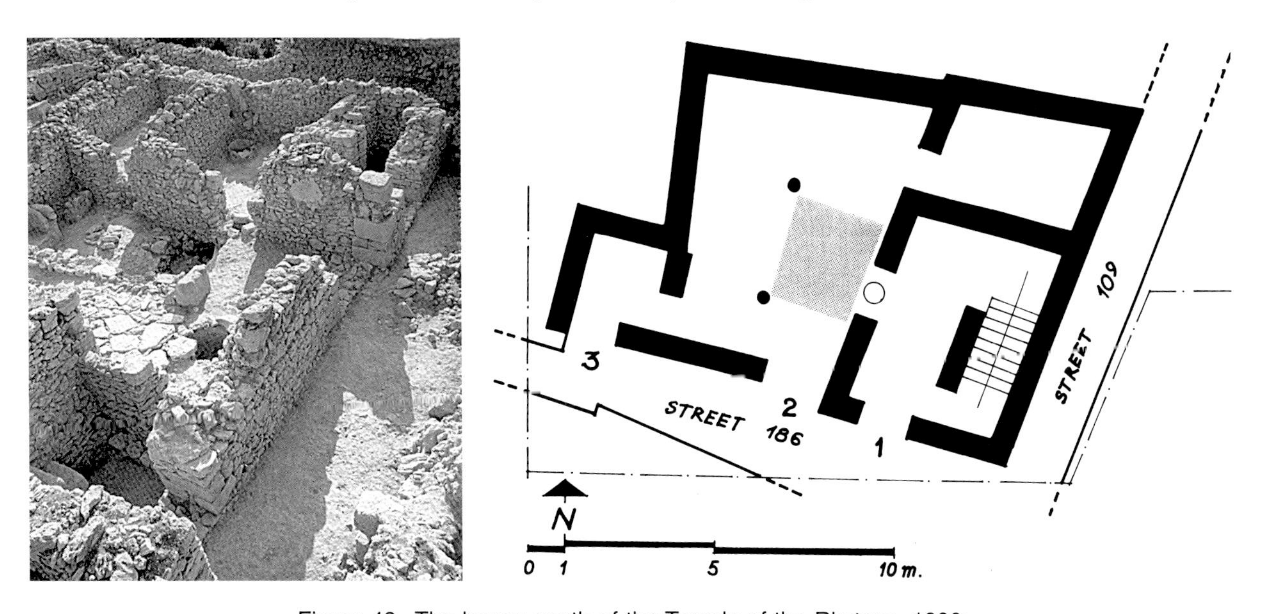

Figure 48. The house south of the Temple of the Rhytons, 1990:
a. looking east; facade on street 186; b. schematic plan, with entrances to the three zones:
(1) private; (2) professional; and (3) commercial.

In its final state, it had a more elaborate, L-shaped plan, divided into two clearly distinct parts, each with its own entrance from the street and with a connecting passageway on the inside. The domestic living area to the east has an entrance with a well and a stairway that leads to a garden, surrounded by rooms with utilitarian functions, and to a funerary zone with a tomb (pillaged), and storerooms with silos dug into the floor.

This was the layout of House B in its final state; however, when it was initially constructed, before the mid-13th century B.C.E., it was designed as a much larger house, with a more balanced layout. The need to compress family living space at the end of the 13th century in order to accommodate the growing urban population led to dividing the house into two, thus modifying the initial plan. The whole southern part and its storerooms was isolated, and a stairway was added to create another house (C) on the south, with an entrance on street 1288 to the east.

The southern part of the block is divided in two by a dead-end lane (1228) that penetrates deep into the center and ends in a courtyard. On the eastern side is an entrance to House D, which is built on a benched slope below the level of House C. The house is badly preserved and difficult to analyze. A stone slab from an oil press has been identified in it.

On the west side of the dead-end lane is an entrance to House E, the western part of which extends beyond the excavated area. There are entrances, a stairway, and rooms, in which personal belongings were found. The objects, including a stone roller for a flat mud roof (no. 55), have been studied for the way in which they fell from the living quarters on the floors above. They were found between the rubble from the ceilings and the rubble of the roof over the second floor.

Along street 35, at the south of the block, is a complex (G) that included artisan's installations (e.g., a stone basin) and an area (F) on the other side of the dead-end lane that was used for various purposes during the Late Bronze Age. At first, it housed an oil press equipped with a pressing room, an oil press, and a courtyard with a hearth; this installation may have been operated by the Temple of Rhytons on the opposite side of street 35. It seems, however, that the oil press no longer existed during the final phase, when the area may have been a garden or perhaps merely an empty lot.

Southern Block

The Temple of the Rhytons and Its Annexes

Below the level of street 35 is a building that has been identified as a cult site on the basis of its plan and the objects discovered in it (*Figs.* 44, 47). Due to the large number of rhytons (used for libations during ceremonies: see no. 37), it has been named the Temple of the Rhytons. Its architectural features are akin to a well-known type of Late Bronze Age sanctuary in the Near East, especially in Cyprus and Palestine.

The vestibule leads indirectly through a corridor to the main hall, the entrance of which is in the northwest corner. The shape of the hall is nearly rectangular, 6 × 7 meters. In the northeast corner is a small sacristy: benches line the northern and western walls, and there is a stepped platform in the center of the eastern wall, perhaps a stand for the statue of a deity.

What makes this cult site exceptional is that it is right in the middle of a residential district. The adjacent buildings in the northeast part of the block are probably not ordinary houses. There are connecting passageways to the temple, and the houses were no doubt related to it.

These structures can be dated to Late Bronze II, and the temple was in use until the end of the city's existence. The temple furnishings were scattered in the looting that accompanied the downfall of the city and were found near the temple grounds. They include rhytons (e.g., no. **37**), a cult stand (no. **41**), and a stone statuette of the god El (no. **13**).

The House South of the Temple of Rhytons

There is not a single passageway connecting the temple and the annexes in the north of the block to the structures that occupy the southern part, which are of a totally different nature. Slightly lower down, in the southeast corner, stands a house with three doors facing south onto street 186, and with its back against the temple and its annexes (*Figs.* 44, 48). This house is an excellent example of a certain type of dwelling and provides information on daily activities in Ugarit in the early 12th century B.C.E. On the ground level, it is divided into three distinct areas, different in size and character and linked to each other by openings inside the complex. In the opening between the private (1) and the professional (2) areas is a well, accessible to the family and to the workers.

(1) The entrance to the private family part of the building is on the east and leads into a vestibule, where there is a stairway (the first flight of nine stone steps has survived). It is likely that the living quarters upstairs extended over the whole surface area of the building. There is no burial vault.

(2) The door in the center gives access to the area where the artisan and professional activities took place. A pavement of large, uneven stones has survived, and at least a part of this paved area must have been open to the sky. At the rear, to the right, is an entrance to a room with very high walls. There are no windows in this room, at least none that has survived. There may have been small skylights under the ceiling to let in light and air, but it is equally possible that this was a windowless storage room.

(3) Finally, on the west is a small area of 10 square meters, linked on the inside to the central area but also having its own access from the street. This was probably the business premises, a sort of shop.

Selected Bibliography

1982, 1983, 1987, 1990, See the "Rapports . . ." in *Syria*.

1987, *RSO III*, pp. 11–128; Yon (M.), Lombard (P.) and Renisio (M.), "L'organisation de l'habitat: Les maisons A, B et E," pp. 129–56; Calvet (Y.) and Geyer (B.), "L'eau dans l'habitat," pp. 157–95; Salles (J.-F.), "Deux nouvelles tombes de Ras Shamra," pp. 197–212; Callot (O.), "Les huileries du Bronze Récent," pp. 213–48; Mallet (J.), "Le temple aux rhytons."

1992, Excavation Report 1992, by J. Mallet, "La maison au sud du temple aux rhytons" (unpublished, archives of the French mission).

1996, Yon (Y.), "The Temple of the Rhytons," in *Ugarit, Religion and Culture (Proceedings of the International Colloquium "Ugarit and the Bible," Edinburgh, 1994, in Honour of J. Gibson)*. N. Wyatt, W. G. E. Watson, J. B. Lloyd, eds. Münster, pp. 405–22.

2001, Mallet (J.) and Matoïan (V.), "Une maison au sud du 'temple aux rhytons', fouilles 1997–1990," in *RSO XIV*, pp. 83–180.

Access to the City from the South

From the City Center, the tell gradually slopes down to the districts known in excavation reports as the South Central and "Main Street" districts.

Excavations in this area began in 1986 and are still underway. Apparently, there are some fine-quality buildings in this area, the homes of high-ranking officials with links to the royal family and important political functions. The extensive archives found in the House of Urtenu in the South Central district (see below, p. 87), for instance, support this understanding of the area during the last period of the city's history.

Unlike the northern limit of the tell, which is so eroded in some places that cliffs have formed over the Nahr Shbayyeb, the relatively regular slope to the south continues all the way to the Nahr ed-Delbeh (see *Fig. 1*). The presence of orange groves in the southern area of the tell makes it difficult to examine the surface contours (see *Fig. 3*). The northern edge of the groves is marked by a stone

Figure 49. Intersection of "Main Street," looking south, 1994.

wall constructed without mortar and a row of tall cypress trees, and alongside them a road runs a few meters from the current excavations (1994).

The excavations are uncovering new residential quarters that are interesting in themselves, but even more the examination of the topography on this part of the site has shed light on the question of access to the city in ancient times, even if it has not totally resolved the point. The study of this zone will continue in the coming years.

As we have seen above, the Royal Zone had its own fortified entrance on the west, but when we began our research in 1978, no other entrances to the city were known. Because of the erosion of the tell on the northern edge, it is unlikely that an access from the north will ever be identified. But recent research indicates that one of the main access roads to the city was the approach from the south.

This large road must have first crossed the Nahr ed-Delbeh, the river that separates the tell from the plain to the south. The exploration of this stream in 1990 led to the discovery of the vestiges of a major engineering structure (see p. 89).

The groves make it impossible to locate the place where the road entered the city, but excavations since 1992 on the southern slope to the north of the groves have begun to uncover a wide avenue coming from the south, which is designated "Main Street" in the reports (see *Fig. 13*).

Main Street District

The excavation of a depression in the tell, where we were hoping to find the access road from the south, has in fact revealed a wide thoroughfare (3018), known as "Main Street." At one major intersection, this wide street crossed streets that ran east–west. Main Street is considerably wider (4 meters wide) than the other streets of the city, which average between 1 and 2.5 meters. It is lined with buildings of unusually fine architectural quality and, judging from the remains of walls that are being exposed, the buildings are likely to be quite large.

At the northwest corner of the intersection, there is a long, unbroken facade that has several doors with jambs of ashlar blocks (*Fig. 49, on the right*). On the northeast of the intersection is the corner of a building that, based on the quality of design and size of the remains that have been uncovered, looks promising (*Fig. 49, on the left*). Fifteen meters of its north–south facade have already been exposed, but no door has yet been found. Along the east–west facade on the street perpendicular to Main Street is a very large door (2 meters wide) with double rabbet jambs and a sill made of an enormous monolith.

The lower part of the wall, 1 meter thick, was carefully constructed of ashlar blocks, on which horizontal beams were fitted: there are distinct traces of dowels and their holes. Blocks of the superstructure tumbled down to the south in a heap that blocks the eastern part of the intersection. The structure shares the characteristics of the most carefully constructed buildings in the city (such as the House of Yabninu). This is undoubtedly an important structure, but nothing more can be said about it until the excavations have been extended farther north and east.

Given the state of excavation work, we do not yet know the exact route of these streets. However, it is already clear that Main Street leads north to the western part of the large Plaza (which is as yet uncleared), the eastern part of which has been cleared in the middle of the South City Trench (see below, p. 91, and above, *Fig. 13*). Two hundred meters to the south, the road aligns with the axis of the bridge across the Nahr ed-Delbeh (see p. 89). Insofar as the perpendicular streets are concerned, their extensions are found in the excavated zones nearby, in "South City" to the east and "South Central" district to the west (see *Fig. 13*).

South Central District

The House with Stone Troughs

Between Main Street and the site of the House of Urtenu, a sounding was undertaken in 1986 and continued in 1988 and 1992. It has revealed some fine-quality utilitarian buildings, combining ashlar and rubble construction. There are several buildings (none of which has been totally cleared) on a street running approximately southeast to northwest and widening into a small, rectangular plaza.

Some of the most interesting buildings located to the south and west of this excavation site may be related to the House of Urtenu complex. These contain utilitarian facilities such as a silo, drainage wells, and jars. Behind a row of small rooms with carefully constructed, thick walls, are open areas with single and double stone troughs (perhaps water troughs for horses). There is a stairway in the southeast, of which several steps of the first flight have survived. But because the remainder lies outside the excavation area, we cannot yet fully grasp the plan of these complexes. It is likely that the exploration of the House of Urtenu on the west will enable us to link these two sites and better determine the relationships among the various buildings.

Figure 50. The House with Stone Troughs, looking north, 1988.

Figure 51. South Central District, the House of Urtenu, with the tomb in the foreground, looking northeast,1994.

The House of Urtenu

A few dozen meters to the west, nearly a hundred tablets of major interest have been accidently discovered in 1973 in a rubble heap (*tas de déblais* in the reports) left during the building of a modern military bunker on the southern part of the tell. The texts were all published in 1991 in *RSO VII*.

This part of the tell was under modern military control for several years, and access to it was impossible prior to 1986, when the bunker was demolished and a systematic excavation was begun.

The excavations underway are gradually unearthing what appears to be a large house of very fine quality, the extent of which has not yet been determined (*Fig.* 51). There is a large, carefully constructed, stone burial chamber, but, unfortunately, it was pillaged in ancient times (a hole pierced by the looter in the center of the covering is visible). The excavations will continue, but it is still too early to determine the size and layout of the rest of the house.

Several hundred tablets, some in Ugaritic but mostly in Akkadian (ca. 80%), were found in this house. In terms of their quantity and quality, these are archives of major importance. The excavations will enable us to identify the strata in which these documents were found and to pinpoint the exact location of the archive, which we have only rarely been able to do elsewhere on the site.

All of the tablets mentioned in the reports (the 1973 tablets already published, those found between 1986 and 1992 whose study is underway, and those found in 1994) belong to the archives of the same house, though they were apparently stored in different places.

We can only approximate the proveniences of the documents found in 1973 because the construction of the modern bunker destroyed part of the center of the house. The 1986–92 texts were found in the part of the house northwest of the bunker, scattered throughout several rooms and on top of the ruins of the walls between them. This leads us to conclude that they fell from a floor above. On the other hand, the majority of the 1994 tablets were found southeast of the bunker in a room (2135) approximately 4 × 2.50 meters in size, located east of the tomb. Some of them were discovered in a sort of niche made in the construction of the wall; in other cases, they appear to have fallen from the level of these niches.

The tablets already studied include royal letters and commercial correspondence, lexical documents, mythological fragments, administrative texts, and so on. It is still too early to describe the contents of the tablets found in 1994, which are in the process of being restored and deciphered. Nonetheless, it already seems possible to identify the owner of this house at the beginning of the 12th century B.C.E. as a man named Urtenu, a person of high social standing already known to us from other texts.

Selected Bibliography

1985, Yon (M.), "La ville d'Ougarit au XIIIe s. av. J.-C," *CRAIBL*, pp. 705–21.
1987, Yon (M.), et al., *Syria* 64, "Rapport . . . ," pp. 184–91.
1990, Yon (M.), et al., *Syria* 67, "Rapport . . . ," pp. 18–28.
1992, 1994, "Rapports de chantier 1992 et 1994," Matoïan (V.), Lombard (P.), Breuil (J.-Y.), and Marchegay (S.) (unpublished, archives of the French mission).
1995, Lombard (P.), "Contexte archéologique et données épigraphiques. Quelques réflexions sur l'interprétation du gisement de 1973–1992," in *RSO* XI, pp. 227–38.

Publication of the texts

1991, Bordreuil (P.), et al., *RSO* VII, *Une bibliothèque au sud de la ville: *Textes de 1973*, Paris.

[2005] The excavation of the House of Urtenu was completed in 2005, and the publication of the archaeological remains is underway. The many texts discovered there are partially published: the texts from the salvage dig of 1973 appeared in *RSO* VII (1991) and the texts from the excavations of 1986–1992 in *RSO* XIV (2001). The publication of the large number of texts from the 1994–2002 seasons is currently in preparation. The area just to the east of the House of Urtenu known as the "Chantier Grand-rue" (Main Street) became the object of renewed excavation in 2005 and the southwestern portion of a large, well-constructed building was uncovered.

1999, etc., Calvet (Y.) et al., "Rapports de chantier" (unpublished archives of the French mission).
2001, Arnaud (D.), dir., "Les textes de la maison d'Ourtenou trouvés en 1986, 1988 et 1990," in *RSO* XIV, pp. 235–422.
2004, Calvet (Y.), in *Aux origines de l'alphabet, 2004* [see p. 26 above], p. 94.

The Southern Bridge/Dam

The area all around the city, particularly the two stream beds, have recently been explored systematically with an eye to discovering points of access to the city other than the fortified entrance on the west of the palace, which clearly was not designed for general public use.

Little can be ascertained regarding access from the north. The extreme erosion of the tell has turned the northwestern boundary into a cliff, and the northeastern part is largely covered by huge heaps of debris from early excavations. However, exploration to the south has yielded far more satisfying results.

Orange groves conceal the topography of the base of the tell on the south (*Fig.* 3), but we have been able to study the bed of the stream known as (Nahr) ed-Delbeh. The flow of coastal rivers exhibits a striking contrast between the summer, when they are dry, and the rainy seasons, when they are full, sometimes to the point of overflowing. Over time, the stream bed erodes, and steep banks are formed, which can make it difficult to ford the stream, especially when transporting heavy material such as building stones, timber, merchandise from the port, and all of the supplies necessary to satisfy the needs of a city's large population.

Beginning in 1984, a foundation of large ashlar blocks that aligns with the axis of Main Street, on

Figure 52. A pier of the bridge/dam on the Nahr ed-Delbeh, south of the city, 1990.

the south bank of the Nahr ed-Delbe, was explored (*Figs.* 1, 13, 52). The pier can be reached by walking around the east side of the grove and proceeding down to the river. Additional excavations in 1992 showed that it was in fact a pier, with a triangular tip pointing upstream, made of enormous stone blocks and carefully assembled, using large dovetail cramps (which were probably of wood).*

One can also see, on the upstream side, vertical dowels that, along with movable wooden beams, were used to dam the stream. The upper course of the pier, which is missing, must have been the base on which the planks of a bridge lay.

This structure, then, was a large bridge that also functioned as a dam, and it was thus used both as the base for an approach from the south across the deep riverbed and to retain water when the heat of the summer began drying up the river and lowering the water table.

Erosion has led to the total disappearance of the foundation on the north bank (the tell side), but excavation in the alluvia of the south bank may reveal whether there are any remains of the scaffolding to the south or remains of other intermediary piers.

*A tentative restoration (in *Barrages-antiques*, p. 76, fig. 39) was made in 1990, before the wedge-shaped, upstream end of the pier had been discovered. The restoration was modified by the excavators in 1992.

Selected Bibliography

1990, Calvet (Y.), "Un barrage antique à Ras Shamra," in *Colloque Techniques . . . Damas* 1987, pp. 487–99.

1992, Calvet (Y.) and Geyer (B.), *Barrages antiques de Syrie*, Lyon, pp. 69–77.

1992, Calvet (Y.) and Geyer (B.), "Rapport de chantier 1992" (unpublished, archives of the French mission).

[2005] In 2002, exploration of the bridge/dam located south of the city over the Nahr el-Delbeh was renewed and the southern pier was uncovered; the channel between the two piers discovered to date measures 1.65 meters. We may assume that a third pier was located to the north, that it has been eroded away, and that the northern channel would have been of roughly the same width as the one defined by the piers that have been preserved.

2002, Geyer (B.), "Rapport de chantier," Unpublished archives of the French mission.

South City Trench

East of the tell's geographical center and the City Center excavations lies a long trench that has been designated the "South City Trench." Although excavated in 1959–60, it was only briefly mentioned in the reports. Nearly 20 years later, erosion had caused damage to some of the remains, yet they were so spectacular that an extensive study of the architecture was resumed in 1978. We are therefore able to propose plausible restorations, but we must remember that the excavation often went well below the ancient ground level, which makes it difficult to distinguish between rubble stone walls and foundations.

The descriptions and analysis of this area are based on the studies published in 1983 and 1994 in *RSO* I and X, which provide an important perspective on city planning and domestic architecture at Ugarit. As is the case for the Residential Quarter and the City Center, the excavated area is not a section of the city in the structural sense of the term but a portion of the city that has been artificially exposed by excavating a trench.

The trench covers about 5,700 square meters, its length oriented approximately north–south for more than 190 meters, with an average width of 30 meters from east to west (*Figs.* 53–54). Groups of buildings are separated by a fairly dense network of streets of varying widths, which can be linked to streets uncovered in other excavated zones nearby. Midway down the slope, west of block VIII, a vast open area that was probably a "Plaza" in the last phase of the city's history has been cleared (the western side has not yet been excavated).

The network of streets delimits 14 blocks, numbered I to XIV in the recent publications of this area, only one of which (block VI) has been entirely cleared on all sides. The others lie partially outside the excavation zone. Thirty-seven houses have been identified.

Figure 53. The South City trench, looking south, 1978.

Block I, on the northern edge of the slope, is relatively poorly preserved, but it seems possible to identify the elements of a single house (with the main entrance to the east, a stairway, and a funerary zone with a small tomb). Only the southwest portion of **block II**, across a street and a small

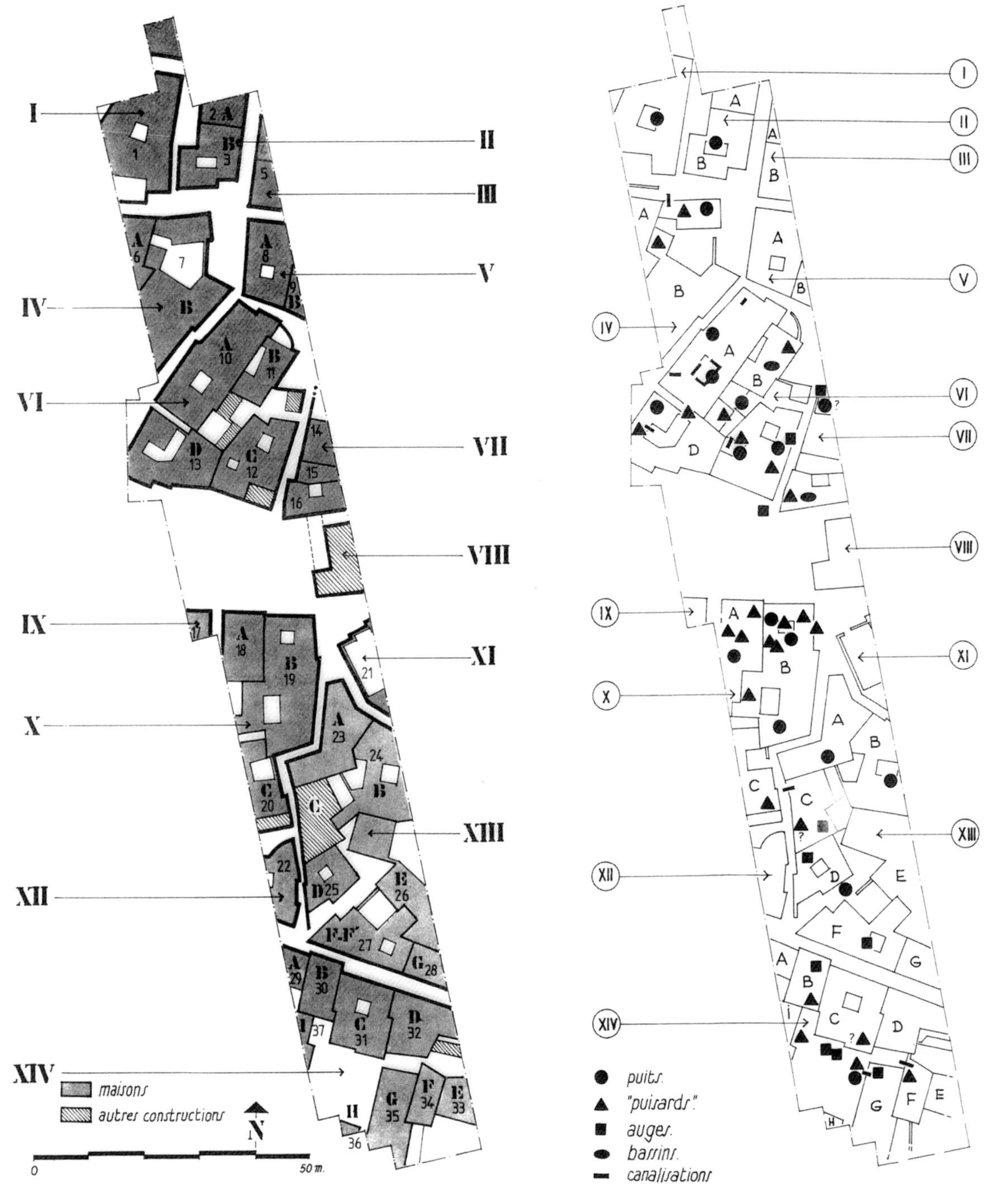

Figure 54. South City Trench: *RSO* X, 1994, p. 371, figs. 270–71:
left: top plan of the blocks of houses; *right*: location of the utilitarian installations.

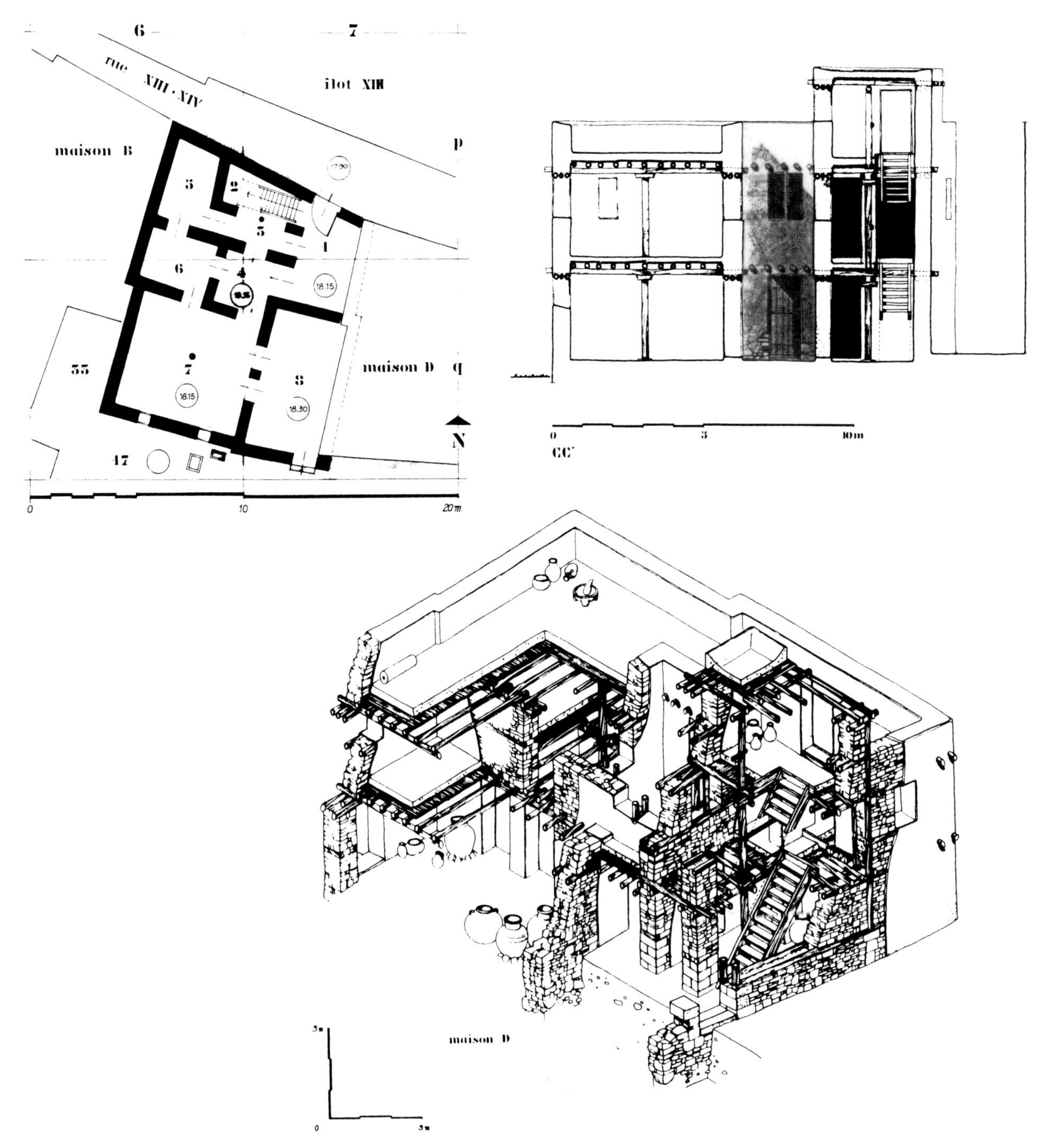

Figure 55. South City Trench, Block XIV, House C: *RSO* X, 1994, pp. 348–50: *top left:* schematic plan; *top right:* north–south section; and *bottom:* an axonometric reconstruction as viewed from the northeast.

plaza from block I, is visible (there is a house with a funerary zone and the beginning of another house to the north). Most of **block III**, on the other side of the street to the east of block II, is still hidden beyond the eastern baulk.

There is a street running east–west (between blocks I–III and IV–V) that is probably an extension of street 35 in the City Center and perhaps also of a street in the South Acropolis Trench. To the south, 250 square meters of **block IV** have been cleared, and two complexes have been identified that may in fact be two parts of a single large house (with rooms reflecting farming activities to the north and the owner's house to the south), but the plan is not complete, because the complex extends into the western baulk.

On the other side of a small plaza formed by the street running north–south is **block V** (*Fig.* 56), which extends into the eastern baulk. One can see the remains of almost all of an entire house with an entrance to the west, a stairwell nearby, another entrance to the funerary zone with the family tomb, and an oil press.

Farther down along the street (between IV and VII) is **block VI**, the only complete block exposed by this trench and the largest block known so far, covering an area of 740 square meters. Four different complexes have been identified in this block. The house to the northwest (house A, published in *RSO* I) has its main side facing the street to the west and is of excellent architectural quality. It preserves the usual features of Ugaritic domestic architecture: entrance with stairway, central courtyard with well, storage area, independent funerary zone, etc. The other houses in the block are of lesser quality. On the edge of the large Plaza (VI–X), on the southeast side of VI C, is a shop. A careful analysis of the floor plans of the buildings in this block has clearly indicated that there were no living quarters on the ground floor. This further supports the hypothesis already formulated in respect to other residential areas of the city that living quarters were located on the second floor.

Only small portions of **block VII** (opposite block VI) and **block VIII** (at the edge of the large Plaza) are inside the edges of the trench. Block VII is not well preserved. Block VIII, which consists of two adjacent spaces, does not have the usual features of Ugaritic domestic architecture, but excavations will have to be extended to the east before we can propose an interpretation.

On the southwest corner of the Plaza is a small portion of **block IX**. The funerary zone of a house with an ashlar-block tomb has been unearthed.

Along the south side of the Plaza stands **block X**, separated from block IX by a dead-end lane. House A is on the northwest end and House B on the northeast. House B is designated the "House of Literary Tablets" in the reports because of the discovery of important documents in the northern area. It is a house of fine architectural quality covering nearly 270 square meters of space. There are several entrances. The entrance on the north, on the Plaza, leads through a vestibule to a stairway located near a small courtyard; an entrance to the east, also with a stairway, leads to workshops (olive press, silo) and from there to a large courtyard (perhaps with porticoes on two or more sides). The third entrance, on the south, leads to commercial zones. The presence of stairways and the structure of the walls indicate that there was at least one upper floor, perhaps even two.

The texts found in this house are the usual kind of documents in Ugaritic and Akkadian, but there are also Babylonian literary texts, including the story of the Flood (*Gilgamesh*) and a collection of proverbs (known as "Wisdom Literature"). Many of the tablets were found in several rooms in the north end of the house but at several different depths, while others were found on the Plaza outside. It is possible that some of the older archives had been discarded, while others were stored on the second floor and then scattered when the second floor collapsed.

On the south of House B is the edge of another house (entrance and stairway); the rest of it is hidden in the western baulk. On its south is a space that opens onto a small street and has no communicating passageway into the interior of the house; it is possible that this space was a chariot shed rather than a shop.

There is an edge of a space, probably unroofed, that appears in the eastern baulk at the entrance to the street leading south from the end of the large Plaza, and we labeled this area block XI.

South of block X are the partial remains of **block XII**, which was cleared for an area of 80 square meters, though this is insufficient for a thorough analysis.

Continuing to the south of blocks IX–XI, one reaches the large **block XIII**. Its boundaries to the north, west, and south are visible, but it extends into the baulk to the east. More than 950 square meters have been cleared so far, but the ruins are in fairly poor condition, and the depth of the excavation, conducted well below the floor level in many areas, makes it difficult to interpret. In the last phase, it is very likely that some public passages

Figure 56. South City Trench, Block V, looking southwest,1979.

were put to private use. For instance, the long dead-end lane to the northwest and another to the west were probably used this way.

Out of the five or six houses that appear to be distinguishable, the small house to the north (A) is the best preserved. It was designated the "House with the Chariot Crater" in the reports (because of a Mycenaean crater of Pictorial style found in an earlier level). It is a small building with a pentagonal plan that could almost be reshaped into a triangle; the entrance is in the northern room. This house is well situated at the intersection of several streets, which suggests that it was a shop. The rest of the building, linked to this space by two doors, probably had a professional function of some kind—but not a commercial purpose, for whatever was sold in the shop was probably produced in this part of the building. The living quarters were upstairs and were reached by a stairway on the south. The owner in the last phase may have enlarged his property by adding the plots to the south, where he erected outbuildings.

The plan of the incomplete house (B) to the east is not clear. It has a very large built tomb with a corbeled vault.

The building to the west (C) does not seem to have been used as a house in the last phase but may have been a sort of "house of the dead" (*RSO* X, p. 74). The two tombs in it have some unusual characteristics. The one in the north has a long dromos (2.6 meters), open to the south and without steps, that is nearly as wide as the chamber. The other is no doubt more recent. It is covered by five parallel stone beams, each 2.6 meters long.

To the south of this building is a small house (D, 65 square meters) that is poorly preserved but easy to restore because it has a typical floor plan with a central courtyard.

The southern part of block XIII, along the street that runs from east to west between this block and block XIV (referred to as "Smith Street" in the reports) is not very easy to interpret. In any case, the new proposals do not correspond to the interpretations posited by the excavators.

In House E, the eastern part of which is missing, a few elements can be grouped together. It includes a tomb covered with flagstones and several rooms that are difficult to analyze in their present state. To the south, House F covers a surface of about 190 square meters. The fact that it underwent profound modifications over the course of its history and the fact that many trenches and excavations have penetrated well below floor level only make its analysis all the more difficult. At the southeast end of the block is the funerary zone of a house (G), the rest of which is still in the baulk.

This is where the house that in the earlier reports was designated the "House of the Bronze Smith" is located (but with a different division of houses, grouping together elements of E, F, and G). The discovery of bronze slag and some bronze artifacts (in E), along with two exceptional hoards of jewelry and statuettes in bronze, silver, and gold (nos. 14, 15), stated as having been found in a "cache" (in F), led the excavators to identify this zone as a metallurgical workshop.

This interpretation, however, lacks sufficient basis. To begin with, it is unlikely that activities producing smoke and pollution would have been located in such a highly populated area. Moreover, the slag may simply have been part of the soil rubble, and the bronze tools could have belonged to the owner of the house, along with the gold jewelry and the iron chisels found with them. The precious objects discovered well above ground level probably fell with the floor above, where they had been kept.

Block XIV is located on the other side of "Smith Street," on the southern end of the excavation area. Its eastern, southern, and western limits are unknown. At least nine houses have been identified. They are more or less complete and evidence the usual features and layout of Ugaritic domestic architecture.

House C is a typical example (*Fig.* 55). Its dimensions are modest (less than 140 square meters) and it has a fairly square, regular plan around a central courtyard. It is known in the reports as the "House of an Artisan" because five stone weights, a chisel, and a bronze needle were found in it. It opens to the south onto a nearly square open space that served as a semipublic plaza for the houses around it. It is also equipped with a well.

Selected Bibliography

1960, Schaeffer (C.), "Résumé de la XXIIe campagne de fouille à Ras Shamra–Ugarit, 1959," *AAAS* 10, pp. 133–58.

1961–62, Schaeffer (C.), "Résumé de la XXIIIe campagne de fouille à Ras Shamra–Ugarit, 1960," *AAAS*, 11–12, pp. 187–96.

1979, Courtois (J.-C.), *UF* 11, pp. 108–11.

1983, Callot (O.), *RSO* I, *Une maison à Ougarit*, Paris.

1994, Callot (O.), *RSO* X, *La tranchée "Ville sud,"* Paris.

South Acropolis Trench

To the east of the South City Trench, on the slope descending from the acropolis (see below, p. 106), another trench was dug between 1961 and 1964 (*Fig.* 57); it is conventionally designated the "South Acropolis Trench" and is situated in quadrants B–C (cf. *Figs.* 1, 13).

The main point of interest in this sector was the discovery of important texts concerning religion and divination (tablets, liver models, etc.). These epigraphic finds and some of the most significant artifacts were promptly published, but the architectural remains have only figured in brief reports. No overall study of the district was made by the excavators, other than recently: in *RSO* IV, a few aspects of a building labeled the "House of the Magician-Priest," which yielded a series of so-called "para-mythological texts," sacrificial rituals, and an extraordinary series of clay models of livers and a lung inscribed with markings that reflect a diviner's interpretation of this organ, were studied. Some of the models have accompanying Ugaritic texts (see below, p. 100).

The northern part of the trench is partly covered with the remains of a settlement dating to the 1st millenium B.C.E. (on the Persian period settlement, see p. 103). The whole area must have

Figure 57. South Acropolis Trench, looking to the southeast, 1986.

served as a quarry for construction material during the Persian Period, and most of the Bronze Age buildings are severely damaged.

The organization of this vast zone is not well known. It was destroyed in antiquity, and the excavated ruins have deteriorated since the 1960s. Nonetheless, judging from current observations and a reading of the excavation archives, the area was apparently a Late Bronze Age urban district much like the others recently studied to the west (City Center and South City). Some places, named after the remarkable documents discovered in them have become well known in the archaeological literature. Until a systematic on-site study is resumed, we will have to limit ourselves to a brief description of a few of these sites.

Like the Residential Quarter, the City Center, and the South City Trench, this trench is not a district in the urban-planning sense of the term; it is a convenient name for an archaeological division. Several streets running east and west, approximately following the contours of the levels, served to delimit blocks with the usual type of domestic dwellings. Despite the deterioration, some portions of streets running north to south are still visible. For example, the street that is a continuation of "Mot Street" (named by the excavator after Mot, the god of death) in the acropolis runs through the northern part of this area.

We will describe this area from north to south.

Tombs

On the top of the slope, right next to the acropolis district, which was excavated in the 1930s, some tombs were also explored. They date to the Middle Bronze Age and Phases 1 and 2 of the Late Bronze Age.

The tombs yielded a good number of bronze objects, including weapons, tools, and utensils, and a quantity of ceramics (no. 28) typical of these periods. Among the notable finds were a Cypriot rhyton in the shape of a bull (no. 39) from tomb 3464 and an ivory statuette of a kneeling musician playing cymbals (no. 24), in a style that was common throughout the Levant and Egypt.

The House of Patilu-wa

A gold ring inscribed with the name Patilu-wa in Hittite hieroglyphs (no. 59) was found in one of the houses in a block to the north of the trench. The house, which has therefore been designated the House of Patilu-wa or Patili, opens to the west onto a street that descends from the acropolis (the continuation of Mot Street). Apparently the house of a fairly wealthy family, it has the usual features of Ugaritic domestic architecture, with a courtyard, a fine funerary chamber of ashlar blocks, a stairway leading to the living quarters above, a storage area with jars, and so on. Also found in the house were bronze tools and ceramics of high quality, in particular, Mycenaean craters, one of which bears an exceptional illustration of a hunting scene with lions and stags.

Various Houses and Cultic Places

Nearly twenty meters south, to the east of a street that continues down the slope, is an architectural complex that has been identified (*Fig. 58a*) but has not yet actually been studied in detail. It seems to be composed of two adjacent houses, with a single connecting passageway inside, but the state of preservation is so poor that any interpretation remains hypothetical.

The buildings have been named after objects discovered there. The one to the north has been designated the "House of Agipshari," and the other, the "House of the Priest Containing Inscribed Liver and Lung Models." Alternate names appearing in the reports are the "House and the

Library of a Hurrian Priest," the "House of the Magician-Priest," and the "Annex Library of Medico-Magic and Literary Texts," or "Lamashtu."

The House of Agipshari

To the north, stretching from east to west, is a nearly rectangular house (with the exception of the southeast corner, where rooms from the adjacent house impinge on the rectangular shape). According to the schematic plans of the excavators, there is an entrance to the west, but it is also possible that there was another to the north. This house presents the usual features of Ugaritic architecture: a courtyard, a storage area with large jars, a funerary zone with a stone burial chamber that has niches in the walls, and what might have been an adjoining enclosed garden to the east. Here we find another instance of a well, with the opening and curb-stone built into an interior wall so that it was accessible from both sides. There is a stone trough on the western side.

A clay vase in the shape of a lion's head (no. **36b**) was found in a small room to the north. On it is a dedication in Ugaritic that refers to the son of Agipshari (who might have been the owner of the house) and invokes the god Reshef. The two conic Mycenaean rhytons found in the southern part of this house, which are characteristic cult objects, may actually have come from the adjacent building to the south that clearly has a sacred function.

The House of the Priest Containing Inscribed Liver and Lung Models

According to the excavators' plan, this appears to be a nearly rectangular building with a slight extension to the northeast where two rooms jut into the adjacent house. Unfortunately, the central part and all of the southeast are so damaged that it is impossible to establish the plan.

Some unusual objects were found in two small rooms to the northeast. There is a connecting passageway from the room to the west (identified by the excavator as a cella and measuring 4.5 × 3.5 meters) to the other room, in which a funerary chamber is located (tomb 3709; *Fig.* 59).

In the cella, where they had fallen or were buried in a pit, a wide variety of artifacts related to religion and ritual were discovered. They include tablets in Ugaritic on magic, rituals, and mythology; a dozen texts in Hurrian (hymns and lists of gods); 2 texts in Akkadian; 20-odd objects linked to divinatory practices; clay models in the shape of sheep livers (no. **42**); and one model in the shape of a lung (the lung and five livers bear inscriptions); two hemispheric bowls in gold and electrum; a musical instrument (an ivory clapper of Egyptian type); and a painted pottery mug (no. 35) illustrated with a scene that should be a scene of an offering to the god El, with a bird, horse, and fish symbolizing the elements of air, earth, and water. In the adjacent room was a tomb, on top of which was found a "libation stand" (no. **40**) depicting the god Baal and various animals in relief (stags, bull, ibex, birds, etc.).

Little can be said about the overall plan of the building. In the northwest there is an entrance, from the street to the west, leading into a vestibule. There is also an indoor connecting passageway to the adjacent building to the north. Apparently, the paved courtyard provided access to the rest of the house.

Lamashtu

In the southwest corner, there was a long, narrow room (10 × 2.5 meters) that yielded about 70 tablets in Akkadian (scattered in the room itself and nearby, including on the street). There are private and royal letters, economic and legal texts, as well as about 50 texts that reveal various aspects of Babylonian learning: lexicographic lists, literary texts, numerous magical or medico-magic texts, including a version of the *Lamashtu* tradition (a

Figure 58. South Acropolis Trench: Block including the House of Agipshari and the House of the Magician-Priest with the *cella* in which tablets were found: **a.** schematic plan; **b.** cella where the models and tablets were discovered; after *RSO* V 1, p. 296; and tomb 3709 from the excavations of 1961.

Lamashtu was a female demon who attacks all life forms, particularly newborn babies and their mothers), texts concerning birthing rituals, eye treatments, and more.

The nature of this exceptional collection of documents suggests the presence of a cult site, but we will have to await further investigation before we can provide a description of its extent or analyze its structure.

An Artisan Quarter (?)

There are several blocks in the middle of the trench with structures that have yielded a large number of bronze tools and utensils (pliers, knife blades, needles with eyes) and a jar with objects in electrum or gold (a rhyton, bowls, pins, dagger, etc.). The excavators concluded that this quarter housed an artisan district where metalsmithing and fabric work was carried on.

While it is clear that there were artisan installations here, as elsewhere in the city, a detailed study of this area will have to be undertaken before we can determine whether this was specifically an artisans' district or whether these objects are simply some of the tools and belongings that one would expect to find in an ordinary quarter where private dwellings and artisan workshops stood side by side.

Tomb 4253

Finally, in the southern part of the trench, there is a house dating to the end of the Late Bronze Age that has not yet been totally exposed. It contains one of the very few undisturbed tombs on the tell from this period. The tomb yielded several skeletons and a large number of funerary deposits: Syrian pottery (no. **28**), imported vases (Mycenaean and Cypriot), alabaster vases, faience objects (notably an Egyptian bowl decorated with fish: no. **48**), three bronze daggers, and two gold headbands. The rubble construction is of average workmanship. This, then, is a good example of an ordinary building of a well-equipped house, complete with a family tomb.

Selected Bibliography

1963, Schaeffer (C.), "La XXIVe campagne de fouille à Ras Shamra . . . ," *AAS* 13, pp. 123–34.

1966, Schaeffer (C.), "Neue Entdeckungen und Funde in Ugarit (1962–1964)," *Archiv für Orientforschung*, 221, pp. 132–33.

1969, Courtois (J.-C.), "La maison du prêtre aux modèles de poumon et de foies d'Ugarit," in *Ugaritica* VI, pp. 91–119. Cf. J.-C. Courtois, 1979, *SDB*, pp. 1267–79.

1985, Courtois (J.-C.) in Pardee (D.), *RSO* IV, *Les textes para-mythologiques de la 24e campagne*, Paris.

[2005]

2000, Pardee (D.), *Les textes rituels*, *RSO* XII, Paris.

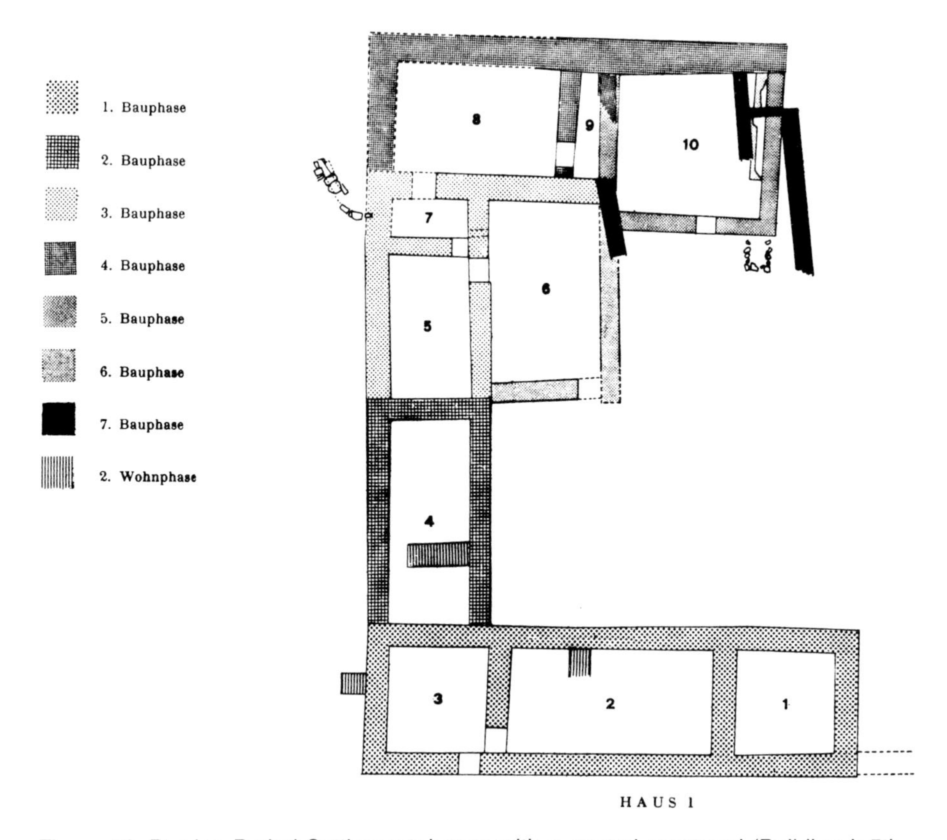

Figure 59. Persian Period Settlement: house with a central courtyard (Building I: 5th century B.C.E.). After R. Stucky, *Leukos Limen*, 1982, pl. 51.

Persian Period Settlement

In the northern part of the South Acropolis Trench, several buildings were excavated that date to a period much later than the city of the Late Bronze Age on the tell.

The tell had been abandoned for nearly seven centuries when, at the beginning of the 5th century B.C.E., a few houses were built on the summit during the era when coastland Syria was part of the Persian Empire. The settlement lasted until around 350 B.C.E. The damage that this area's construction caused to the Late Bronze Age buildings went well beyond the site itself to the surrounding areas, which were robbed for stone to use in the construction. The settlement consisted of several houses (now severely damaged) that reveal no organized urban planning. The best preserved is a house (*Fig.* 59), about 55 × 35 meters, that seems to be made up of a group of rooms around a central, pebble-paved courtyard.

To the north and to the south of these structures, burials were found both in sarcophagi and in cists that also reused architectural materials from the Late Bronze Age.

A 1982 final publication gave general currency to the Greek name *Leukos limen* as a designation for the levels of the 5th-century B.C.E. discoveries on the tell. This is a descriptive term, however, meaning "white harbor," that some Greek writers of the late Roman period (e.g., the *Stadiasmos*) used to refer to the port of "Minet el-Beida" (same meaning in Arabic), which has striking white limestone cliffs; it does not fit the farming settlement located nearly a kilometer inland.

Apparently, there are some traces on the tell, and nearby, of a settlement from the Roman period, but no installation of any significance has been identified.

Selected Bibliography

1982, Stucky (R.), *Leukos Limen*, Paris.

[2005]

2004, Siegert (S.), "Une inscription phénicienne trouvée à Ras Shamra (fouille 1963)," with *Appendice* by M. Yon, in *RSO* XIV, pp. 231–34.

Sondage SH: A Major Stratigraphic Sounding

Proceeding east from the City Center toward the acropolis and the major temples, one walks along a deep excavation; this is *Sondage SH*, the deepest stratigraphic sounding on the tell (*Figs.* 60, 61; *see also Figs.* 8, 9). The sounding reaches down to the earliest levels of occupation, the Neolithic levels (see p. 15).

Several soundings have been undertaken at different spots on the tell, including the acropolis area and the garden of the Royal Palace (cour III), each with an eye to providing a comprehensive history of the site by digging through levels of occupation from the surface down to virgin soil. The entire history of the site and its occupation, as it has been presented by the excavators, is based on the characteristic features of each level reached in these soundings. The phases corresponding to the different levels are numbered from I to V, beginning with the surface level and working down to the Neolithic period (8th millennium B.C.E.; see the chronological table on p. 24).

The earliest sounding dates to 1935. It was located between the temples of Baal and Dagan (and has since been refilled). That sounding reached bedrock at a depth of 18.55 meters and revealed evidence of human occupation extending back to the Neolithic period (level V).

Other soundings were undertaken thereafter to confirm these findings and to provide additional information. Some of these probes also went down

Figure 60. *Sondage SH*, as viewed from the west. In the background is the temple of Baal, 1994.

to bedrock, but the limited surface area that they covered restricted the scope of the conclusions that can be reached.

Sondage SH, the most impressive of these soundings, was conducted between 1962 and 1976 underneath the levels of the 2nd millennium B.C.E. The location was on the slope to the west of the acropolis, just before one reaches the entrance to the enclosure around the Temple of Baal. Because this sounding covered a larger area than the others—about 24 meters from north to south and 12 meters from east to west on the upper level, and 35 square meters at the bottom—the observations that can be made are all the more significant.

The spot chosen for *Sondage SH* was a place where the two most recent levels (the Late Bronze and Middle Bronze Ages) had been removed by earlier excavations in the acropolis area. Stratigraphic examination thus began with level III (Early Bronze Age) and reached down to level V (Prepottery Neolithic) on virgin soil 15 meters below the conventional zero level, which was set in 1962 on the eastern edge of the sounding.

The successive levels (*Fig. 61*) show the evolution of civilizations on the tell from the 8th to the 3rd millenium B.C.E., revealing progressive technological development and many cultural changes. The first inhabitants were farmers who also practiced hunting and fishing. The use of stone for building, the first ceramics, and the appearance of animal husbandry characterize the second phase of the Neolithic period, ca. 7000. After the appearance of copper metallurgy, the 3rd millennium B.C.E. (Early Bronze Age) witnessed the development of metal industry (bronze); at the same time, the settlement began to take on an urban character (narrow streets, rampart), prefiguring the urban development of the 2nd millennium.

Figure 61. *Sondage SH*: the northern face.

Selected Bibliography

1961, Schaeffer (C.), "Les fondements pré- et protohistoriques de Syrie du Néolithique précéramique," *Syria* 38, pp. 7–22.

1962, Schaeffer (C.), "Les fondements pré- et protohistoriques . . . ," *Syria* 39, pp. 147–50.

1979, Courtois (J.-C.), in *SDB*, cols. 1130–50.

1992, Contenson (H. de), *RSO* VIII, *Préhistoire de Ras Shamra*, Paris.

The Acropolis and the Great Temples

Heading east from the Royal Palace, with the excavated zones of the south slope on one's right, one reaches the highest part of the tell. This area was explored between 1929 and 1937 and was designated the "acropolis" (quadrant B, *Figs. 1* and *62*) from the beginning. Following the street that runs from the Palace, and ascending a few steps, one enters the Temple of Baal.

At the summit of the tell and on the northern slope are heaps of excavated material from early excavations in this area. The excavation dumps create mounds to the north of the Temple of Baal that rise above the level of the acropolis and alter the appearance of this quarter by inverting its relief. The visitor should also try to imagine how the district would look without the highly noticeable rubble wall running north to south. This was built in the 1930s to run the small railway used to carry the dumps away to the northern border of the tell (it is the long branch visible just left of the Temple of Baal on the 1936 plan, *Fig. 62*).

The two monumental temples are built according to identical plans, and each was surrounded by an enclosure delimiting the sacred area. Their towers stood high above the ancient city of Ugarit. Linking the two temples are two streets running approximately east to west ("Dagan Street" and "Library Street"), and they also separate blocks of buildings.

The building known as the "House of the High Priest" (or the "Library of the High Priest") is situated between the two temples. The great mythological texts (no. 1) were found in it, promptly attracting attention to the site in 1930. Also found were a group of bronze tools (no. 63) inscribed with dedications that were instrumental in deciphering the Ugaritic language. To the south, immediately below the level of the temples, lies a large residential area that was excavated in the 1930s (see *Fig. 62*) but has never been studied in detail.

The monuments and objects found in this area of the acropolis have been mentioned in many reports, but the architecture and urban planning of the area have not been analyzed. The study of the two temples was recently resumed, and the results will be published in a forthcoming report.

The Temples

Judging from the remains of the two temples, they must have been spectacular structures, dominating the city and the surrounding plain.

The steles found inside the temple enclosures or in their immediate environs were the only clues to the identity of the gods who were worshiped there. The temple to the west seems to have been reserved especially for the worship of Baal. The large stele labeled "Baal with Thunderbolt" (no. **18**) and an Egyptian stele bearing a hieroglyphic dedication to "Baal of Sapan" (no. **17**) were discovered here, along with the image of a goddess, probably Anat, Baal's sister and ally. The other temple was in all probability the site of Dagan worship. Two steles with Ugaritic inscriptions dedicated to Dagan were found in the precinct (no. **19**); other divinities may also have been worshiped here, however.

The Temple of Baal

Although the Temple of Baal is the better preserved of the two temples, it had been looted in antiquity. More recently, at the beginning of the 20th century, a Turkish governor severely damaged the temple in his search for treasure. Many architectural components and objects were thrown out of the temple, down the slope to the west, probably

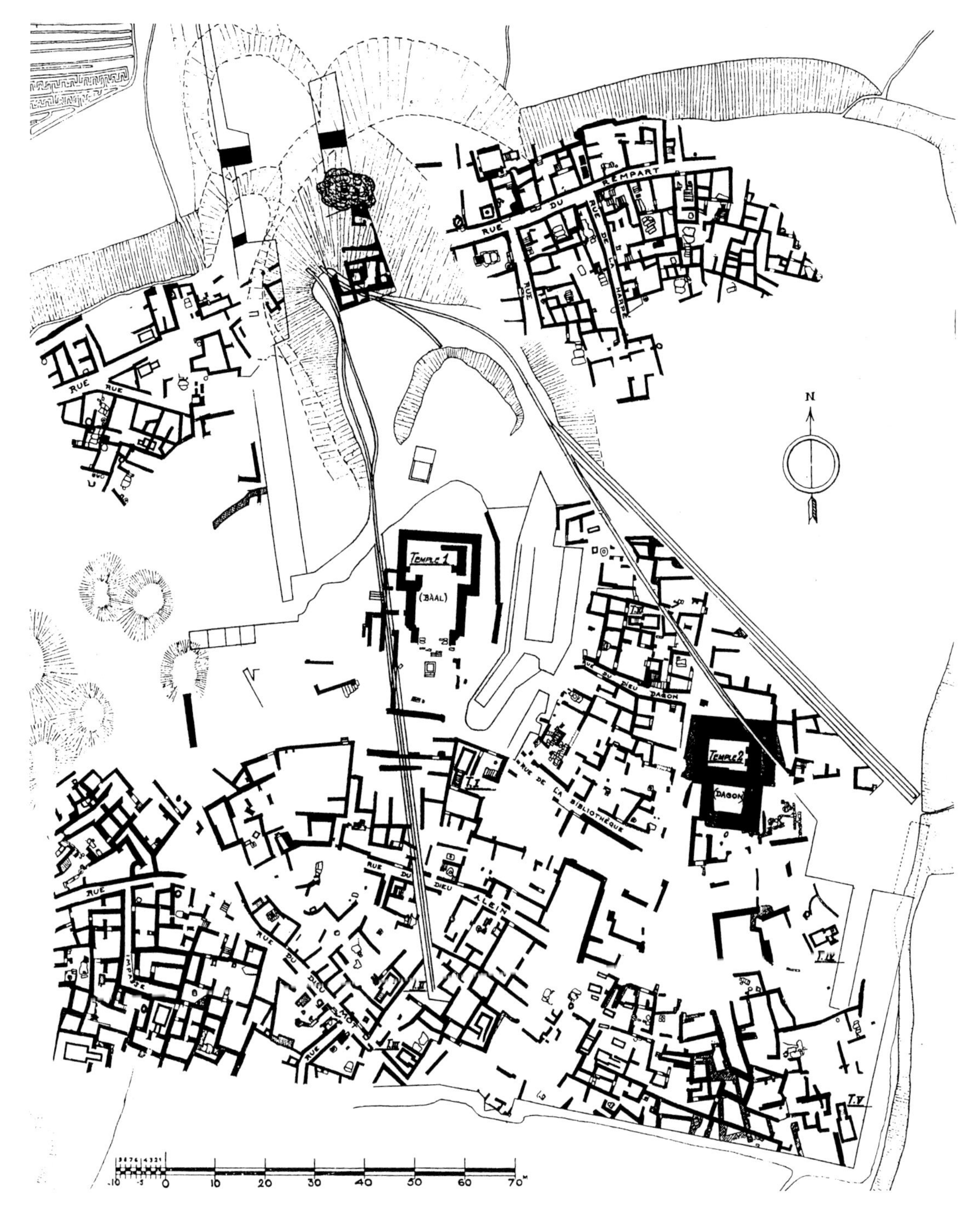

Figure 62. Plan of the Excavations on the Acropolis and the Lower City. After C. Schaeffer, *The Cuneiform Texts of Ras Shamra–Ugarit*, The Schweich Lectures of the British Academy, 1936, London.

at this time. The stele of "Baal with Thunderbolt" (no. 18), for example, was found on this slope. In addition to earlier looting and damage, the excavation in the 1930s went well below the floor level of the temple, so it is now extremely difficult to grasp the design of the building at first sight.

The temple and its enclosure cover an area of about 850 square meters. The enclosure is partially preserved on the east, southeast, and southwest sides. From the city, one climbs a stepped street (some of the steps have survived) to a gate on the western side of the enclosure wall. The severely

Figure 63. The Temple of Baal and its precincts, as viewed from the stepped street that ascends to it from the west.

damaged structures on the left of the entrance were probably utilitarian annexes.

The door leads into the courtyard, situated in front of the temple itself. Nearly in line with the axis of the temple's entrance, in front of the entrance, are large stone blocks that were part of a square altar (2 meters in width), with two steps on its southern side. The altar was still largely intact when it was discovered but has since been destroyed. Next to the altar are a few large stone boat anchors (limestone blocks or blocks pierced with one to three holes), weighing as much as 600 kilograms. They were probably brought to this location by sailors as votive offerings to Baal.

The entrance to the temple is on the south. The foundations are strong, and the preserved lower part of the walls is made of large well-assembled ashlar blocks. The building was a rectangle, 16 × 22 meters, composed of two adjoining, rectangular rooms of different sizes: a vestibule to the south and a rectangular room or "cella" to the north, with a door between the two rooms and a stone sill, the blocks of which have collapsed. A stairway led from the courtyard to the vestibule, which provided access to the temple's "cella."

To the right, upon entering the temple, one can see an enormous foundation made of ashlar blocks that supported the first flight of a stairway along

Figure 64. The Temple of Baal on the Acropolis, looking toward the Mediterranean Sea from the northeast, 1991.

the eastern wall. It is possible that there was a niche (perhaps for a cult image) framed by the stairway's posts on the ground floor. Some of the steles that were excavated in the temple and its environs must have come from this room.

In addition to this flight of stairs, on the eastern side of which the base has survived, there are structural traces along the northern wall and some elements on the western side indicating that there were two other flights of stairs continuing along these sides. These stairways led to an upper terrace, where ritual ceremonies took place, as described in the Ugaritic text in which King Keret offers a sacrifice "on the summit of the tower."

The presence of these stairways enables us to posit a restoration for this part of the sacred building. It would have had the form of a tower, some 18 to 20 meters high. Because the acropolis itself rises nearly 20 meters above the surrounding plain, the terrace would have stood 40 meters above the plain. Moreover, because it was situated less than a kilometer from the sea, it would have been visible from a great distance and must have served as a landmark for sailors entering the port. The terrace could also have served as an observatory from which it would have been possible to communicate with the port of Minet el-Beida and the Ras Ibn Hani settlement with fire signals. The 17 stone anchors found in the temple precinct (including four incorporated into the construction of the temple itself) bear witness to the gratitude of sailors who had reached safe haven at the port and to the connections between the Baal sanctuary and maritime affairs. In the Late Bronze Age, the economy of Ugarit thrived on agricultural production and prosperous maritime trade. Baal was the protector of the kingdom, god of agricultural fertility (according to the mythological texts; see below, "House of the High Priest"), and benefactor of commercial enterprises.

Baal's power was thought to extend over the land, where, as the storm god, he was responsible for bringing the beneficial autumn rains that nourish plants and crops until harvest and gathering time in the spring. After spring comes the dry season and struggle with the extreme heat that leads to the death of nature (see no. 1, "The Conflict between Baal and Mot").

As storm god, Baal lived on the summit of Mount Saphon (Jabal al-Aqra, see *Figs.* 2 and 6), a mountain in the north that dominates the landscape of Ugarit from afar, except in the summer, when it often disappears in the haze. As storm god, Baal also controlled the fate of those who traveled the seas, which is borne out by the votive offerings of anchors in his temple.

The stele known as "Baal with Thunderbolt" (no. 18) offers a good illustration of Baal's position in the kingdom. It was found during excavations in 1932 on the slope below the temple, but its original location was certainly inside the temple. At once threatening and serene, Baal stands on a double base bearing the symbols of the two realms over which he exercises power: the mountains and the sea.

The Middle Bronze Age Necropolis

To the east of the Temple of Baal is a long, deep trench where excavations were conducted in 1931 (and partially filled in thereafter). Below the upper level, which corresponds to the last phase of the city, several layers of superimposed tombs were discovered.

This necropolis, used during the first two centuries of the 2nd millennium B.C.E. (Middle Bronze Age) provided an abundance of ceramics and bronze objects, which bear witness to a remarkable mastery of metallurgical techniques.

The House of the High Priest
(or the Library of the High Priest)

Between the two temples stood several buildings, but only the eastern part, next to the Temple of Dagan, has survived (the rest disappeared in the excavation of the Middle Bronze Age necropolis). The most noteworthy building was discovered in 1929 and is known as the "House of the High Priest" (or the "Library of the High Priest"). Despite its damaged state, it is clear that this building has the usual features of Ugaritic domestic architecture in the Late Bronze Age, with an entrance vestibule, stairway, paved courtyard, well, and so on.

The house has yielded some of the most important objects for understanding the history of the city, including a cache of 74 weapons, utensils, and bronze tools (a hoe and four adzes with dedicatory inscriptions on them that were used in 1930 to decipher Ugaritic; see no. **63**), and also a series of tablets with mythological poems, which have made possible the recovery of ancient Ugaritic literature.

Baal, god of the storm and of plant life, the symbol of agricultural abundance and of the kingdom's power, is the central figure in the poems that constitute what is known as the *Baal Cycle*: "Baal and the Sea," "Baal and Anat," "the Palace of Baal," and "The Conflict between Baal and Mot" (no. **1**). He is the protagonist of all sorts of adventures that probably coincide with the yearly cycle of seasons, linked at every point to the specific conditions of the Mediterranean climate and crops. He appears alongside other deities: his sister and ally, Anat; Mot, god of death; Yam, god of the sea; and the entire Canaanite pantheon, including El, the father figure (cf. no. **13**).

There are also tablets that recount the "Birth of the Beautiful and Graceful Gods" (that is, sons of El—a myth linked to the introduction of agriculture), the "Wedding of the Moon" (perhaps a myth linked to marriage and fertility), and some that are devoted to other supernatural entities, such as the Rephaim (translated as "ghosts" or heroes").

Other poems feature characters from Canaanite legend: the story of King Keret and his family misfortunes illustrates the kindness of the gods to the king; the story of the hero Danel, the mythical symbol of the righteous sufferer, and of his son Aqhat highlights the opposition between wisdom and power and warns against a lack of moderation.

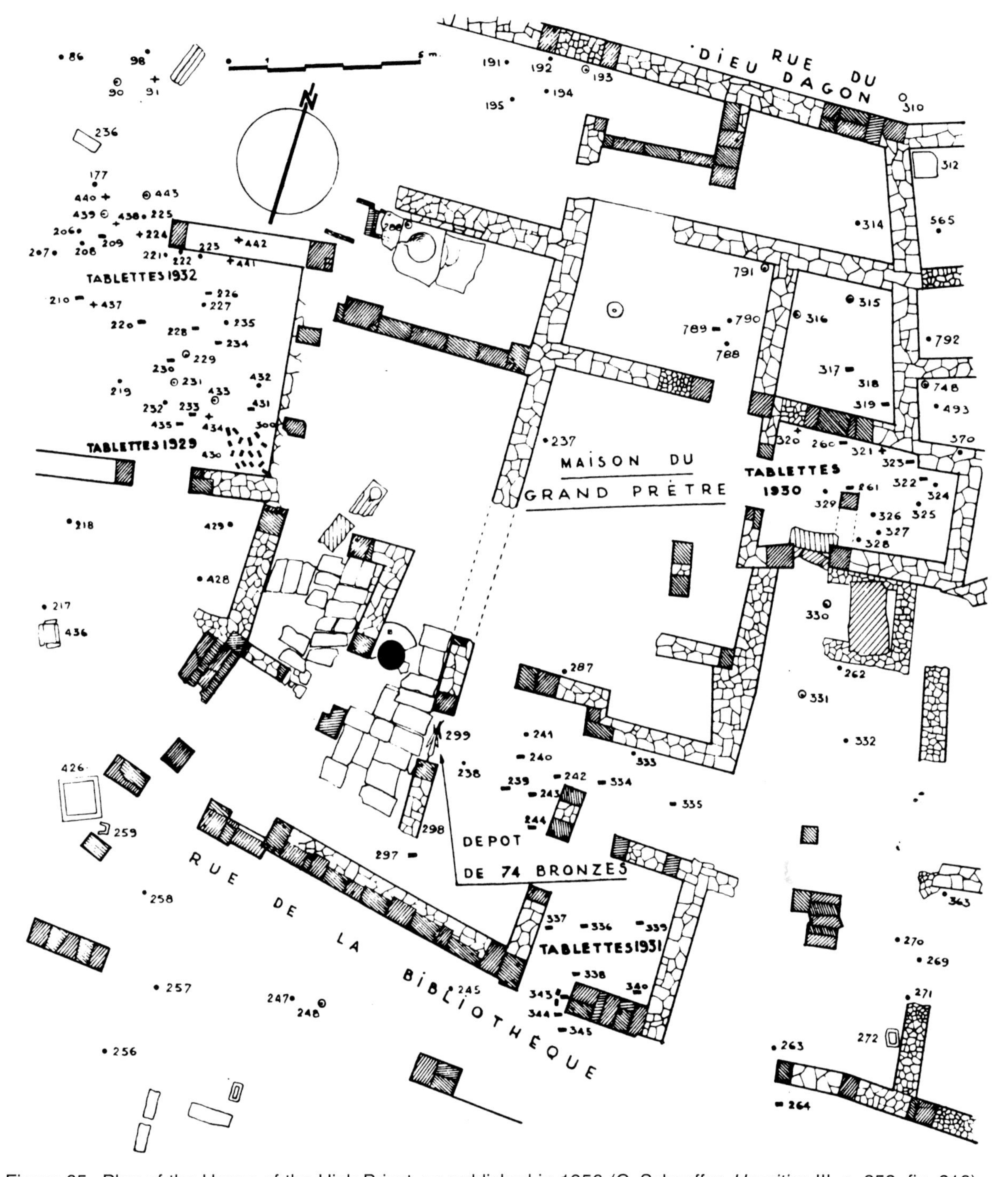

Figure 65. Plan of the House of the High Priest, as published in 1956 (C. Schaeffer, *Ugaritica* III, p. 252, fig. 216).

The Temple of Dagan

To the east of the House of the High Priest is the second temple on the acropolis. This one faces south, like the Temple of Baal, but is less well preserved. All that remains is the base, with its huge foundation walls in the form of a glacis, which indicates that perhaps the first phase of construction was in the Middle Bronze Age. But the date of its construction is still being discussed.

From the layout of the foundation, we can reconstruct the temple as having a plan similar to the plan of the Temple of Baal. It included a vestibule to the south that led to a rectangular room. Because the superstructure has disappeared, the varying thickness of the foundations is evident. They are wider (up to 4 meters) where they serve as benching walls on the sides where the temple dominates the slope to the north and to the east. The foundations are wide enough for two or three flights of stairs leading to the upper stories. The first flight began in the southeast corner and continued along the eastern wall, between it and another wall parallel to it. The second flight was

Figure 66. The Temple of Dagan and the enclosure for steles on the southeastern edge of the temple precinct, 1989.

incorporated into the north wall. There was probably a third flight, as in the Temple of Baal, although no remains of it have survived; it might have been set on a buttress in the southwestern corner.

The temple was erected in a protected space formed by the northern and western walls of the temple itself and the enclosure wall to the south and the east.

In the courtyard in front of the entrance (that is, within the sacred area), two steles were found (one of which is incomplete) on which there are dedicatory inscriptions to the god Dagan in Ugaritic (no. **19**); the complete stele has a rectangular tenon for fitting into a socketed base. To the southeast of the temple (*Fig.* 66), against the eastern side of the vestibule is a platform with stone blocks that have a long mortice cut into them. This installation is not a water channel (or "a cult arrangement in relation to the temple," as the excavator suggested), nor are they watering troughs for animals; instead, they are the socketed stone bases in which the steles with tenons were set (same type as the Dagan steles), and the arrangement that resulted would have been comparable to the installation found in the "Obelisk Temple" at Byblos.

On the basis of the two steles, this temple has been attributed to the god Dagan. Some scholars have questioned this attribution, claiming that Dagan is an eastern Syrian god, foreign to the Levant. However, Dagan clearly had a place in Ugarit. Judging from the god-lists, his place in the pantheon was far from insignificant, because his name appears between El and Baal, and he is frequently mentioned in the Ugaritic ritual texts as a recipient of offerings.

Quarter to the South of the Acropolis Temples

A relatively large area on the southern slope of the acropolis below the temples was excavated in 1935 and 1936, but it has not been studied thoroughly, and thus we can say little about the organization of the district or the architectural features of the buildings. Basically, it was a crowded residential area with streets that the excavators named after the mythological texts that had just been translated ("Mot Street," "Alein Street," etc.).

The tombs that were discovered there obviously belong to the houses in which they were constructed, but the outlines of the houses themselves have not yet been determined in detail.

A large number of objects were found in this area (no. **12**), and some of them immediately attracted attention due to their intrinsic quality and their connection with the nearby Temple of Baal. The two best-known works of art are a gold patera with the scene of a royal hunt on it and a gold dish decorated with animals (nos. **56**, **57**). These were found in a building 30 meters southwest of the Temple of Baal, although the find-spot was probably not their place of origin.

Two sculpted stone steles were uncovered in two different houses slightly down the slope to the southwest. They are known as the "stele of homage to the god El" and the "stele of the oath."

Selected Bibliography

The Temples and the Library of the High Priest

1929, etc., Schaeffer (C. F.-A.), "Rapport . . . ," *Syria* 1929, etc.

1949, Schaeffer (C. F.-A.), *Ugaritica* II, pp. 1–130.

1979, Courtois (J.-C.), in *SDB*, cols. 1150–1202.

1991, Yon (M.), "Stèles de pierre," in *RSO* VI, pp. 271–344.

Ugaritic Texts and Language

The following is a selection of a few foundational texts selected from the abundant literature written on the subject.

The First Copies of the Tablets

1929, Virolleaud (C.), "Les inscriptions cunéiformes de Ras Shamra," *Syria* 10, pls. 40, 51–75.

Decipherment

1930, Dhorme (E.), "Première traduction des textes phéniciens de Ras Shamra," *Revue Biblique* 40, pp. 32–56.

1930, Bauer (H.), *Entzifferung der Keilschrifttafeln von Ras Shamra*, Halle, 1930.

1931, Dhorme (E.), "Le déchiffrement des tablettes de Ras Shamra," *Journal of the Palestine Oriental Society* 11, pp. 1–6.

Ugaritic Texts

1963, Herdner (A.), *Corpus des tablettes en cunéiformes alphabétiques* . . . (= CTA), Paris.

1974, Caquot (A.), Sznycer (M.), and Herdner (A.), *Textes ougaritiques*, I: *Mythes et légendes*, Paris.

1979, Caquot (A.), in *SDB*, cols. 1362–1403.

1992, Bordreuil (P.) and Pardee (D.), in *Anchor Bible Dictionary* 6, New York.

1995, CAT = Dietrich (M.), Loretz (O.), and Sanmartín (J.), *The Cuneiform Alphabetic Texts from Ugarit, Ras Ibn Hani and Other Places*, Münster (new edition of *KTU* = *Die keilalphabetischen Texte aus Ugarit* I, Kevelaer/Neukirchen-Vluyn, 1976).

Figure 66bis. Model of the Temple of Baal, viewed from the west: proposed reconstruction (in *Aux origines de l'alphabet*, 2004 [see p. 26 above], p. 271, model by F. Laliberté after O. Callot) [2005].

The Lower City

To the north of the tell, below the acropolis, is an area of living quarters that was excavated from 1935 to 1937. It has been designated the Lower City because of its position in relationship to the acropolis (*Figs.* 68, 69). The presence in the middle of this area of a large mound created by excavation dumps from the acropolis delimits two zones: the Lower City West (or "site A" in the early reports) and Lower City East (sometimes called "site B" in the reports). By 1938, the focus of investigation had moved to other areas that were thought to be more promising, such as the northwest part of the tell, where excavations eventually uncovered the Royal Zone. These northern areas were published in brief reports, but no architectural or stratigraphic analyses were carried out.

Due to the discovery of Middle Bronze Age tombs in deeper levels, the excavator dated this district quite early (the area is known sometimes as the "Hyksos Quarter," after the Asiatics who settled in Egypt around the Nile Valley at this time). He recognized that it was reoccupied in the

Figure 67. The Lower City West, as viewed from the west, 1989. In the background are the Alawi Mountains.

Late Bronze Age, but even the date of the buildings visible on the surface was not determined.

A new study of the eastern section of the Lower City, begun in 1994, has already led to the conclusion that, as one might have expected, this quarter presents the same organizational and architectural features as the other districts on the tell. The buildings unearthed by the excavations date to the Late Bronze Age, and here as elsewhere some of the structures were significantly altered during the last phase of the city (about 1200 B.C.E.). But deep soundings below these levels have allowed us, as we hoped, to reach the earlier Middle Bronze Age levels and the tombs that belong to this period.

These areas, as they appear in their final state, were built on benched terraces on land that slopes up from the edge of the tell to the heights occupied by the temples. A street known as "Rampart Street" runs parallel to the edge of the tell, from west to east on either side of the mound created by the dumps. It delimits a series of blocks of buildings to the north, though the boundaries of these blocks are not well defined; and, to the south, "Rampart Street" delimits other building complexes on streets heading up to the acropolis.

The Late Bronze Age houses are built using the usual techniques, combining rubble construction with ashlar blocks (for door jambs, the base of walls,

Figure 68. The Lower City East as viewed from the Acropolis, with a view of the groves in the background, to the north of the tell, 1994.

and so on), and feature the same spatial design, with courtyards, tombs, stairways, and so on. The quality of the construction varies widely, with well-built, well-designed buildings adjacent to mediocre houses.

The Lower City West

Excavated in 1935, the Lower City West is the quarter that can be seen on the left when one heads from the center of the tell toward *Sondage SH* and

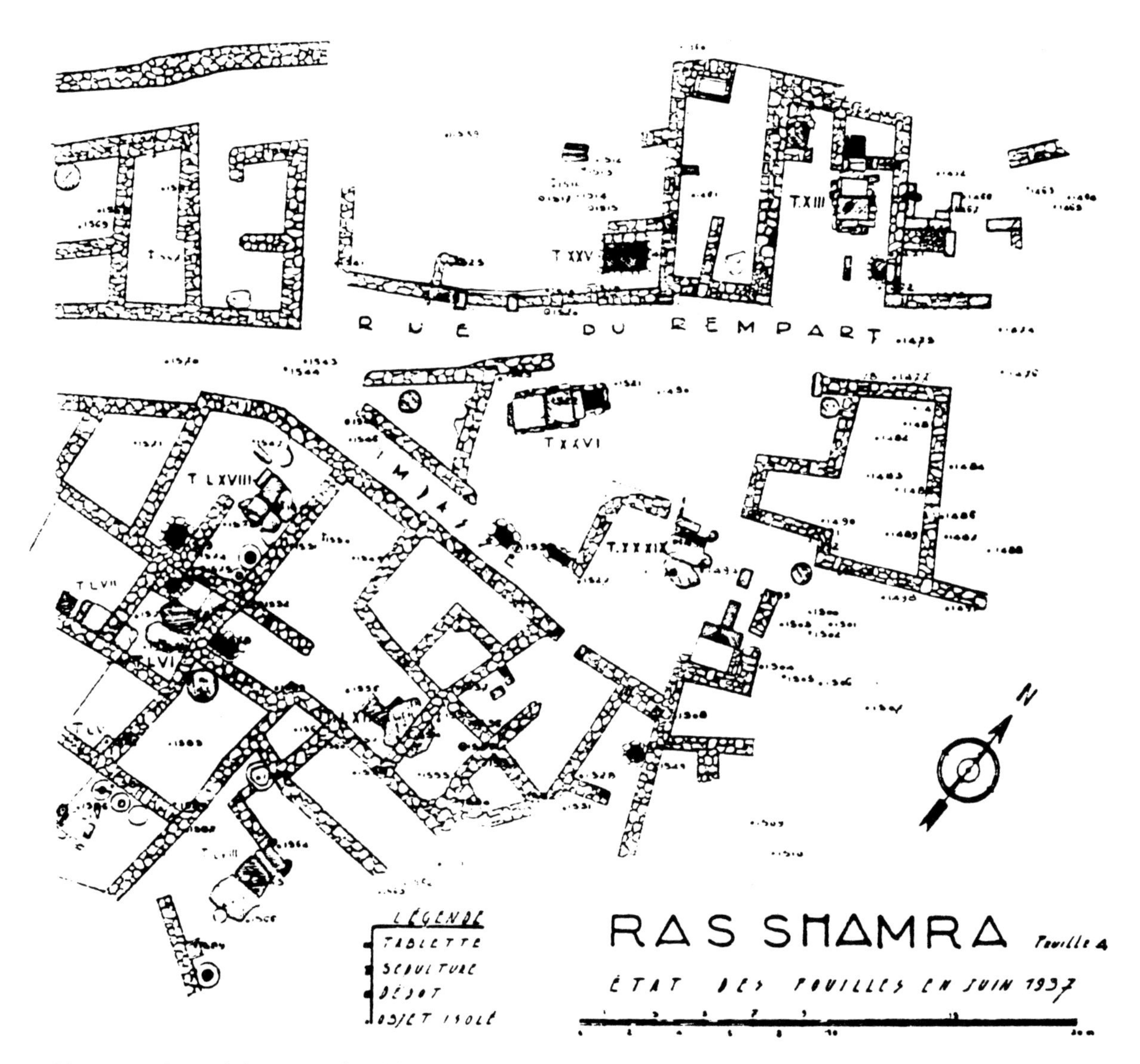

Figure 69. Plan of the Lower City West in 1937, as published in *Syria* 19 (1938) 217, fig. 16 ("chantier A").

the Temple of Baal. The excavated section, today destroyed by erosion, occupies nearly 2300 square meters. Because the study of this area has not been resumed, what we are reporting here is based on succinct, early reports.

The Late Bronze Age

Apparently, the quarter is mainly composed of Late Bronze Age buildings with tombs. Some of the tombs were not pillaged. This is the case for tomb XIII, which was found in a house north of Rampart Street and was still covered with a stone slab. In the eastern wall of the funerary chamber, an ossuary was containing the remains of 44 persons was found. On the ground, more than 100 vessels of local or foreign (Cypriot, Mycenaean) manufacture were scattered, along with bronze, ivory, and stone artifacts dated to the Late Bronze Age.

The reports also mention some objects discovered in this area that we now know should be linked to ritual ceremonies: two cone-shaped Mycenaean rhytons and a Mycenaean rhyton in the form of a hedgehog(?). A small, fragmentary group with two faience figures on a horse-drawn chariot (no. **46**) was also found here.

Figure 70. The Lower City East. Facades of houses on "Harpé Sword Street," as viewed from "Rampart Street," looking northwest, 1994.

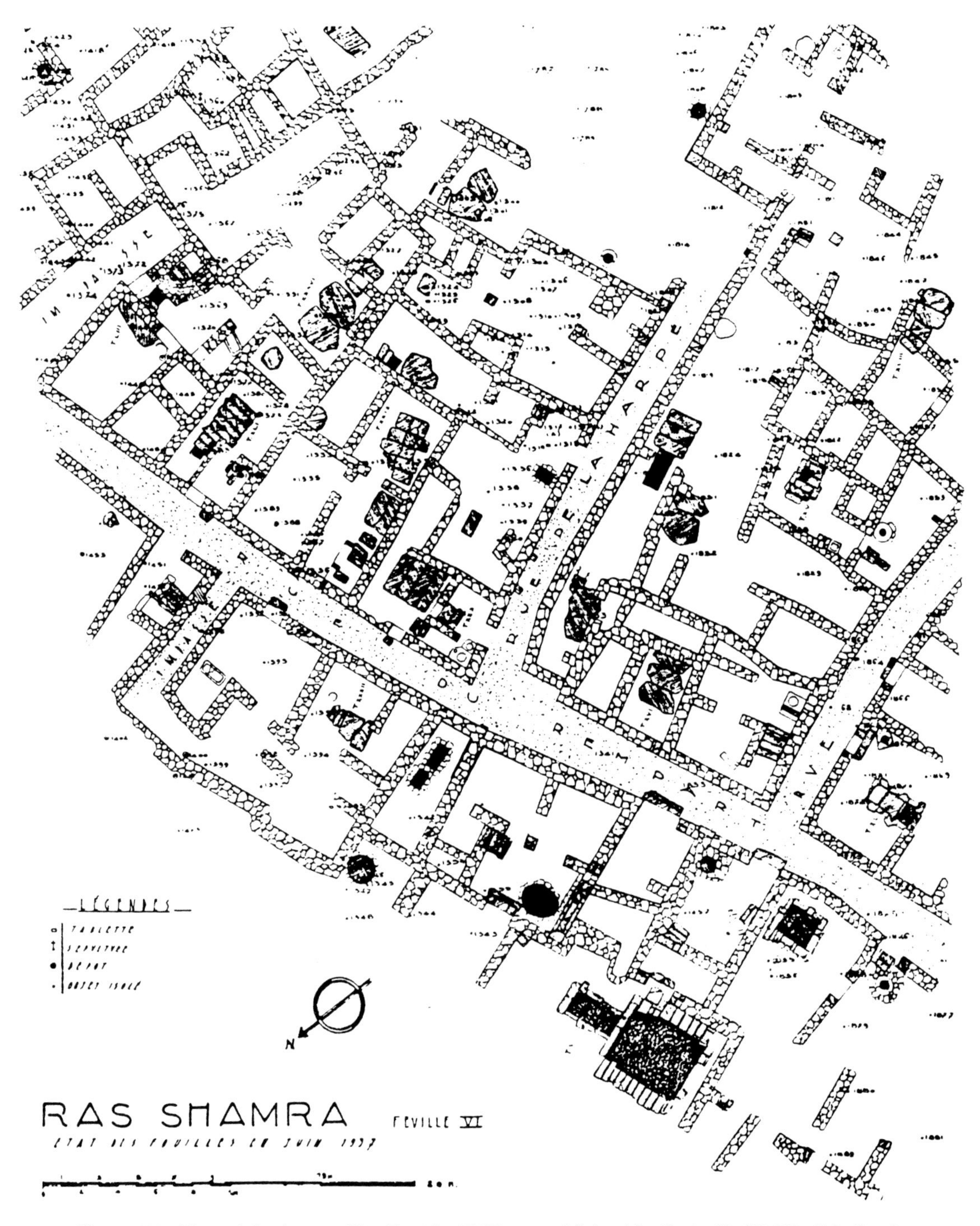

Figure 71. Plan of the Lower City East in 1937, as published in *Syria* 19 (1938) 198, fig. 2. Note the orientation of the plan: north is at the lower left.

The Middle Bronze Age

The excavation reached Middle Bronze Age levels at some spots and, in particular, uncovered several tombs with material typical of this period.

Lower City East

This quarter, excavated in 1936 and 1937, is located to the north of the temples and below them.

The Late Bronze Age

The area explored is larger than the one in the west and clearly reveals elements of city planning. This area yielded a wide variety of objects and other finds, sometimes of high quality (such as a bronze bull, no. **65**).

Rampart Street, which traverses this zone from east to west, is still visible today, as are the buildings on both sides, and in some cases the remains are preserved relatively high. On the northern side were large houses of fine quality. On the southern side, the quarter is divided into blocks by perpendicular streets that ascend to the acropolis. A wide western street was excavated for about 20 meters, but part of it today is covered by the excavation dumps. The second street that runs from north to south is known as "Harpé Sword Street" (because of the discovery of a bronze sword of this type, no. **61**). It extends across two blocks of houses that have relatively well-preserved walls. At the corner of Rampart Street and Harpé Sword Street is one of the best-preserved complexes, and study of it was resumed in 1994, revealing a residence dating to the Late Bronze Age (*Fig. 70*).

Middle Bronze Age

The deep excavations of 1937 reached five intact funerary chambers dating to the Middle Bronze Age (Tombs LIII–LVIII). A wide variety of objects were found, including bronze tools and weapons, and ceramics characteristic of what is called the Hyksos Period.

Selected Bibliography

1936, 1937, 1938, Schaeffer (C. F.-A.), "Rapport . . . ," *Syria* 17, pp. 105–47; 18, pp. 125–54; 19, pp. 197–255.

1979, Courtois (J.-C.), in *SDB*, cols. 1202–8.

1994, Castel (C.), Field Report, "La ville basse Est" (unpublished, archives of the French mission).

[2005]

2004, Castel (C.), "Naissance et développement d'une maison dans la 'Ville Basse' orientale d'Ougarit (fouille 1936)," in *RSO* XIV, pp. 41–64.

The East Terrace

In 1950 and 1959, two narrow, east–west trenches were dug for a length of 50 meters on the slope to the east of the acropolis, but no systematic study was conducted. Although we cannot present a complete picture of this area, we do know that it has streets and houses with the same architectural features as other Late Bronze Age areas of the city.

The excavation inventories mention some interesting objects from this area, notably a complex vase in alabaster in the shape of a small figure carrying a jar. This vase was found inside a large jar containing the remains of a child's corpse—providing evidence of a funerary practice rarely attested at Ugarit.

The House with Jars

The excavation of this architectural complex in 1959 uncovered the storage rooms of a house and a portion of a street (*Fig. 72*). In the jars found here were clay bullas (a bulla is a kind of "label"). These were inscribed with cuneiform signs and/or had impressions of stamps or cylinder seals on them.

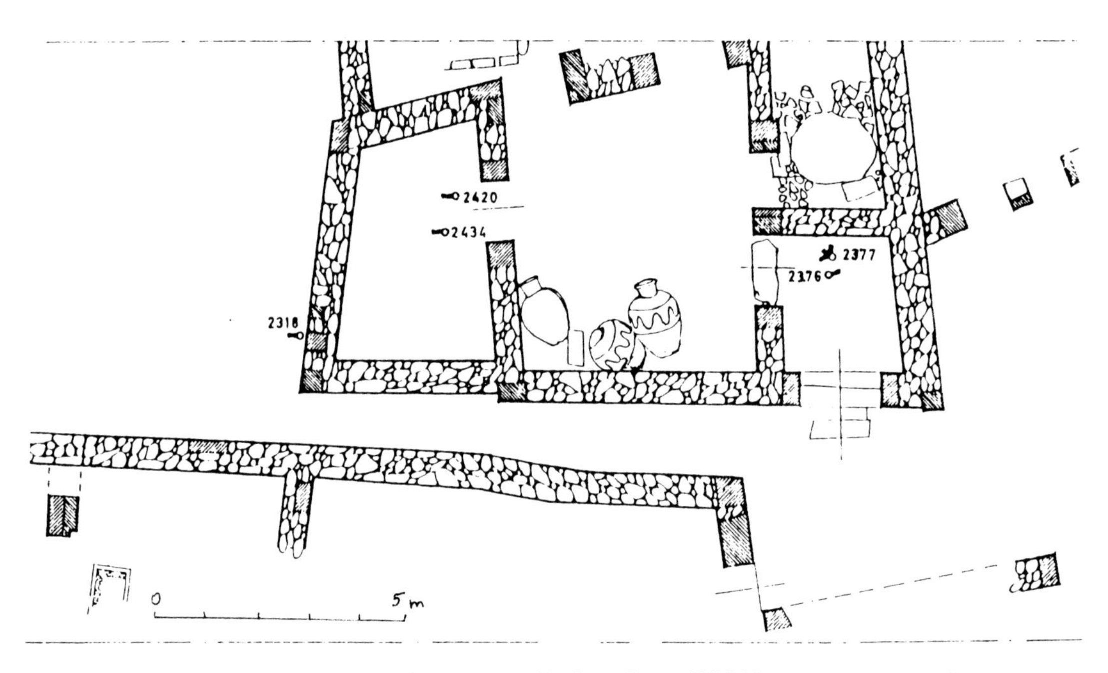

Figure 72. The East Terrace: the House with Jars. From *RSO* V, 1, 1989, p. 282, fig. 35.

Selected Bibliography

1951, Schaeffer (C. F.-A.), "Rapport," *Syria* 28, pp. 19–20.

1960, Schaeffer (C. F.-A.), "Résumé des résultats de la 22e campagne de fouille . . . ," AAAS X, pp. 133–58.

Chapter 3

Artifacts Illustrating Official and Everyday Life

A visit to the ruins on the tell of Ras Shamra as they now appear would offer only a partial picture of the actual city life of ancient Ugarit. Missing would be the colors that painted the city's houses, the variety of furnishings, the sounds of everyday life, the activity on the streets, and everything else that gave it the character of a vibrant and densely populated capital. To a great extent, a picture of life at Ugarit must be supplied by one's imagination, because only a small part of the ancient reality has been recovered. Nevertheless, in addition to the architectural ruins, many objects allow us to comprehend more of the life of the city's inhabitants. And a visit to the ruins must be combined with a visit to the museums to which many of the significant artifacts have been transferred.

Certain Ugaritic objects of gold and ivory are examples of Syrian art at its zenith. The royal palace, the temples, and some tombs that were not pillaged have provided a very rich trove of artifacts: imported luxury ceramics and stone, faience, ivory, and metal objects. But many other objects deserve to be mentioned, not so much for their aesthetic value but for their significance in other respects. Their message is no more explicit than the thousands of inscribed tablets discovered on the tell; these too are mute but decipherable if one interprets them accurately. Certain religious objects have helped in locating cultic installations, and the modest domestic artifacts that have been recovered in large quantities have greatly enhanced our ability to trace the activities of everyday life.

The various objects discovered in the course of 60 years of excavations reflect the kind of operations that took place in the local workshops of potters, stone cutters, and scribes, and they attest to developments in metal, ivory, and faience craftsmanship. The artifacts provided by the excavations include all sorts of diverse objects that were imported to Ugarit, revealing the cosmopolitan character of the emporium. The local residents came into direct contact with foreign people, because sailors and merchants from Greece, Cyprus, the Levant, Egypt, Anatolia, and the Euphrates regularly visited Ugarit. Their ships and caravans transported expensive cargo, sometimes from great distances—ivory from India or Africa, lapis lazuli from Afghanistan, amber from the Baltics—but also perishable consumer products such as textiles, grain, wine, and perfume, from which archaeology has only been able to recover the containers, and even then, only in the best of circumstances.

Of all the objects that have been recovered, we are able to present here only a selection that is representative of the various areas on the tell where they were discovered or that aided in defining the architectural space in which they were found. These are truly exceptional finds, while others more mundane are important precisely because of their banality, testifying to the life-style of the general population living in the second-millennium city.

These preserved objects are housed, sometimes exhibited, in museums and reserves in Syria (Damascus, Aleppo, Latakia, Tartous) or in France (the Louvre). Some recently discovered are presently under restoration in the workshops of the Damascus Museum. Taken as a whole, these artifacts constitute an imaginery museum of Ugarit in this book.

recto **1** verso

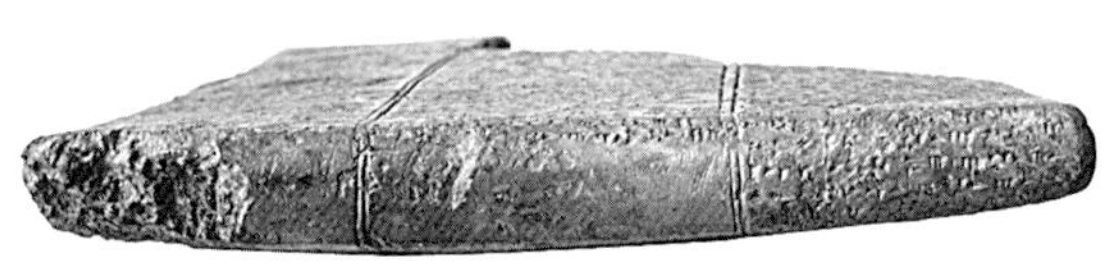

edge

a **2** b

Transcription of alphabetic cuneiform signs
(after *Le Monde de la Bible*, 1987, p. 27).

Tablets Written in Ugaritic (Alphabetic Cuneiform)

[H = height, W = width, D = depth, L = length]

1. An Ugaritic mythological poem: *The Conflict between Baal and Mot* RS 2.[009]+5.155

1930 and 1933, the Acropolis, the High Priest's Library. Louvre Museum AO 16636

H 27 cm, W 19.5 cm, D 3.8 cm. Incomplete clay tablet (with part of the text missing). The tablet has a lengthy, 3-columned text on both sides. It recounts the battle between the gods Baal and Mot (the personification of death). The text must be interpreted as an agrarian myth, the image is of Baal's annual disappearance, which symbolizes the power of nature. As the various agricultural images demonstrate, the heat of the summer causes the god to vanish. In the end, however, Baal returns in a tempest, evoking the image of the storm that brings the rains of autumn.

– ***Bib.***: *Syria* 12, 1931, pp. 193–224 ; 15, 1934, pp. 226–43; A. Herdner, CTA, 1963, 6; A. Caquot, M. Sznycer, and A. Herdner, *TO Mythes*, 1974, pp. 223–71; *KTU* (1976), 1.6.

2. Ugaritic abecedaries

The writing system consists of 30 cuneiform signs that were impressed on soft clay. Several abecedaries have been recovered at the site and are generally considered to be documents with a pedagogical function. The abecedaries typically assume the common form and proportions of rectangular Ugaritic tablets, the lone exception being the examplar recovered from the Royal Palace. This one is quite elongated (see no. **2a**).

a. 1948, the Royal Palace, northwest entrance hall. RS 12.063

Damascus Museum (inv. 3561)

H 5.2 cm, W 1.7 cm, D 1.6 cm. A clay tablet of elongated form, featuring the inventory of alphabetic signs, and written from left to right on three lines.

– ***Bib.***: *Syria* 28, 1951, pp. 22–23.1A; C. Virolleaud, *PRU* II, 1957, 184; *KTU* (1976), 5.7.

b. 1955, the House of Yabninu (South Palace), room 204. RS 19.031

Damascus Museum (inv. 5018)

H 3.7 cm, W 5.2 cm, D 2.1 cm. A rectangular clay tablet, featuring the inventory of alphabetic signs, and written from left to right on four lines.

– ***Bib.***: *KTU* (1976), 5.12.

[2005] Unique at Ras Shamra, an abecedary organized according to the order typical of the South-Arabian tradition was unearthed in the House of Urtenu (RS 88.2215). A similar abecedary had earlier been discovered at the Palestinian site of Beth-Shemesh, but all other abecedaries from Ras Shamra discovered to date reflect the standard Phoenician–Hebrew order that was adopted by the Greeks and that has endured to our day. See P. Bordreuil and D. Pardee, in *RSO* XIV, 2001, pp. 341–48, no. 32.

3

4

recto

5 verso

6

Tablets Written in Other Languages

3. The General's Letter (Akkadian) RS 20.033

1956, the Residential Quarter, the House of Rapanu, room 6. Damascus Museum (inv. 5290)

H 13.3 cm, W 10.4 cm, D 3.7 cm. A clay tablet broken at the bottom. It is inscribed on both sides in a compact syllabic cuneiform script. It contains the report of an envoy of the Ugaritic king (whose name is not given) to the general of the army, Sumiyanu, who is responsible for organizing the defense of the kingdom along its frontier with the neighboring kingdom of Amorites/Amurru. In the first publication of the letter (1968), C. Schaeffer suggested that the king in view was Niqmaddu III, and the date of the events in question approximated 1200, which would correspond well with the rest of the archives discovered in Rapanu's House. More recently, I. Singer has proposed a much earlier time for the letter, coinciding with the Amarna period (14th century B.C.E.). In this letter there is an allusion to the threat of conflict between Egypt and Hittite Syria, and the dates that have been proposed rely on this allusion. However, there is no evidence to prove one date more likely than the other.

– **Bib.**: J. Nougayrol, *Ugaritica* V, 1968, pp. 69–79 (cf. comment by C. Schaeffer, pp. 640–95, fig. 22, 22 A–G; S. Izre'el and I. Singer, *The General's Letter from Ugarit: A Linguistic and Historical Reevaluation of RS* 20.33, 1990).

4. Beya's Letter, Chief of Pharaoh's Guards (Akkadian) RS 86.2230

1988, South-Central Sector, the House of Urtenu, room 2053. Damascus Museum (inv. 7767))

H (preserved) 6.2 cm, W 7.2 cm, D 2.3 cm. The upper part of a clay tablet written in syllabic cuneiform. There are only remnants of the address and greeting formula on the recto. The letter, which can be dated to the first years of the 12th century, is addressed to Ammurapi, king of Ugarit, from Beya, a person attested in other documents, who eventually was appointed to a position of power in Egypt.

– **Bib.**: D. Arnaud, in *Syrie, Mémoire* . . . , 1993, pp. 248–49, no. 222. **[2005]** D. Arnaud, in *RSO* XIV, 2001, pp. 278–79, no. 18.

5. Tablet containing bilingual maxims in Akkadian and Hurrian RS 15.010

1951, Royal Palace, room 53 (east archives). Tartous Museum (inv. 511)

H 5.7 cm, W 10 cm, D 2.6 cm. Rectangular clay tablet written horizontally in syllabic cuneiform on the recto and the top of the verso. It consists of an Akkadian version and another in Hurrian. It contains extracts from an anthology of ethico-religious maxims probably derived from a treatise concerning "appeals to the gods."

– **Bib.**: J. Nougayrol and E. Laroche, *PRU* III, 1955, pp. 311–24, pl. 106; cf. C. Schaeffer, *Ugaritica* IV, p. 316, fig. 119.

6. Tablet in Cypro-Minoan RS 17.006

1953, Residential Quarter, found on the surface. Damascus Museum (inv. 4515)

H (cons.) 4 cm, W 4.2 cm, D (max.) 1.8 cm. Small, incomplete clay tablet, almost square, bulging on both sides. One side is well preserved, but the surface of the other side is damaged. On both sides is a text written in linear, Cypro-Minoan characters. The lines are delimited by horizontal markings. The contents remain enigmatic because, unfortunately, it is not yet possible to decipher Cypro-Minoan.

– **Bib.**: O. Masson in *Ugaritica* III, 1956, pp. 233–46, pl. 8–9.

7

8

9

10

11

Seals and Scarabs

7. A royal tablet with seal impression (Akkadian) RS 16.146+161

1952, Royal Palace, Court IV (central archives). Damascus Museum (inv. 4261)

H 12.3 cm. W 8.9 cm, D 3.4 cm. A clay tablet written in syllabic cuneiform. At the top of the recto is the seal impression of the king of Amurru. The tablet describes the trousseau (ivory furniture and objects, gold and bronze tableware, and precious textiles) of Queen Akhatmilku, daughter of the king of the Amurru, for her marriage to Amishtamru II, the king of Ugarit (approx. 1250).

– **Bib.**: J. Nougayrol, *PRU* III, 1955, pp. 182– 86, pl. 11, fig. 14; cf. SDB, col. 1182, fig. 912.4 (seal only).

8. An Ugaritic cylinder seal (along with a modern impression) RS 4.021

1932, Minet el-Beida, trench 25.IV, topographic point 1. Louvre Museum AO 15772

H 2.2 cm, Diameter 1.2 cm. Black steatite. Fine engraving but rather poor relief. Cylinder with longitudinal piercing. The scene is a chariot hunt, shown in full profile. One can see only one wheel of the chariot (with four spokes) and one horse. In the chariot is a warrior who holds the reins around his waist, wearing an Egyptian-style crown and pulling his bow. Opposite the charioteer is a large rearing lion. The horse is portrayed as leaping over a corpse lying on its back. Behind the chariot is one eagle, and another eagle hovers over the team of horses.

– **Bib.**: P. Amiet, *RSO* IX, 1992, p. 131, no. 302.

9. A modern impression of a Cypriot cylinder seal RS 20.039

1956, Residential Quarter, edge of a blind alley northwest of Rapanu's House. Damascus Museum (inv. 2648)

H 2 cm, Diameter 1.3 cm. Soapstone. Cylinder with longitudinal piercing. The engraved scene has several figures, monsters (man with a bull's head), and animals (lions, an ibex) crowned with various astral emblems, a winged solar disk, and a head encircled with sun rays. This cylinder was imported from Cyprus.

– **Bib.**: P. Amiet, *RSO* IX, 1992, pp. 187–90, no. 452.

10. Scarab of Amenophis II, Pharaoh of Egypt, written in Egyptian hieroglyphic RS 16.094

1952, Royal Palace, room 44, northwest of Garden III (along with the ivory objects nos. 21, 22).

Damascus Museum (inv. 2585)

H 7.4 cm, W (cons.) 2.6 cm, D 2.7 cm. Glazed shale. Broken along a tubular perforation that runs the entire length of the insect. The text comprises nine lines of Egyptian hieroglyphic. The scarab records the marriage of Pharaoh Amenophis III to Queen Tiy.

– **Bib.**: P. Krieger, in C. Schaeffer, *Ugaritica* III, 1956, pp. 221–26, fig. 204.

11. Stamp seal of Mursili II, King of Hatti, written in Hittite hieroglyphic and Akkadian RS 14.202

1950, Royal Palace, southeast edge of Court I. Damascus Museum (inv. 3562)

Diameter 5.1 cm, D 1.4 cm. Chlorite. Engraved text. Double-convex stamp once attached to a metal mounting (now lost). At the center is a Hittite hieroglyphic cartouche bearing the monogram of King Mursili and framed by the sign "the Great King" beneath the winged solar disk. Around this design in two concentric circles are the following lines of Akkadian cuneiform: "Seal of Mursili, the Great King, the King of the Land of Hatti, the favorite of the storm god Manuzi, son of Suppiluliuma, the Great King, King of Hatti, the hero" (translation by Salvini).

– **Bib.**: C. Schaeffer, *Ugaritica* III, 1956, pp. 87–93; M. Salvini, in *Syrie, Mémoire . . .*, 1993, p. 248, no. 221.

12

13

Stone Statues

The excavations at Ras Shamra have not yielded many statues of stone. One interesting group is the Egyptian statues that were found mainly on the Acropolis in the 1930s and have been dated to the Middle Kingdom period. As for local craftsmanship, there is very little for us to assess. From the Late Bronze Age, an outstanding example is a statue made of local stone that was discovered in 1988, which we propose is a representation of the god El. This small object may be a replica of another much larger statue. The quality of execution and its apt proportions suggest that there was a tradition of sculpture at Ugarit that required the highest degree of skilled labor.

12. Egyptian basalt statue (without a head) of Princess Chnumet RS 3.336

1931 Acropolis, to the south of the High Priest's Library. Aleppo Museum 7378

H (preserved) 35 cm, Black polished basalt. Egyptian statue from the Middle Kingdom. The statue is missing its top, which was broken (intentionally?) off at the torso. It represents a female seated on the traditional cubic seat, with her two hands resting on her knees. She is clothed in a long tunic, and her feet are resting side by side on the base, which bears a hieroglyphic inscription that is repeated on both sides of the feet. The text reveals the name Chnumet, the daughter of Amenemhat II. Princess Chnumet-Nefret-Hedjet, the princess "of the beautiful crown," was the wife of Sesostris II. But according to the tutelary, this statue dates prior to her marriage, to approximately 1920 B.C.E.

– **Bib.**: *Syria*, 13, 1932, p. 20, pl. 14.1 (cf. *Ugaritica* IV, pp. 212–13, fig. 19).

13. Limestone statue of the god El RS 88.070

1988, City Center, in a dump near the Temple of the Rhytons Latakia Museum

H 25 cm, W 12 cm, D 11 cm. Limestone. Traces of bitumen are evidence that attachable parts (arms and eyes) that are now missing were once fastened to the statue. An old man sits on a high-backed, armless chair with his two feet resting on a small footstool. He is wrapped in a long, rolled-edge, bordered (wrap-around) cloak. He wears a headdress shaped like an oval tiara. The two missing arms may have been similar to the arms of statue no. **14**. It appears that they were crafted separately (in wood? in ivory?) and fastened with bitumen to the statue. The same goes for the eyes, which may have been composed of inlaid shell. The armless chair is similar to a type of furniture found in Egyptian tombs (e.g., Tutankh-Amun) and on frescoes from the New Kingdom.

– **Bib.**: M. Yon and J. Gachet, *Syria* 66, 1989, p. 349; [2005] M. Yon, "El, père des dieux," *Mémoires et Monuments Piot* 71, 1991, pp. 1–19; M. Yon, in *Syrie, Mémoire . . .*, 1993, pp. 224–25, no. 173.

14

15

16

Metal Statues

Paradoxically, appreciably more metal figurines have been found in the excavations at Ugarit than stone figurines. These objects were hidden or they escaped detection because of their small size. Thus, they were missed in later looting and pillaging of metal for smelting. In most cases, the metal statues were made of bronze and covered with gold.

14. A bronze and gold statue of the god El — RS 23.393

1960, South City, block XIII, court 38, topographic point 2755 (found with no. **15**).

Damascus Museum (inv. 3573)

H 13.5 cm. Bronze covered with gold leaf. An old man is seated and wrapped in a long, bordered, rolled-edge cloak, with sandals on his feet. On his head is a Syrian version of the Egyptian *atef* headdress. The lateral horns (now missing) were fastened on two mortises above the ears. The statue's right hand is stretched out in a gesture of benediction, while the left hand once held an object (now missing). The statue was designed to sit on a bench (now missing), to which it was fastened with a tenon. It is the same type as the stone statue shown in no. **13**, and it undoubtedly presupposes the same archetype.

– ***Bib.***: C. Schaeffer, AAS, 1961–62, p. 191, fig. 6; D. Collon, in *Au pays de Baal* . . . , 1983, pp. 154–55, no. 171.

15. A bronze and gold statue of the god Baal — RS 23.394

1960, South City, block XIII, court 38, topographic point 2755 (found with no. **14**).

Damascus Museum (inv. 3372)

H 12.2 cm. Bronze covered with gold leaf (which now covers only the head). The figurine represents a young man standing in the position of a warrior who is ready to strike. His feet are bare, and he is clothed in a short loincloth. His headdress is a high tiara. His posture and costume identify him as the god Baal, as he appears on numerous items from Ugarit (figurines, jewelry, steles), particularly on the stele "Baal with Thunderbolt" (cf. no. **18**).

– ***Bib.***: C. Schaeffer, AAS, 1961–62, p. 191, fig. 6; D. Collon, in *Au pays de Baal* . . . , 1983, pp. 154–56, no. 172.

16. Bronze (and gold?) statue of a seated goddess — RS 9.277

1937, the Royal Precinct, the "Hurrian" Temple. — Louvre Museum AO 19397

H 24.8 cm. Copper metal, probably once covered with gold. The gold leaf appears not to have covered the back of the statuette, which was made by casting, then bent to fit on a seat of some sort. Figurine of a female in a long dress bordered with thick braiding, above which the breasts were exposed. The garment's weave is fashioned in a sort of slanted cross-grid or angled, checkered work. The arms are bent at the elbow and stretched out. The right hand is open; the left undoubtedly once held an object (now missing). The head is in round relief with large sockets that held the eye inlays, which were fashioned in another material (now missing). The body is flat, the outline is extremely elongated, and the feet are positioned side by side on a base. Considered by the excavator to be Hurrian. He dated it to the 19th–18th centuries B.C.E.

– ***Bib.***: C. Schaeffer, *Syria* 19, 1938, pl. 34; *Ugaritica* I, 1939, pp. 128–40.

17

18

19

20

Stone Stelae

17. Stele of Mami with a dedication to Baal of Saphon in Egyptian hieroglyphic RS 1.[089]+2.[033]+5.183
Louvre Museum AO 13176

1929, 1930, 1933, Acropolis, Temple of Baal.

H (restored to) 42 cm, W 25 cm, D 7.3 cm. Sandstone imported from Egypt. Incomplete, but partially restored. Stele with an arched pediment, with the anterior side entirely decorated. The design is divided horizontally in two sections. In the upper space is a scene, along with five vertical lines of hieroglyphic. In the lower space are six horizontal bands containing hieroglyphic text. The scene is of two figures facing each other on either side of a libation altar. The inscriptions read: on the left, "Baal of Saphon"; on the right, "Mami, royal scribe and attendant of the royal domain." The stele dates to the beginning of the 19th Dynasty.

– **Bib.**: C. Schaeffer, *Ugaritica* I, 1939, pp. 39–41, fig. 30 ; M. Yon and A. Gasse, in *RSO* VI, 1991, pp. 284–88.

18. The so-called stele of "Baal with Thunderbolt" RS 4.427

1932 Acropolis, on the slope to the west of the Baal Temple. Louvre Museum AO 15775

H 142 cm, W 50 cm, D 28 cm. Limestone. Stele with a curved pediment and slight narrowing at the base. The anterior side is bordered by a small band that delimits the decorated panel (Champlevé decoration). It shows a young man striding to the right, standing on a double base. His feet are bare, and he is clothed in a simple loincloth. He wears a tall headdress from which spiral curls of hair are hanging. We assume that this figure is Baal. His right arm is raised and holds a club in a menacing gesture, and his left hand holds a lance. The point is stuck in the ground, and the shaft has leafed branches. In the space beneath his left arm is a small base with a standing figure wearing a long robe: probably the king in priestly dress. The two superimposed bases under the feet of the god exhibit schematic motifs symbolizing the sea (incised undulating lines) and mountains (undulating lines in relief). Both represent the domains of Baal.

– **Bib.**: C. Schaeffer, *Syria* 14, 1933, pp. 122–24, pl. 16; *Ugaritica* II, 1949, pp. 121–30; M. Yon, in *RSO* VI, 1991, pp. 294–99; in *Syrie, Mémoire . . .* , 1993, pp. 224–25, no. 173.

19. Stele with a dedication to the god Dagan in Ugaritic RS 6.021

1934, Acropolis, court of the Temple of Dagan. Louvre Museum AO 19931

H 87 cm, W 38 cm, D 15.5 cm. Local limestone. Stele with arched pediment. The anterior side has no image but does feature three lines of text engraved in the stone in alphabetic cuneiform, a dedication to the god Dagan. The stele was found along with another fragmentary stele bearing a similar dedication.

– **Bib.**: C. Schaeffer, *Syria* 16, 1935, pp. 155–56, pl. 31; M. Yon, P. Bordreuil, and D. Pardee, in *RSO* VI, 1991, pp. 301–3.

20. Stele with an archer god RS 23.216

1960, South City, block V, locus 3. Damascus Museum (inv. 6355)

H 33 cm, W 21.3 cm, D 9.5 cm. Limestone. Stele with arched pediment and slight enlargement at the base. The decoration of the raised edge is marked by incisions, but the quality of the whole is rather mediocre. A figure is striding toward the right, pulling a bow. It may be a representation of the god Reshef(?).

– **Bib.**: M. Yon, in *RSO* VI, 1991, pp. 309–10; in *Syrie, Mémoire . . .* , 1993, p. 226, no. 176.

Drawing by J.-P. Lange

Ivories of the Royal Palace

21. Bed panel of carved ivory RS 16.056+28.031

1952, Royal Palace, room 44 to the northwest of Garden III (along with no. **22**). Damascus Museum (inv. 3599)

H 50 cm, W 100 cm. The panel was found extremely damaged but was patiently restored in the laboratory of the Damascus Museum, using ivory pieces that had chipped off the panel and fallen to the ground below. The sculpted panel is made of rectangular ivory plaques measuring 24 × 10–12 cm cut from an elephant's tusk and assembled with mortises. The panel itself comprises eight vertical plaques, surmounted by one long, horizontal plaque. The six central vertical plaques are sculpted in low relief on both sides. The two plaques at each end portray carved palmettes à jour.

On side *a*, the plaques picture the king in his war activities and on a hunt. Side *b* portrays the life of the royal couple; in the center plaque, a goddess is suckling two infants. On both sides, the long horizontal plaque is decorated with hunting scenes. Comparison with Egyptian parallels (the furniture of Tut-Ankh-Amun, for example) shows that this part of the bed was at the foot.
– ***Bib.***: C. Schaeffer, *Syria* 31, 1954, pp. 51–59; J. Gachet, *Répertoire des ivoires et des os travaillés d'Ougarit*, Mémoire 1984, Université de Lyon (unpublished), pp. 139–70; A. Caubet and F. Poplin, in *RSO* III, 1987, pp. 285–87, fig. 17. **[2005]** J. Gachet, *RSO* XVI, cat. nos. 269–71 (in press).

22. Head of a young man (a god?) in ivory, inlaid with metal and stone (?) RS 18.221

1954, Royal Palace, room 44 (along with no. **21**) Damascus Museum (inv. 3601)

H 15 cm, D 10 cm. Head in the round, made of elephant tusk. It portrays the head of a young man with a headdress in the form of a cap, the tip of which is missing. The headdress is provided with mortises probably intended to permit the insertion of a pair of divine horns. The headdress was covered in gold. The eye-socket (the inlay of which is partly missing) is in bronze. The forehead is edged with semicircular ringlets of silver inlaid with gold.
– ***Bib.***: C. Schaeffer, *Ugaritica* IV, pp. 25, 27, 34–36, figs. 24–26; *AAS*, 1954–55, p. 151, pl. 2. **[2005]** J. Gachet, *RSO* XVI, cat. no. 408 (in press).

22

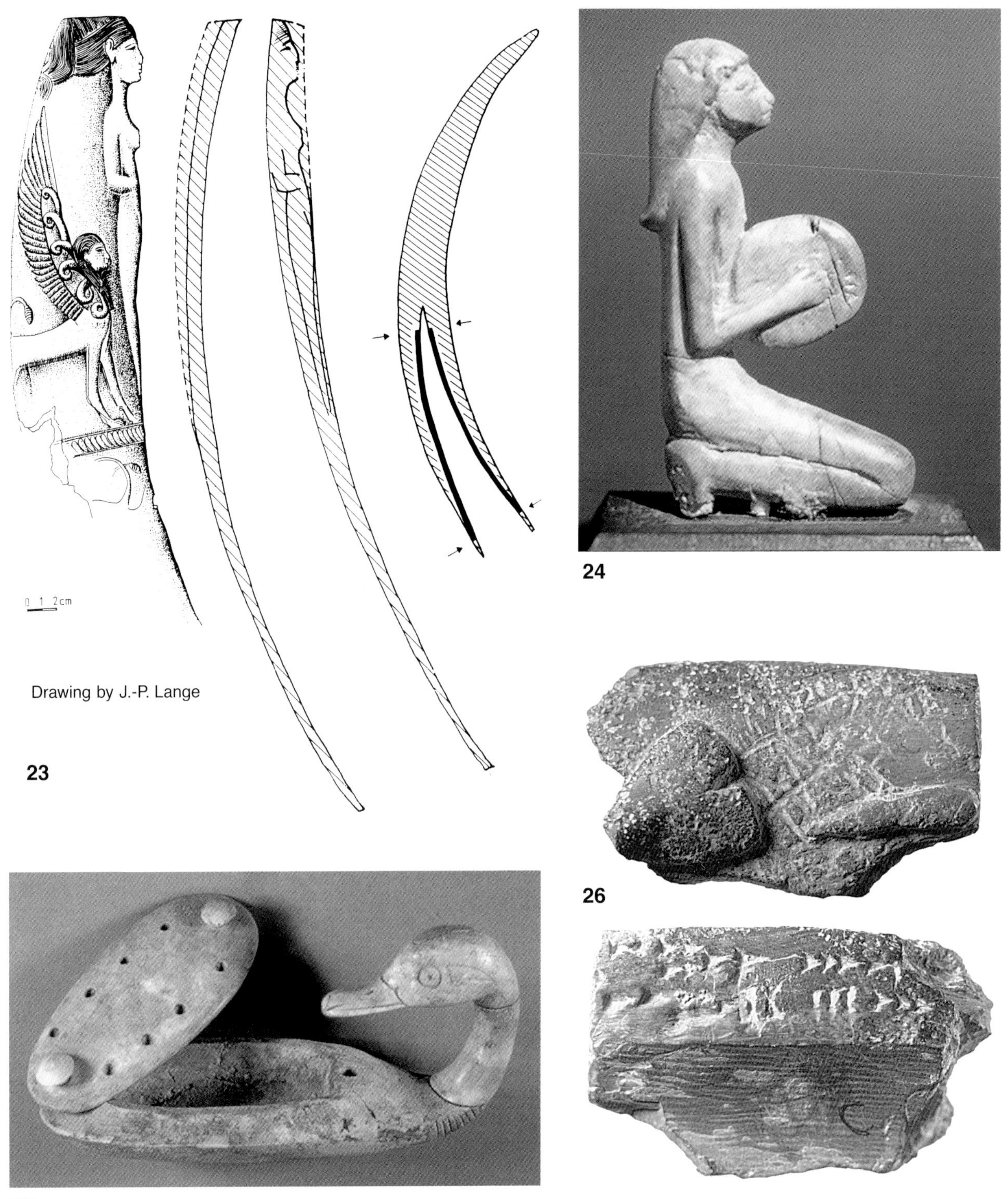
0 1 2cm
Drawing by J.-P. Lange
23
24
25
26

Objects of Ivory

J. Gachet, *RSO* XVI, cat. nos. 386, 409, 22, 615 (in press)

23. Olifant

RS 16.404

1952, Royal Palace, pavilion 86 to the northeast of Garden III. Damascus Museum (inv. 7360)

H ca. 60 cm, Diameter at opening 11 cm. Cut from the hollow part of an elephant's tusk. It is adorned with the sculpted relief figure of a naked woman with her hands holding her breasts and flanked on either side by a sphinx with wings unfolded.

– **Bib.**: C. Schaeffer, *Syria* 31, 1954, pp. 62–63; A. Caubet and F. Poplin, in *RSO* III, 1987, p. 287, fig. 19.

24. Miniature figurine of a musician

RS 24.400

1961, South Acropolis, tomb 3464. Damascus Museum (inv. 3602)

H 5.4 cm. Sculpted in the round in hippopotamus ivory (this object is similar to a small lyre-player found at Kamid el-Loz, Lebanon, also carved from the tooth of a hippopotamus). This miniature figurine represents a kneeling person, sitting on his/her heels, holding either a tambourine or a pair of cymbals.

– **Bib.**: C. Schaeffer, *AAS* XIII, 1963, p. 132, figs. 12–13; J. Gachet, in *Baal et Astarté*, no. 180; A. Caubet, "La musique à Ougarit," *CRAIBL* 1987, pp. 731–54.

25. A duck-shaped cosmetic box with lid

RS 3.235

1931, Minet el-Beida, depot for the precinct, to the west of the great tombs. Louvre Museum AO 14779

H 7.6 cm, L 14.5 cm, W 5.4 cm; lid: L 9 cm, W 4.2 cm, D 0.6 cm. The container was carved from a hippopotamus's canine tooth in the form of a duck, with its head turned and facing backward. The elongated body has a flat bottom, but the neck and the head of the duck were carved separately and fastened onto the body by pins. A mortise on the rim permitted the insertion of an ivory button that passes through the lid as a fastener. The lid has traces of blue paint. The box was a container for personal luxury items. The tombs and houses of the wealthy in this city yielded numerous examples of this type of box, both complete and fragmentary. There is also a brief reference to "twenty cosmetic boxes in ivory" in a tablet listing the trousseau of queen Akhatmilku (cf. no. **4** above).

– **Bib.**: C. Schaeffer, *Ugaritica* I, 1938, p. 31; *Syria* 13, 1932, p. 6, pl. 8.2.

26. Miniature liver model designed for divination

RS 20.401 Ac

1956, Royal Palace, room 81 to the west of court V (southwest archives). Damascus Museum (without number)

H (cons.) 4.6 cm, W 2.8 cm, D (max.) 2.1 cm. Liver model carved out of ivory (incomplete, burned, and blackened). What remains is part of the right lobe, on which appear two rectangular lobes that are joined at the top. On the lower side is an inscription in Ugaritic. A group of similar items, badly damaged by the palace fire, were also found with tablets. These were identified recently as miniature liver models. Others in terra-cotta or metal served in divination (see no. **42** below).

– **Bib.**: Inscriptions: M. Dietrich and O. Loretz, *Die Elfenbein-Inschriften*, Alter Orient und Altes Testament 13, 1976, p. 8, pl. 3:E 20 (= KTU 6.49 ; TEO, p. 264). Identified as livers: J. Gachet, in *RSO* XI, 1995, p. 257, fig. 3c. **[2005]** J. Gachet and D. Pardee, "Les foies d'ivoire inscrits," in *RSO* XIV, 2001, no. 46, pp. 199 and 215.

27

28

29

Syrian Pottery

Local pottery constitutes more than 95% of the ceramics found in the excavations of the last period of Late Bronze Age Ugarit (13th century), and very fine, imported ceramics from the Aegean or Cyprus (see here nos. **32–34**) make up the remainder of the tableware of the houses. The few tombs of the period that were not plundered reveal that local tableware was also manufactured regularly for use as funerary items. The majority of these are plain ceramic without decoration (here nos. **27–28**), but in addition to these mundane products, pottery decorated with brown paint was also manufactured by local specialist workshops. Simple geometric decorations were the most frequent, but stylized vegetable and even animal motifs, such as goats, stags, birds (see no. **29**), and even exceptionally complex scenes (see no. **35**) have been found.

27. "Clepsydra" or shower vase — RS 81.509

1981, City Center, House E, room 1201. — Latakia Museum

H 19.5 cm, Diameter (max.) 18 cm. Fine plain buff pottery with burnished surface. Jug with a large, ovoid body. The opening is narrow, contracting to a small hole 1 cm in diameter. The bottom is pierced with 22 small holes to form a strainer. The narrowness of the opening does not permit filling by any means other than plunging the vase entirely into a large container full of water. It holds about 1 liter. The function of this sort of vase is obvious. The container remained full if the opening was sealed with one's thumb to prohibit the entrance of air; the liquid could not flow out through the bottom. When the thumb was removed (allowing air to enter the jug), the water could flow out through the bottom, creating a type of shower head.

This object matches the definition of a *clepsydra* mentioned by ancient authors (Hieron): in its primary sense, the term *clepsydra* is not restricted to a measure of time. What we have here is an instrument used for washing, like a shower in a bathing installation (or shower stall). This was an object of everyday life, but only in a relatively refined context. This vase was found with other personal funerary objects fallen from the upper floor of a house of medium status in the city center. Other examples (e.g., RS 30.325) show that this was not an uncommon item in homes at Ugarit.

– ***Bib.***: M. Yon, P. Lombard, and M. Renisio, in *RSO* III, 1987, p. 106, fig. 87; P. Lombard, ibid., pp. 351–57.

28. Plain stemmed cups — RS 26.427–430

1963, South City, tomb 4253 (from right to left and from top to bottom 430, 427, 429, 428). — Latakia Museum

Dimensions: 427: H 7.7 cm, Diameter 16.4 cm; 428: H 86.5 cm, Diameter 22.2 cm; 429: H: 8.8 cm, Diameter 17.8 cm; 430: H 10 cm, Diameter 17.9 cm. Buff pottery, bell-shaped cup, with conical pedestal.

– ***Bib.***: L. Courtois, in *Ugaritica* VI, 1969, p. 129, figs. 5C (427), L (428), H (429), G (430).

29. Bird-decorated jug with pointed base — RS 79.034

1979, City Center, House E, room 1201. — Latakia Museum

H 28.7 cm, Diameter (max.) 13.4 cm. Red pottery, buff slip, red and black painted decoration. Jug with a narrow neck, ovoid body, and pointed base. Decorated with small birds in a horizontal band of metopes. Like the shower vase (no. **27**), this jug was one of the furnishings in a private home.

– ***Bib.***: M. Yon, P. Lombard, and M. Renisio, in *RSO* III, 1987, p. 107, fig. 87.

"Deposit of 80 jars," Minet el-Beida, excavations 1931
(cf. C. Schaeffer, *Syria* 16, 1923, pl. 3.3; *Ugaritica* I, 1939, p. 31, pl. 9).

All sorts of products that were traded throughout the eastern Mediterranean required storage or shipping containers of wood, straw, textiles, pottery, and so on. Archaeology has yielded only containers that were made of indestructible materials such as clay, which was used to make commercial jars. It was necessary that the jars' openings be relatively narrow so that they could be easily sealed hermetically. Their dimensions and shapes had to be such that they could be transported and stacked in the hold of a boat or in a warehouse. Many of these ceramic pots were found in the city on the tell of Ras Shamra as well as in the warehouse at the port of Minet el-Beida and served for exporting or importing grain, which is easily pourable, and liquid food products, such as oil and wine, in large quantities.

Commercial jars

30. Canaanite jar RS 3.257

1931, Minet el-Beida, "deposit of 80 jars." Louvre Museum AO 14876

H 52 cm, Diameter 35 cm. Syrian pottery. Short cylindrical neck, two loop handles at the top of the body. This example is representative of 80 jars found carefully arranged in a port warehouse (see also the photo opposite). Each jar was propped up against another.

– ***Bib.***: C. Schaeffer, Syria 16, 1932, pl. 3.3; *Ugaritica* I, 1939, p. 31, pl. 9; A. Caubet, in Catalogue *Pharaonen und Fremde Dynastien im Dunkel*, Vienna, 1994, p. 259, no. 356; M. Yon, "Ougarit et le port de Mahadou / Minet el-Beida," *Acts of the Conference Ras Maritimae Nicosia 1994*, 1997.

31. Minoan stirrup-jar RS 3.[570]

1931, Minet el-Beida, deposit 213. Louvre Museum AO 14932

H 49 cm, Diameter 32.5 cm. Coarse, dark red pottery with white painted decoration. Imported from Crete. Jar with ovoid body, spout on shoulder and stirrup handles (false neck) on the top.

– ***Bib.***: M. Yon, in *Au pays de Baal . . .*, pp. 167–68, no. 187 (with bibliography).

30

31

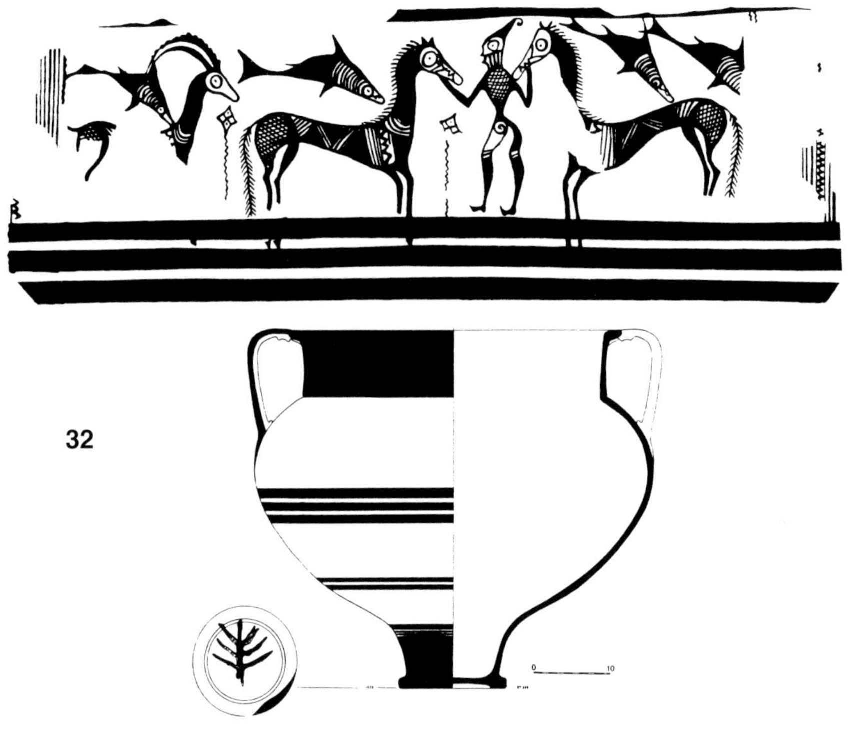

32

33

34

Imported Pottery from the West

Great quantities of Mycenaean and Cypriot pottery from the Late Bronze Age have been found at many sites in Egypt and the Levant, especially at Ugarit. Some vases, such as small juglets with a narrow mouth, circulated as containers for precious goods: perfumes, scented oils, and even opium. Others were imported for use as tableware by aristocratic clients. This is the case, for example, with vases for drinking or serving wine. However, despite a fair quantity of Mycenaean and Cypriot vases (whether complete or fragmentary) discovered during excavations at Ugarit, the total number does not exceed 1% of the total ceramic repertoire found in the Late Bronze Age dwellings (cf. J. Y. Monchambert, *Syria* 60, 1983, pp. 25–45). The percentage is slightly higher in the tombs.

32. Mycenaean krater of the "Master of Horses," from Miletus or Kos RS 27.319

1964, South Palace, room 219. Latakia Museum

H 43 cm, Diameter of opening 43.5 cm. Amphoroid krater from the Mycenaean IIIB–IIIC transition. On each side is a scene of a male figure between horses, and large diving dolphins. One side contains an ibex as well. The krater's manufacturing technique and the style of decoration are associated with the Mycenaean "oriental" series. The workshop was probably in the Dodecanese Islands (Kos?) or on the coast of Caria (Miletus?) at the end of the Late Bronze Age (approximately 1200 B.C.E.).

– ***Bib.***: J.-C. Courtois, in *Ugaritica* VII, 1978, pp. 346–50, fig. 54 (cf. *Ugaritica* V, pls. 3–5).

33. Mycenaean shallow bowl RS 4.215

1932, Minet el-Beida, tomb VI (wrongly designated tomb V in *Syria* 1933) Louvre Museum AO 15748

H 6.5 cm, Diameter 23 cm, W (with handles) 27.5 cm. Buff pottery, painted decoration in orange-red. Mycenaean IIIB. Open bowl with ring-base. The interior decoration is a concentric pattern consisting of a band of protomas of highly stylized bulls with protruding horns. This bowl belongs to a group, other examples of which have been found on Cyprus in the region of Citium, some decorated by the same painter (cf. E. Vermeule and V. Karageorghis, *Mycenaean Pictorial Vase Painting*, 1982, p. 176: painter no. **22**; p. 205, V 92).

– ***Bib.***: C. Schaeffer, *Syria* 14, 1933, pl. 10 (bas, gauche); *Ugaritica* II, 1949, figs. 61 A–B, 59 (34), 126 (4).

34. Cypriot juglet or "bilbil" RS 9.378

1937, excavations in the Lower City. Louvre Museum AO 19240

H 15.5 cm, Diameter 8.5 cm. Juglet of Cypriot Base-Ring Ware; light brown pottery, blackish-brown slip; one handle, small ring-base, ovoid body, narrow neck, and flared rim. Many vases of this type were found in tombs or in houses; the type is referred to as "bilbil" (alluding to the sound that liquid makes when it flows out of the very narrow spout) in the reports.

These juglets were used by Cypriot merchants to ship luxury goods to coastal areas of the eastern Mediterranean. Their small dimension and form (with a very small opening) show that they were reserved for precious liquids, designed to be used one drop at a time. The form of the juglet, when turned upside down, very closely resembles the pod of a poppy, which suggests that these juglets may have been produced for shipment of opiated liquids (suggestion by R. Merrillees, *The Cypriote Bronze Age Pottery Found in Egypt*, Lund, 1968, pp. 154–61).

Restored drawing by C. Florimont.

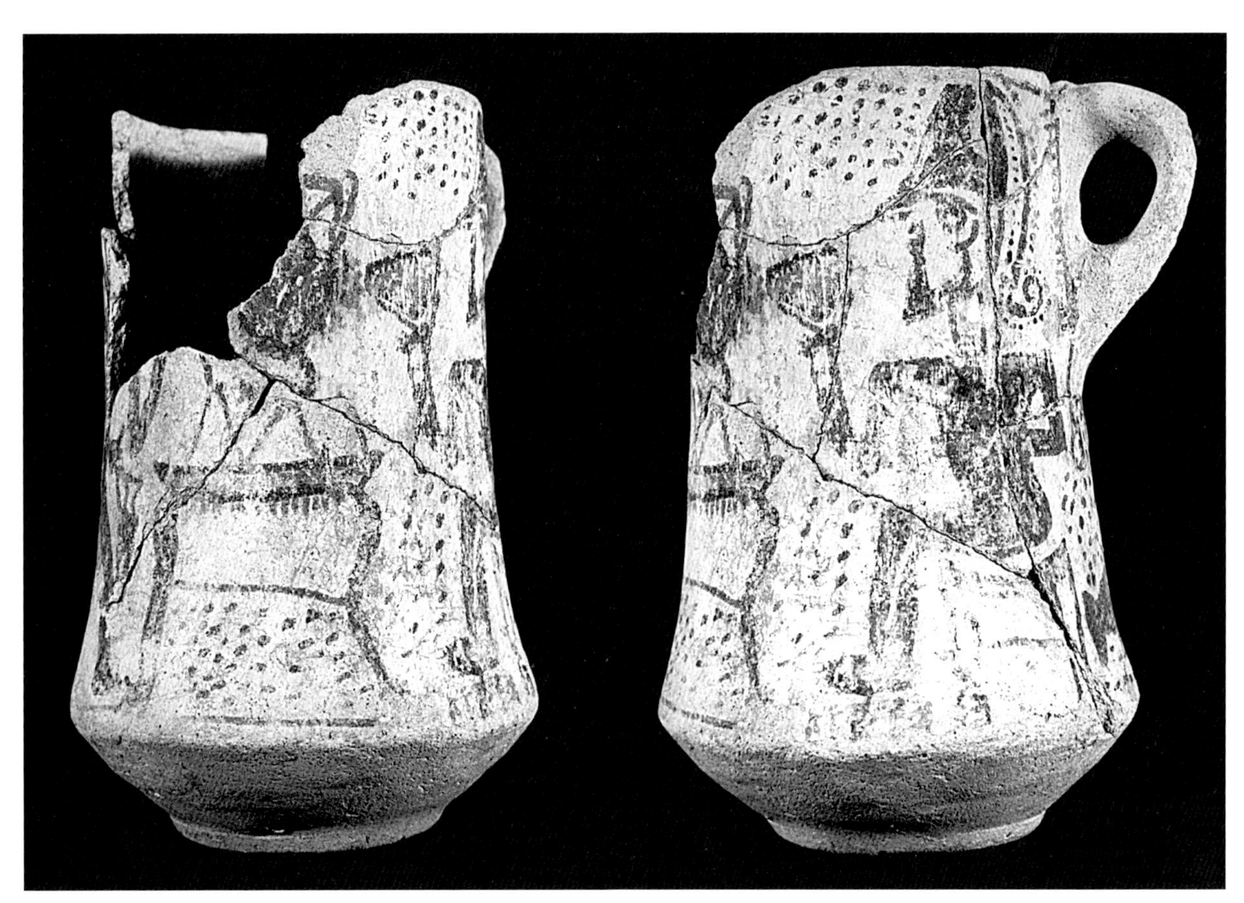

35

Syrian Vessels Related to the Cult

The excavations yielded ceramic objects from several spots on the tell of Ras Shamra or at Minet el-Beida that, either because of their decoration or their form and function (nos. 37–39), do not appear to have been used for common, everyday domestic purposes. In several cases, the context is obviously religious, as in the case of the divination items found with the cup illustrated in plate no. 35. In other cases, these special vases aided the excavators in recognizing (or confirming) the religious function of the architectural and archaeological environments in which they were found: in other words, they aid in the identification of cultic places. In other instances, they accompanied the dead in the tombs. Some of these objects are from local workshops (nos. 35–36, 40–41); others were imported (nos. 37–39).

35. Decorated mug, scene of an offering to the god El — RS 24.440

1961, South Acropolis, House of the "Magician-Priest." — Damascus Museum (inv. 6881)

H (restored) 21.5 cm. Gray pottery with pinkish slip, decorated with brown glaze; slightly concave, carinated body; vertical handle. On the body of the vase is a scene with a male figure of venerable status seated on the right. Facing him is another person who is standing and holding a jug (or rhyton?) by the handle. Between the two is a low table bearing food (offerings?). In the remaining space three animals appear: a horse, a fish, and a bird. The religious and magical context (cf. nos. **40**, **42**) in which the vase was discovered confirms that this is a cultic scene with symbolic elements. We propose that this is a scene in which the god El is accepting an offering from an individual, perhaps the king. The three animals are symbolic. They may represent the cosmic elements: land, water, and air. – ***Bib.***: C. Schaeffer, *Syria* 43, 1966, pl. 1; J.-C. Courtois in *Ugaritica* VI, 1969, pp. 111–13, fig. 13; M. H. Pope, "The scene on the Drinking Mug from Ugarit," in *Near Eastern Studies in Honour of W. F. Albright*, Baltimore, 1971, pp. 393–405.

36 a

b

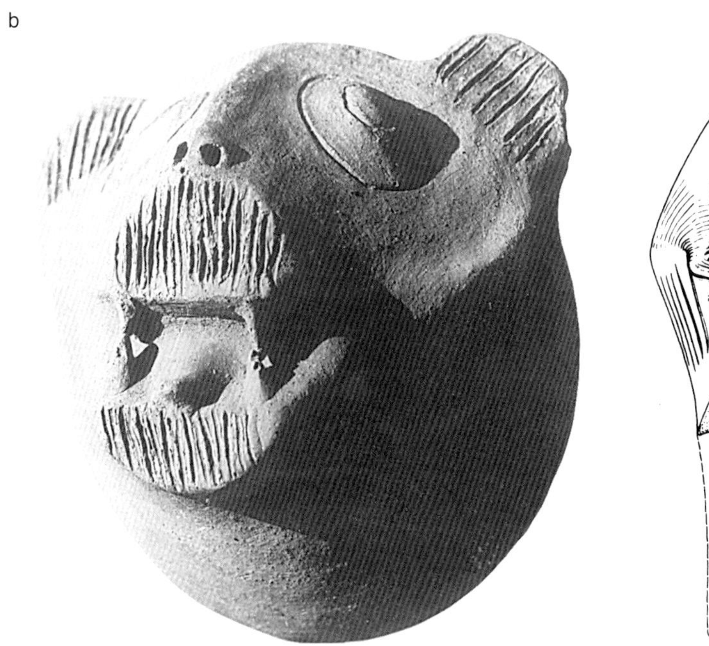

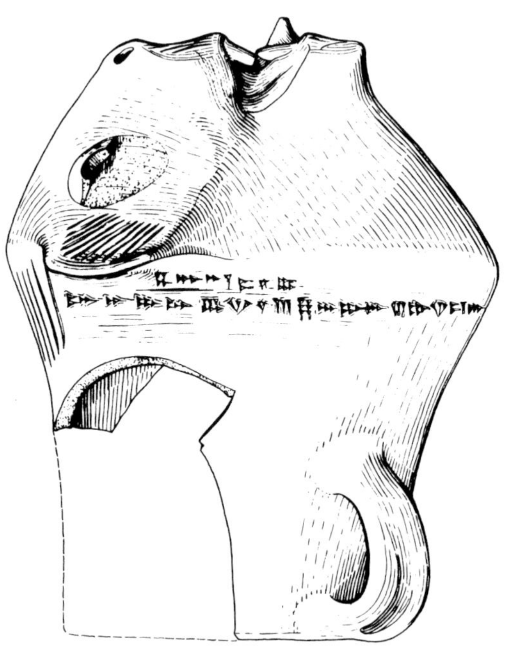

36. Goblets or mugs in the form of a lion's head

The excavations of the city have revealed examples of one-handled mugs with base fashioned in the form of a lion's head with a menacing, open mouth (see one example from the Lower City, found in 1937: C. Schaeffer, *Syria* 1938, pl. 19; another found in 1955: RS 16.052, on exhibit in the Damascus Museum). Despite apparent similarities, the structure and function of these containers prevent their confusion with other animal-headed objects, such as rhytons that have pierced bases (and which are not *containers* but *funnels* through which liquid flows; see, for example, the animal head in no. 38). However, a difference in function does not necessarily imply a different use (nothing prevents making libations by turning over mugs designed to pour liquid, for example).

a. Mug with inlaid eyes — RS 16.052

1952, Royal Palace. — Damascus Museum (inv. 4217)

H 16.2 cm. Buff pottery manufactured in Syria. The bowl (not pierced) of the mug represents a rather realistic modeled lion's head. The details are incised. The almond-shaped eyes surrounded by a rolled edge were made of an inlaid material that is now missing. The mouth is open.

– **Bib.**: K. Kolmayer, in *Land des Baal*, catalogue d'exposition, Berlin, 1982, no. 128, pp. 139–40; M. Yon, in *Au pays de Baal . . .*, 1983, pp. 171–72, no. 193.

b. Mug with dedication in Ugaritic — RS 25.318

1962, South Acropolis, House of Agipshari. — Damascus Museum (inv. 7034).

H 18.5 cm, Diameter at the opening 10 cm. Pinkish pottery. Wheel-thrown mug; carinated body; bowl (not pierced) modeled in the form of a slightly caricatured lion's head. The details are indicated by rather rigid incisions. The ears are flattened and pinched at the tips. The round eyes (one of which has been pulled out) are shaped in the form of lozenges or pastilles with an oval pupil encircled by an incision. The mouth is open and reveals the feline teeth and tongue. Beneath the handle, at the point of widest diameter, an inscription was engraved in alphabetic cuneiform, prior to baking. The tops of the characters are slanted at the base toward the head of the lion—that is to say, against the functional direction of the vase. The "son of Agipshari" is mentioned, and someone else is offering this vase to the god Reshef.

– **Bib.**: *KTU* (1976), 6.62; C. Schaeffer, *Ugaritica* VII, 1978, pp. 148–54; inscription: M. Dietrich and O. Loretz, ibid., pp. 147–48. **[2005]** D. Pardee, *RSO* XII, 2000, pp. 812–15; M. Yon, "Le lion de Rashap," in *Mélanges P. Bordreuil* (in press).

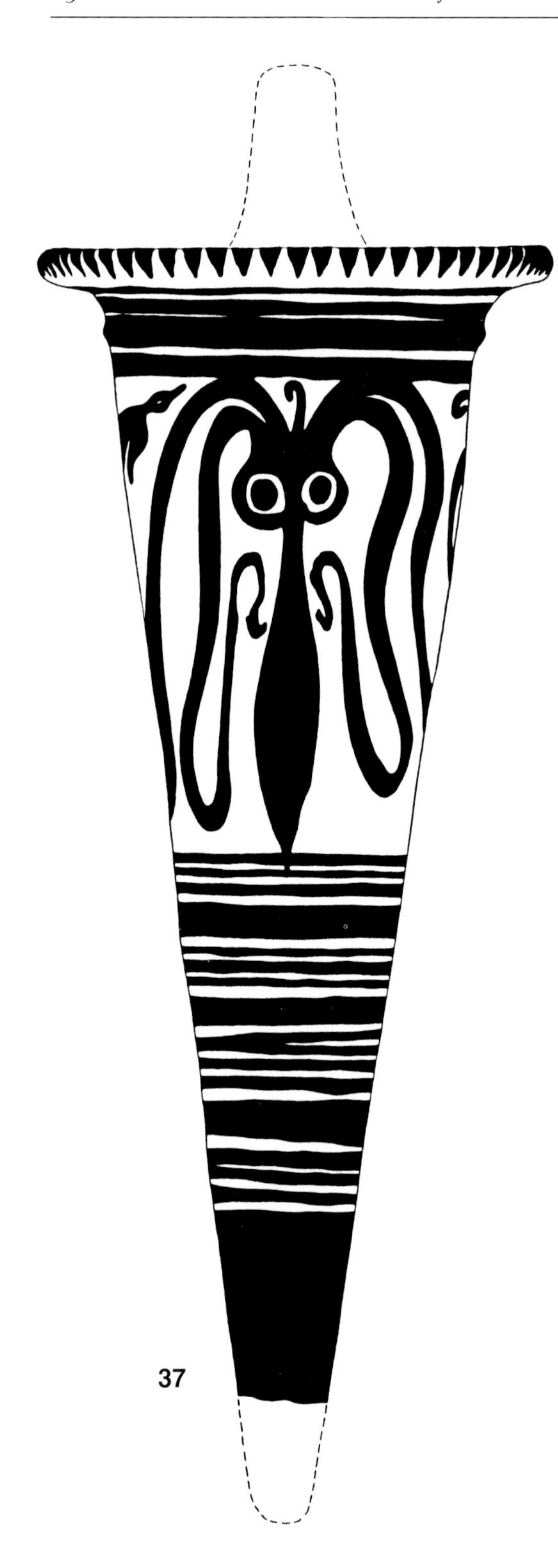

37

38

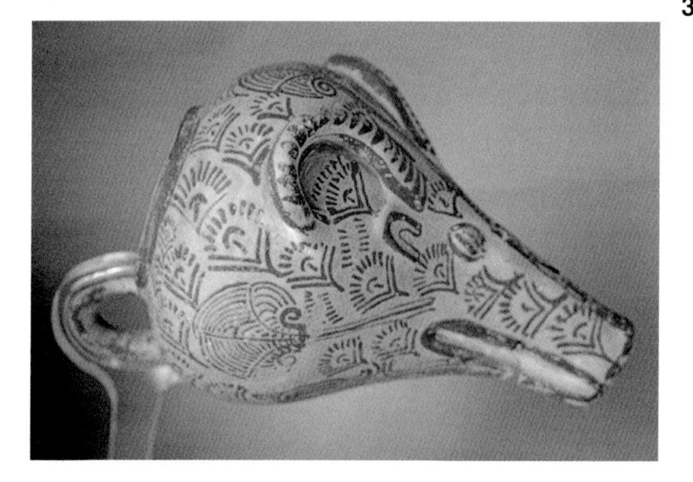

39

Funnels Related to the Cult (Rhytons)

A rhyton is an object made in the form of a funnel that provides one opening for filling and a second opening for pouring. Rhytons were made of metal (silver), ivory, and stone but mostly of pottery. Two types are represented here: rhytons with bodies that are elongated into a conical or ovoid shape and rhytons made in the form of an animal or an animal's head. Nearly all of the rhytons found at Ugarit were manufactured in Cyprus, Mycenae, or Crete, although local workshops occasionally produced rhytons identical to the foreign prototypes, especially the conical or ovoid shapes. As we have seen (no. 36), the Syrian mugs with a lion's head are different from the rhyton type represented by no. 38; their structures are different. These vessels were employed in libation ceremonies, and their presence in a building leads to speculation that religious ceremonies took place inside: 17 examples have been found in connection with the building designated the "Temple of Rhytons" (see no. 37). They have also been found in tombs among the various funerary utensils that accompanied the dead.

37. Mycenaean conical rhyton RS 79.017

1979, City Center, Temple of the Rhytons, room 78. Latakia Museum

H (preserved to 32 cm). Conical rhyton with a vertical handle (missing); imported. Decorated with a stylized octopus, with only four arms represented, two of which surround the body. The free space is filled with motifs of flowers and flying birds.

– ***Bib.***: M. Yon, in *RSO* III, 1987, pp. 347–48, fig. 2, no. 12.

[2005] According to V. Karageorghis (1998), this would be a Mycenaean rhyton created by the "Painter of Swallows," the artist who created six currently known vases, all discovered in the eastern Mediterranean (four on Cyprus, two at Ugarit, including this example).

– ***Bib.***: V. Karageorghis, "Note on a Mycenaean IIIB Rhyton from Ugarit," *Archäologischer Anzeiger*, 1998, pp. 1–3.

38. Mycenaean rhyton in the form of an animal head RS 9.076

1937, Lower East City, "near a tomb." Louvre Museum AO 19932

H 22.5 cm. Grayish-yellow pottery with red paint, polished surface, Mycenaean manufacture. Wheel-made ovoid rhyton with a handle, modeled in the form of a not-very-realistic animal's head (the head of a goat according to C. Schaeffer; but perhaps a bear, lion, or boar). The end is slightly irregular near the base in order to form the snout. Above the forehead are molded arches, but it is not clear whether they represent rounded ears or horns. The eyes were modeled in relief. The surface is elaborately decorated with floral motifs.

– ***Bib.***: C. Schaeffer, *Syria* 19, 1938, pl. 19.2; *Ugaritica* II, 1949, pp. 222–23.

39. Cypriot rhyton in the form of a bull RS 24.435

1961, South Acropolis, tomb 3464. Damascus Museum (inv. 6883)

H 15.5 cm, L 19.2 cm. Handmade brown pottery, with white paint (Cypriot Base-Ring II Ware). Vase in the form of a bull, with two openings: one for filling, in the back; the other for pouring, in the snout.

– ***Bib.***: C. Schaeffer, AAS, 1963, fig. 25; M. Yon, in *Au pays de Baal . . .* , 1983, p. 170, no. 191.

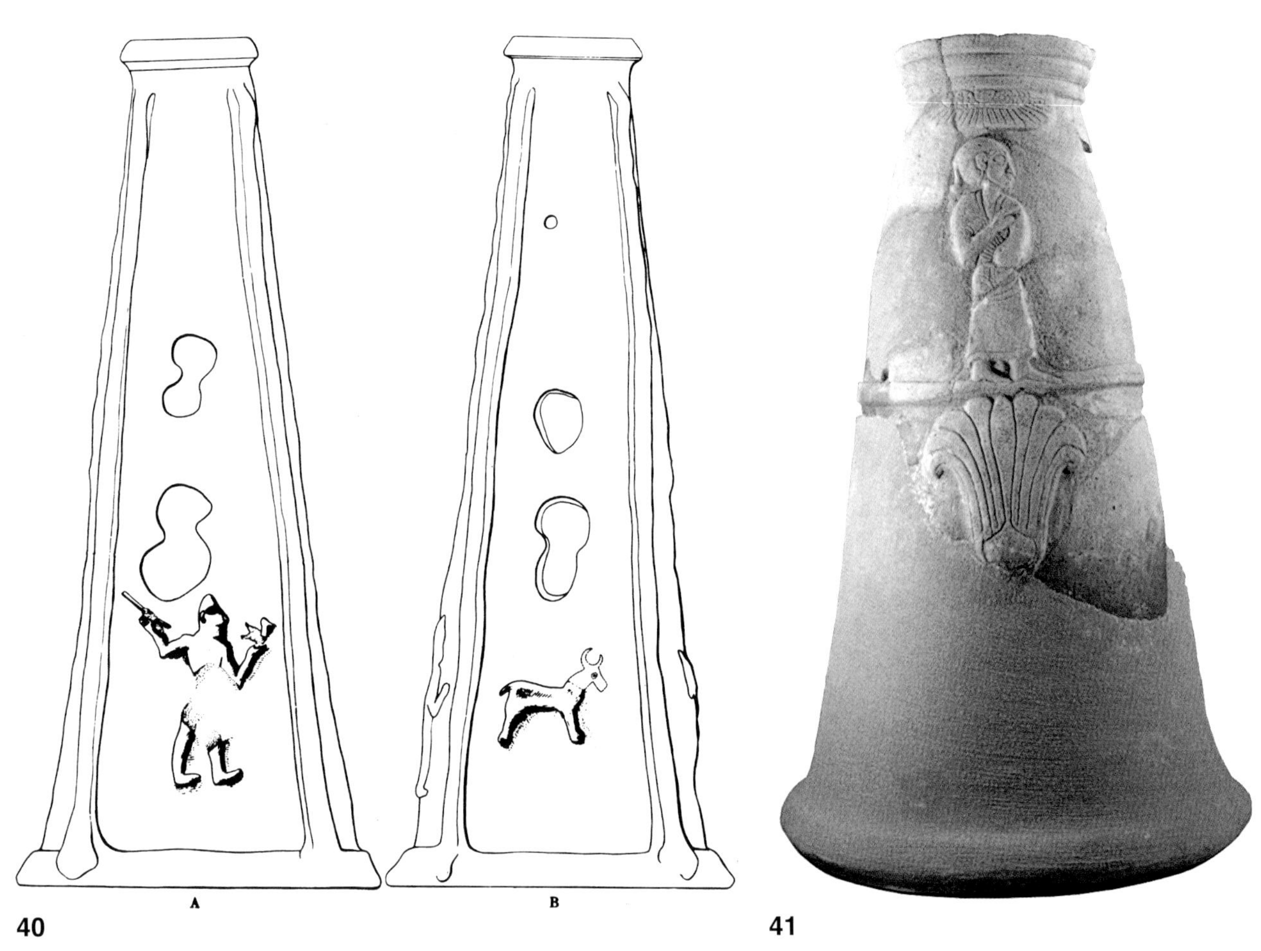

40

Drawing by L. Courtois.

41

Cultic Objects

It has been difficult to ascertain the purpose of these pottery artifacts, which are often quite large. It is possible that the primary function was utilitarian; someone placed it on the fire and used the upper part to hold another container; the holes in the sides allowed the smoke to escape. However, some of these also served a specific purpose as a furnishing in Late Bronze Age sanctuaries. Syro-Palestinian sanctuaries have yielded many examples. The examples that come from a religious context (indicated by other evidence) often feature significant symbols that should be taken into account. This is the case with the two examples from Ugarit presented here. For the sake of convenience, we are using the conventional designation "chimney-pipe" or "stand," neither of which is satisfactory.

40. Libation chimney-pipe: Baal and animals RS 24.627

1961, South Acropolis, House of the Magician-Priest, east of the "Tablet Room." Damascus Museum (inv. 6890)

H 75.5cm, Diameter from 10.5 (at the top) to 35.4 cm.

Truncated conical "chimney" in buff pottery. The surface is divided by large vertical ribs in four panels. Each is decorated. The motifs are in relief on the four sections. One section has a person (the god Baal?) who is ready to strike, striding toward the right, holding a bird. On the other three panels a bull, a stag and bird, and a goat appear.

– ***Bib.***: J.-C. Courtois, in *Ugaritica* VI, 1969, pp. 96–100.

41. Cultic stand or libation funnel: portrait of a priest-king RS 78.041+81.3659

1978 and 1981, City Center, pit to the north of the Temple of Rhytons. Latakia Museum

H (restored to) 60 cm, Diameter 20 (at the top) to approximately 40 cm. Stand or chimney-pipe in the form of a truncated cone, pierced with small openings in the side and with molding at the top and at the base. The surface is divided horizontally into two zones by a horizontal rib at about mid-height. The decoration, in relief, includes motifs superimposed along the same vertical axis. At the top is a solar winged disk, representing divine protection. Underneath, just above the level of mid-height, is a figure in a long dress in profile, walking to the right—a representation of the king in his priestly function (see on stele no. **18**). Beneath the horizontal boundary line is a large palmette, perhaps symbolizing the earth's power over the world of vegetation.

We have found fragments of similar objects (the head of a king, RS 75.247; top parts of a winged disk, RS 24.520) in various places in the city. This demonstrates that their use was more widespread than is at first apparent.

– ***Bib.***: M. Yon, in *RSO* III, 1987, p. 350.

42

43

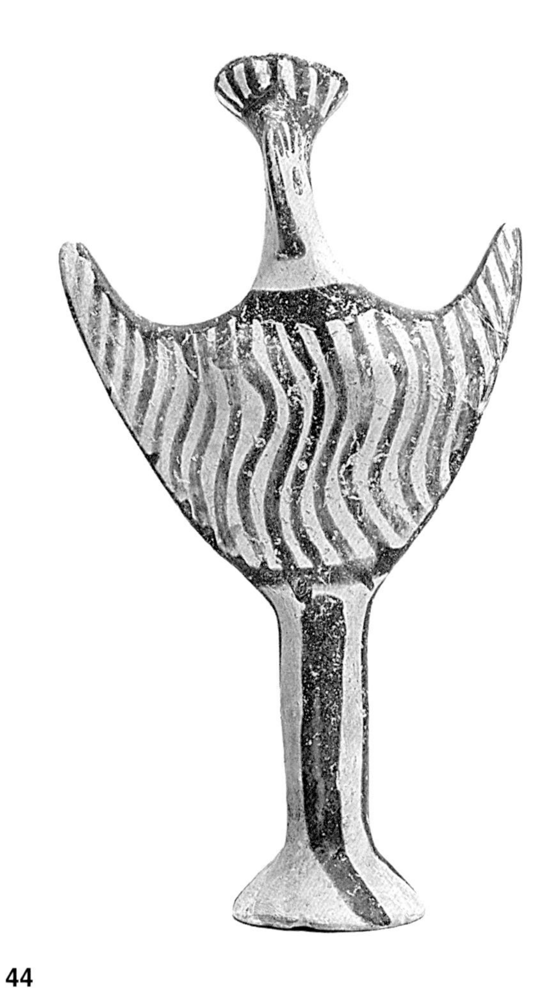

44

Cultic Objects
(Clay Models and Figurines)

42. Terra-cotta liver model used for divination, with an Ugaritic inscription RS 24.326

1961, South Acropolis, House of the Magician-Priest, Tablet Room. Damascus Museum (inv. 6655)

Dimensions 6.5 × 4.5 × 3 cm. A triangular model of a terra-cotta liver. One side is deeply incised; the other has three lines of an Ugaritic inscription in alphabetic cuneiform beginning with the very word *kbd*, "liver." Objects of this kind, miniature imitations of real sheep livers used in the practice of divination, hark back to the hepatoscopy long attested in Mesopotamian traditions (see also the miniature ivory models, such as the example here: no. **26**). Among the clay models found in the so-called House of the "Magician-Priest" were at least five livers that contained an inscription (add RS 24.654 to the four published by Dietrich and Loretz . . .); also a model of a lung (RS 24.277).

– **Bib.**: J.-C. Courtois, in *Ugaritica* VI, 1969, pp. 110, 113, figs. 10.3, 14.3; inscription: M. Dietrich and O. Loretz, ibid., p. 174, fig. 8. **[2005]** D. Pardee, *RSO* XII, 2000, pp. 773–74.

43. Terra-cotta figurine of a nude Ashtarte RS 81.848

1981, City Center, court 1050. Latakia Museum

H (cons.) 9.2 cm, W 3.8 cm. Terra-cotta, Syrian manufacture, broken at base. The figurine was cast in a simple mold that had the relief carved in the interior surface of the mold's hollow. The back was rounded and smoothed by hand. It represents a nude Astarte, with her arms by her side and long curls rolled up symmetrically on her shoulders (the headdress is of the so-called Hathor-type). The presence of these figures in houses reflects the domestic cult.

– **Bib.**: T. Monloup, in *RSO* III, 1987, p. 314.

44. Mycenaean terra-cotta female figurine of so-called Psi RS 3.188

1932, Minet el-Beida, trench 7.IV, point 317. Louvre Museum AO 14837

H 13.8 cm. Grayish-yellow terra-cotta with cream-yellow slip, black paint, Mycenaean manufacture. The figure was hand-modeled in the shape of a schematic female with uplifted arms. These figurines were often found in tombs as one of the personal items accompanying burial.

– **Bib.**: C. Schaeffer, *Syria* 13, 1932, p. 7, fig. 5.

45

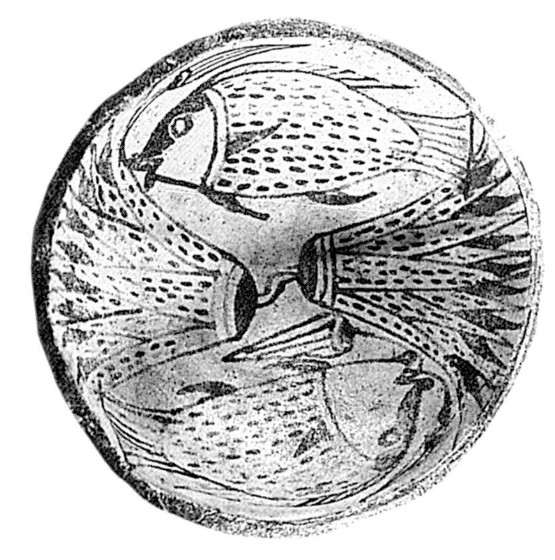

48

46

47

Faience

Numerous objects have been unearthed in the ancient Levant that were usually fashioned by molding and were manufactured from a composition of sintered silicon or quartz, then covered in a colored glaze following a technique that was developed in Egypt. We designate objects made with this technique "faience" (a conventional term that we preserve here for convenience), "frit," or more simply "vitreous material." Some of these objects were actually imported from Egypt, but workshops were also established in the Levant, on Cyprus, and in Ugarit. They have been found everywhere from the Mediterranean to Mesopotamia.

45. Cosmetic ladle — RS 9.795

1937, Lower City, tomb LVI. — Aleppo Museum

L. 15.6 cm. Composition covered with a pale green glaze, molded. The bowl is supported by a hand in relief beneath the bottom at the end of the handle, which terminates in the turned-backed head of a duck. This object belongs to a series of Egyptian cosmetic containers made from precious materials: faience, ivory, alabaster, and, of course, wood. According to its context in tomb LVI, this one appears to date to 1650–1550. It is a prototype, because other examples show that the type becomes more prevalent in the Levant beginning in the 14th century.

– ***Bib.***: C. Schaeffer, *Syria* 19, 1938, p. 241, pl. 22.2; A. Caubet, in *Au pays de Baal . . .*, 1983, p. 172, no. 194.

46. Bearded figures on a chariot — RS 7.090

1935, West Lower City, building area A. — Louvre Museum AO 18522

H figures, 15 cm. Proposed reconstruction of several fragments: two standing, bearded figures with their arms crossed, the head of a horse, the fragments of wheels, and so on.

– ***Bib.***: C. Schaeffer, *Syria* 17, 1936, p. 114, fig. 7, pl. 18.1; *Ras Shamra 1929–1979*, 1979, p. 32, fig. 16.

47. Goblet in the form of a woman's head — RS 4.106

1932, Minet el-Beida, tomb VI. — Louvre Museum AO 15725

H 16 cm. Conical goblet on a small, flared base, with the molded face of a female in relief. The success of this type of vase in the Late Bronze Age is evidenced by the fact that examples have been found from Cyprus to Ur (Lower Mesopotamia).

– ***Bib.***: C. Schaeffer, *Ugaritica* I, 1939, p. 32, pl. 10.

48. Egyptian fish-bowl — RS 26.256

1963, South Acropolis Trench, tomb 4253, no.77. — Damascus Museum (inv. 7119)

H 5.2 cm, Diameter 13 cm. Faience with blue-green glaze design painted in brown-black. Hemispherical bowl decorated with two Nile fish (*tilapia nilotica*) separated by two lotuses on the interior. It belongs to a series of cups of Nun, god of the primordial ocean. These cups are found scattered throughout New Kingdom Egypt and were exported to or imitated in great numbers throughout the Levant. Their symbolic value, linked to the idea of the reappearance of the Nile waters, explains why they were found frequently in tombs.

– ***Bib.***: C. Schaeffer, 1966, p. 132, fig. 15; A. Caubet, in *Au pays de Baal . . .*, 1983, no. 198.

49

50

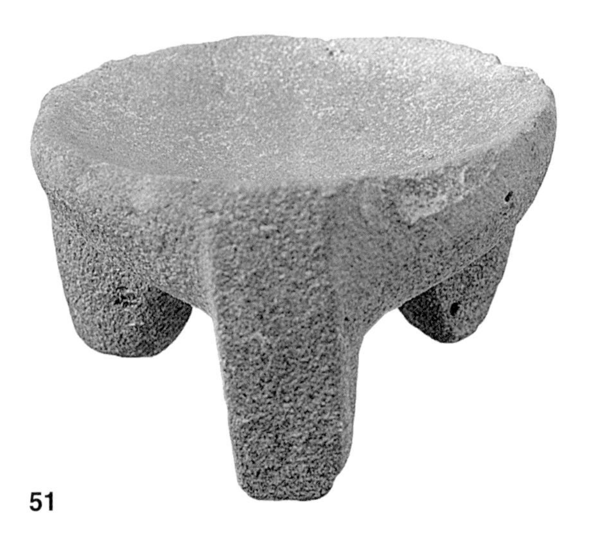

51

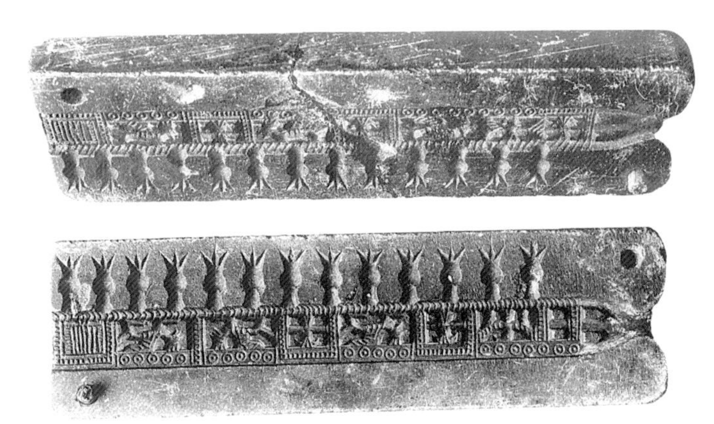

52

Stone Vases and Instruments

49. Fragment of an alabaster vase (for the marriage?) of King Niqmaddu RS 15.239

1951, Royal Palace, room 31 (central archives), topographic point 132. Damascus Museum (inv. 4160)

H (preserved) 17.5 cm, W (preserved) 14 cm. Probably an Egyptian vase, of which only a fragment of the shoulder remains. The engraved design represents a couple under an Egyptian kiosk supported by columns with floral decoration. The entablature features a frieze of ibex heads; these Asiatic animals were substituted here for the usual (Egyptian) upright cobras. The Egyptian hieroglyphic texts preserve the name of the person shown on the left, who is wearing a Syrian-style headdress: he is "the king of the land of Ugarit, Niqmaddu." The woman on the right is in an Egyptian garment. The scene may be King Niqmaddu III's marriage to a princess from Egypt (unless Egyptian fashion was widespread in Levantine courts, in which case the young person may simply be a Levantine princess in Egyptian dress?).

– ***Bib.***: C. Desroches-Noblecourt in C. Schaeffer, *Ugaritica* III, 1956, pp. 164–68, 179–220; C. Ziegler, in *Au pays de Baal . . .* , 1983, pp. 179–80, no. 206.

[2005] According to M. Gabolde (2004), this vase is to be dated to the end of the 18th Dynasty; in his view, it does not commemorate the marriage of a king of Ugarit to an Egyptian princess but is a diplomatic gift that should be interpreted as a sign of good relations between Egypt and Ugarit.

– ***Bib.***: M. Gabolde, in *Aux origines de l'alphabet*, Lyon, 2004, p. 155, no. 140.

50. Alabaster amphora on a matching stand RS 29.128+129

1966, Residential Quarter, topographic point 4704. Aleppo Museum (inv. 6198+6199)

Amphora: H 45.5 cm, Diameter 14 cm; stand: H 14.5 cm, Diameter 19.8 cm. Egyptian amphora with ovoid body, two vertical handles on the shoulder, cylindrical neck, and a tenon under the base. Convex pedestal.

– ***Bib.***: C. Schaeffer, 1954, pl. 5; A. Caubet, in *Au pays de Baal . . .* , 1983, pp. 155–64, no. 183; in *RSO* VI, 1991, p. 239.

51. Basalt tripod mortar RS 79.953

1979, City Center, House C, room 1049. Mission dig-house

H 20.3 cm, Diameter 35.5 cm. Concave bowl on three short legs extending down from the rim. The inner surface is polished from use. Mortars were a common utilitarian piece of equipment found in many houses of the city, used for crushing grain with a stone pestle, many of which have also been uncovered in the excavations.

– ***Bib.***: C. Elliott, in *RSO* VI, 1991, pp. 29, 82, fig. 8.

52. Soapstone mold for casting jewelry RS 8.[541]

1936, Lower City? Aleppo Museum (inv. 4571)

W 25.7 cm, Diameter 4.3 cm. Bivalve mold formed of two rectangular blocks, with mortises for fastening the two blocks together. The engraved band is adorned with birds, sphinxes, and hanging pomegranates. The design permits the two blocks to contact so as to allow molten metal to be poured into the cast. The narrow casting channel is located at one end and is conical in form.

– ***Bib.***: C. Schaeffer, *Syria* 18, 1937, p. 152, fig. 17; 1939, p. 43, fig. 32; M.-J. Chavane, in *Au pays de Baal . . .* , 1983, no. 199 (with an error in the inventory number: confused with RS 19.224).

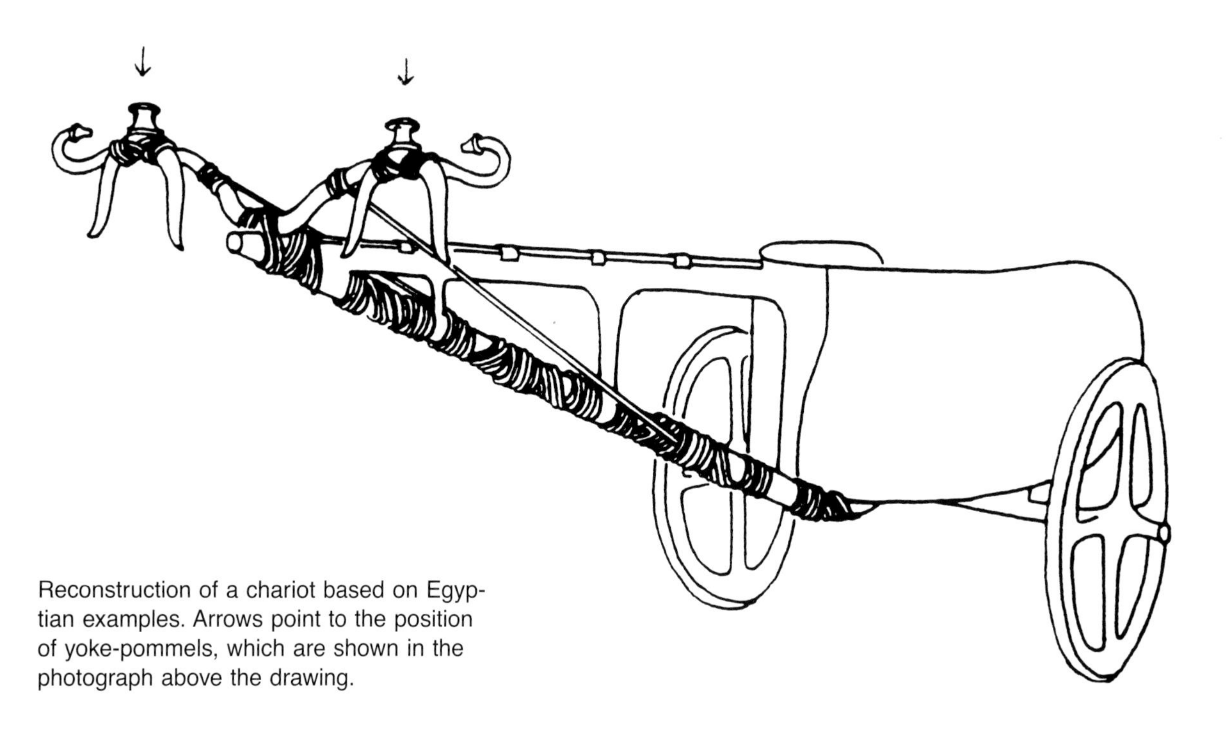

Reconstruction of a chariot based on Egyptian examples. Arrows point to the position of yoke-pommels, which are shown in the photograph above the drawing.

Stone Tools

53. A pair of alabaster yoke-pommels for a chariot yoke RS 94.2013 and 2081

1994, South Central City, House of Urtenu. Mission dig-house

H 5 cm, Diameter 5.2 cm. White alabaster. Components in the shape of a spool designed to be placed on a chariot yoke, as the comparison with Egyptian models demonstrates. Drawing is based on examples found in the tomb of Tut-Ankh-Amun.

Light war chariots with two wheels appeared in the Near East in the 2nd millennium, and Ugarit seems to have played a role in the adoption and propagation of this new technology as far as Egypt. Most of the chariot was constructed of perishable materials, which have not been preserved at Ugarit (wood, leather, rope, etc.). Thus, at Ugarit, chariots are unknown except in representations on other objects (see here, for example, the hunting scenes on a cylinder seal and on a gold vase: nos. **8**, **57**). Archaeology has yielded only the components that were small and made out of hard materials, such as ivory and alabaster.

The fact that the yoke-pommels were discovered in a house attests to the presence of a chariot, which reveals the social status of the owner. Chariots were dismantled (carriage, wheels, axle, and yoke) for storage in the houses; distribution of these small objects throughout various quarters of the city shows that the chariot owners stored their own chariot equipment.

– ***Bib.***: M. Yon, "La maison d'Ourtenou (fouille 1994)," *CRAIBL* 1995, p. 439, fig. 9; for this kind of object, cf. A. Caubet, in *RSO* VI, 1991, pp. 266–67, fig. 1. **[2005]** A. Caubet and M. Yon, "Pommeaux de chars, du Levant à la Mésopotamie et à l'Élam," in *Études mésopotamiennes, Recueil J.-L. Huot*, Paris, 2001, pp. 69–78.

54a

54b
Harvest with a sickle.
Egypt, tomb at Deir el-Medineh, ca. 1250 B.C.E. Drawing after E. Coqueugniot, in *RSO* VI, p. 196, pl. 22.

55

54. Flint sickle blades RS 84.1026+1063+1066+1162+1167+1045 (from left to right)

1984, City Center, House A, sump 1269 of room 1040. Mission dig-house

L (restored) ca. 30 cm. An assemblage of flint blades forming a sickle (this reconstruction is proposed according to actual examples found in Egypt and as represented on the walls of tombs). This type of sickle generally consisted of six or seven blades that were fastened next to each other on a shaft of wood using bitumen as the binding agent, traces of which remain on the back of the blades. The blades are trapezoidal in shape except for the one on the end, which is triangular. The cutting edge preserved traces that, when observed through a microscope, turn out to be fragments left by the cutting of plants such as cereals or reeds. Sickles were agricultural tools, and the fact that such a large number of them has been found in so many houses shows that they were common tools used by Ugaritic farmers of the Late Bronze Age (13th century).

– ***Bib.***: E. Coqueugniot, in *RSO* VI, 1991, pp. 159–63, 197, pl. 23.1; cf. J. Connan, O. Deschesne, and D. Dessort, ibid., pp. 101–2.

55. Limestone roof roller RS 81.236

1981, City Center, House E, room 1050. Mission dig-house

L 63 cm, Diameter 21 cm. This cylindrical roller was cut from rather coarse limestone and is provided with a depression on each end in which a wooden handle could be inserted, so that the stone could be used for rolling. These objects, examples of which were found throughout the entire city, were used to pack the mud clay that was used to cover the flat roofs in order to render it impermeable. Recent excavations show that there was one in almost every house and that they were left on the roofs, from which they had fallen (they were found in the ruins of roofed rooms, not in courtyards). A comparison with similar rollers used today throughout the Middle East indicates that they are generally stored on the flat roofs, which are also used by residents for outdoor activities.

– ***Bib.***: M. Yon, P. Lombard, and M. Renisio, in *RSO* III, 1987, pp. 101–5, fig. 79; C. Elliot, in *RSO* VI, 1991, pp. 34–35, fig. 11.2.

Gold vessels

56. Gold bowl decorated with animals RS 5.032

1933, Acropolis, to the southwest of the Baal Temple (found with no. 57) Aleppo Museum (inv. 5472)

Diameter 17 cm, actual weight 179 grams (approximately 20 shekels). Bowl shaped like a nearly hemispherical skull-cap. The decoration in repoussé (from interior to exterior) is made to be viewed from the exterior. The decoration consists of mythological heroes in a hunting scene in a forest of large, stylized trees. Floral motifs complete the exuberant sign, leaving no empty space. Three concentric registers encircle a navel in the form of a rosette. A continuous spiral band separates the two exterior registers, and another adorns the border. The central register has five ibexes and rosettes; the second register: lions and bulls with a tree and a stylized palmette surmounted by pomegranates on each side; the third register (principal scene) displays one scene with winged monsters and animals (lions, bulls, gazelles) and one scene of a lion hunt on either side of a stylized tree.

– ***Bib.***: C. Schaeffer, *Ugaritica* II, 1949, pp. 1–48, pls. 2–5, 8; R. Stucky, in *Au pays de Baal . . .* , 1983, p. 160, no. 178.

56

57. Gold cup decorated with a royal hunt RS 5.031

1933, Acropolis, to the southwest of the Baal Temple (found with no. 56) Louvre Museum AO 17208

Diameter 19 cm, H 3 cm, actual weight 218 grams (some fragments are missing, but the estimated ancient weight was 30 shekels at 7.5 grams per shekel). Rather flat bowl with carinated contour (flat bottom and vertical border), reminiscent of Egyptian plates. The decoration in repoussé (from exterior to interior) is made to be viewed from the interior and is oriented to the right. The moderation of this composition contrasts with the complexity of bowl no. **56**. The motifs stand out from a plain background. Two concentric registers surround a central motif. The central register contains four aligned ibexes. The outside register is adorned with a hunting scene in which a figure pulling a bow (probably the king) stands in a chariot drawn by two horses. He is followed by a dog and the hunted animals, consisting of two deer, two bulls, and a cow with her calf. The circular composition results in an order so that a mature bull, which leads the animals being pursued, finds itself immediately behind the chariot, which it charges with its head lowered.

– ***Bib.***: C. Schaeffer, *Ugaritica* II, 1949, pp. 1–48, pls. 1, 7; A. Caubet and R. Stucky, in *Au pays de Baal . . .* , 1983, pp. 158–60, no. 177.

57

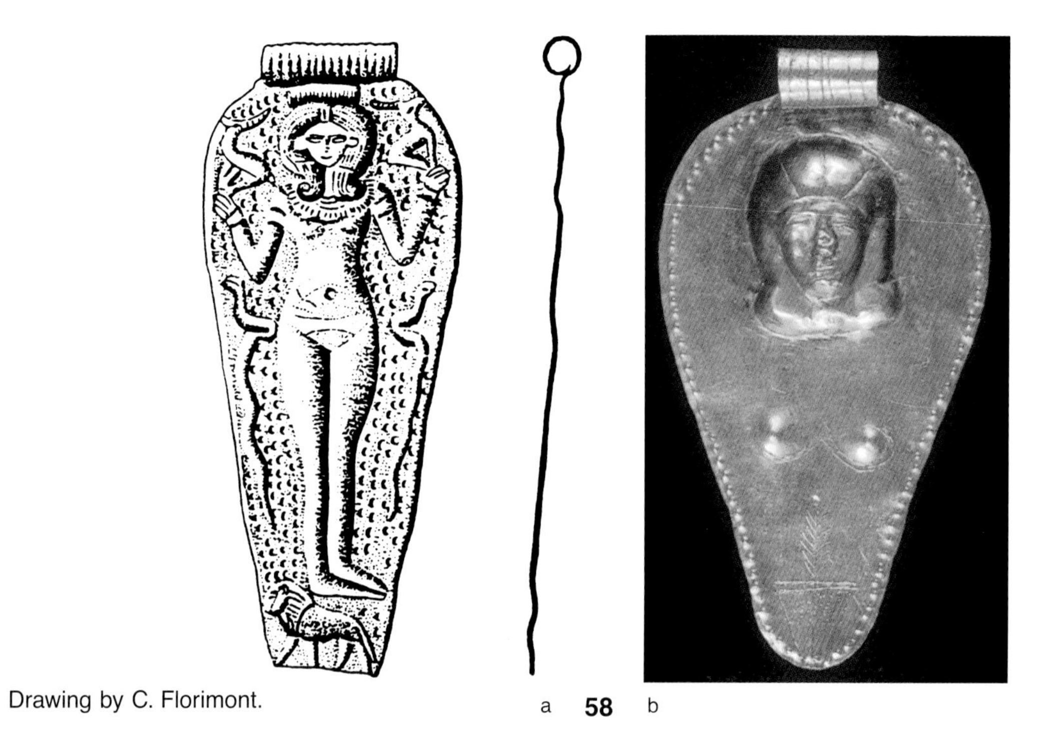

Drawing by C. Florimont.

a **58** b

59

60

Gold Jewelry

58. Gold Astarte pendants

a. 1931, Minet el-Beida, deposit 213. RS 3.185

Louvre Museum AO 14714

H 6 cm. Stamped sheet of gold. Elongated plaque, the top of which is rolled to make a bail. On this pendant is a nude female figure in full face, with a characteristic, Hathor-like headdress (with curled locks on the shoulders). With her hands elevated on each side she holds miniature goats by their hooves. Under her feet, a lion is walking toward the left. In the background, sprinkled with dots, there are serpents on each side of her legs; their heads are level with her belly.

b. 1931, Minet el-Beida, deposit 213 RS 3.184

Aleppo Museum (inv. 4576)

H 7 cm, W 3.9 cm. Elongated plaque, the top of which is rolled to make a bail; bordered with punctate marks. This pendant features the figure of a nude female, of the same general type as no. **58a** but more schematic. The representation is limited to a face, breasts in relief, and an incised sexual triangle.
– ***Bib.***: T. Monloup, in *Au pays de Baal . . .* , 1983, p. 157, no. 175.

59. Gold ring of Patilu-wa, Hittite inscription RS 24.145

1961, South Acropolis, house to the north of the trench. Damascus Museum (inv. 7001)

Diameter 1.8 cm. Gold ring. The flattened top has an inscription in hieroglyphic Hittite that refers to someone named Patilu-wa (or Patili, in some reports).
– ***Bib.***: *RSO* V 1, 1989, p. 298, fig. 39.

Prestige Weapon in Iron, Copper, and Gold

60. A ceremonial axe with lion and wild boar RS 9.250

1937, Royal Zone, Hurrian Temple (surface level). Aleppo Museum

L 19.5 cm, Weight 852 grams. Copper and gold (handle), hardened iron (blade). Axe with a bronze handle, decorated in relief with the figure of a wild boar and two lions' heads that appear to be spitting out the iron blade. The details of the animals and the motifs (rosettes) were made with gold wire that was inlaid by hammering it into grooves prepared on the surface of the solid copper. The motif of an animal spitting out a blade, attested in Iran from the 3rd millennium on, spread thereafter to the west. The decorative floral motifs suggest Aegean influence. This is one of the earliest examples of an item manufactured out of three different metals (14th–13th centuries).
– ***Bib.***: C. Schaeffer, *Ugaritica* I, 1939, pp. 108–25; F. Tallon, in *Au pays de Baal . . .* , 1983, pp. 176–77, no. 203.

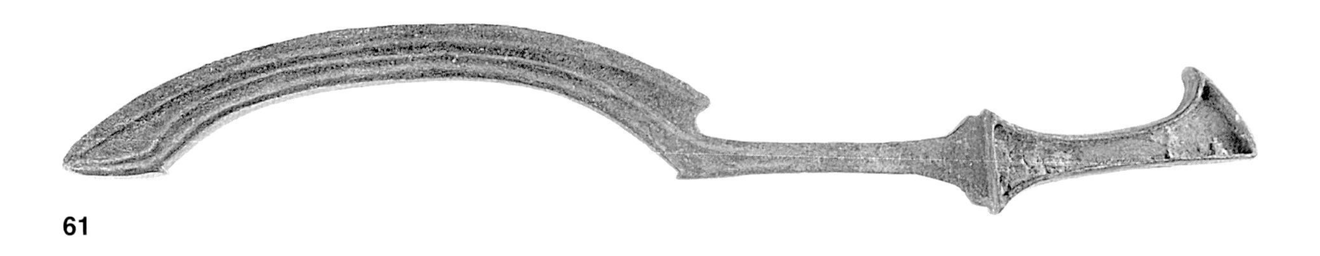

61

62

detail

Bronze Weapons

61. Ceremonial weapon, a so-called *Harpé*-Sword RS 7.036

1935, Acropolis, east Lower City, building area C. Aleppo Museum (inv. 4180)

L 57.7 cm. Bronze, cast in one piece. Weapon with curved blade, the cutting edge of which is on the exterior (the convex side); and long, straight handle. There were once inlays in the handle, now missing.

Weapons of this sort were exceptional and clearly were luxury items. They are relatively rare but are attested from the 3rd millennium on in Mesopotamia (on the "Stele of Vultures," for example), and we encounter examples in the 2nd millennium throughout the Near East, from Bactria to Byblos to Egypt (bearing royal inscriptions). The *harpé*-sword at Ras Shamra, with a blade as long as the handle and cast in a single piece, is characteristic of the Late Bronze Age Levant.

– ***Bib.***: C. Schaeffer, *Syria* 17, 1936, p. 145, pl. 18.2; F. Tallon, in *Au pays de Baal* . . . , 1983, p. 178, no. 204.

62. Sword with a cartouche of Pharaoh Merneptah RS 17.090

1953, Residential Quarter, "House of the Bronze Weapon-Maker," northeast courtyard.

Damascus Museum (inv. 3591)

L 74.4 cm, W (max.) 5 cm. Cartouche 2.9 × 1.5 cm. Cast in bronze cast and engraved. Long blade with a tang and two cutting edges. It is engraved with the cartouche of Pharaoh Merneptah (1224–1204) in hieroglyphic Egyptian. This sword was probably manufactured in Syria (Ugarit?) but was destined for Egypt; weapons of this type were not introduced to Egypt until the 13th century.

– ***Bib.***: P. Krieger in Schaeffer, *Ugaritica* III, 1956, pp. 169–78, pl. 8, figs. 123–24; C. Ziegler, in *Au pays de Baal* . . . , 1983, pp. 178–79, no. 205. [2005] M. Gabolde, in *Aux origines de l'alphabet, Catalogue Lyon 2004*, 2004, p. 108, no. 82.

63

64

65

Tools and Instruments of Bronze

63. Adze inscribed in Ugaritic RS 1.[051]

1929, The Library of the High Priest. Louvre Museum AO 11610

L 23.2 cm, W 6.5 cm. Bronze casting, with engraved inscription. Adze with rounded socket. On the blade is an engraved alphabetic cuneiform inscription that reads "adze of the high priest." It belongs to a hoard of 77 bronze objects, 5 of which (tools) were marked in the same manner. These implements with inscriptions were instrumental in the deciphering of the Ugaritic language (1930).

– ***Bib.***: C. Schaeffer, *Ugaritica* III, 1956, pp. 251–75; D. Arnaud, in *Au pays de Baal* . . . , 1983, pp. 176–77, no. 203.

64. Knife-dagger RS 79.019

1979, City Center, House B, room 1062. Latakia Museum

L 31 cm. Bronze, cast in one piece. The knife consists of a two-edged blade and a handle that was hollowed on both sides in order to hold inlaid material (wood, leather, bone?). The butt is convex. The outer edge is blunt and rather rounded (13th century).

– ***Bib.***: M.-J. Chavane, in *RSO* III, 1987, pp. 364–67.

65. A weight in the shape of a bull RS 8.244

1936, East Lower City, building area IV. Louvre Museum AO 19092

L 17.5 cm, D 7.6 cm, Weight 467.7 grams. Bronze hollow casting made by the "lost wax" method. A weight in the shape of a reclining bull. The thin hooves are bent back, and the small head with large neck is turned slightly to the right. The tail is bent over its back and right haunch. Two symbols are traced on the flank of the animal, both of which are the Egyptian sign for "10," totaling a value of 20 units (2 × 10)—the significance of which we cannot ascertain very well. The weight of the object corresponds to an Ugaritic mina: 50 shekels in this system. The mark 20 must therefore correspond to some other system of measure.

– ***Bib.***: C. Schaeffer, *Syria* 18, 1937, pp. 147–49, pl. 23; M. Yon, in *Syrie, Mémoire* . . . , 1993, p. 230, no. 187.

[2005] E. Bordreuil (2004) has shown that the weight unit consisting of 23.39 g, that is, the weight of 457.8 g divided by 20 ("20" is the number inscribed on this animal's side), corresponds to a double shekel in the Hittite system (here the weight of the individual shekel would be 11.695 g).

– ***Bib.***: E. Bordreuil, in *Aux origines de l'alphabet, Catalogue Lyon 2004*, 2004, p. 139, no. 132.

Object from the Persian Period

66. Bronze bowl RS 6.132

1934, Acropolis, Trench 74, topographic point 18.

Louvre Museum AO 17360

H 8.2 cm, Diameter 11.4 cm. Hemispherical bowl decorated with floral petals in low relief. Persian period, 6th–4th centuries B.C.E.
– ***Bib.***: C. Schaeffer, *Syria* 16, 1935, pl. 30.4.

66

Selected Bibliography and Abbreviations

AAS, later *AAAS* = Reports of the French mission to Ras Shamra in *Annales Archéologiques de Syrie*, later *Annales Archéologiques Arabes Syriennes*, Department of Antiquities and Museums in Syria, Damascus

Anchor Bible = "Ugarit Excavations, Ugarit Texts," in *Anchor Bible Dictionary* 6, pp. 695ff., New York, 1992.

Au pays de Baal . . . = *Au pays de Baal et d'Astarté*, Catalogue d'exposition, Grand Palais, Paris, 1983

BASOR = *Bulletin of the American Schools of Oriental Research*

CRAI = *Comptes Rendus de l'Académie des Inscriptions et Belles-Lettres*, Paris

CTA = A. Herdner, ed., *Corpus des textes cunéiformes alphabétiques déscouvertes à Ras Shamra–Ugarit de 1929 à 1939*, Paris, 1963

H. Klengel, *Syria, 3000 to 300* BC: *A Handbook of Political History*, Berlin, Akademie, 1992 [English edition].

KTU = M. Dietrich, O. Loretz, and J. Sanmartín, *Die keilalphabetischen Texte aus Ugarit*, I, Kevelaer/Neukirchen-Vluyn, 1976. Second enlarged edition: *The Cuneiform Alphabetic Texts from Ugarit, Ras Ibn Hani, and Other Places*, Münster, 1995

"Ougarit," *Monde de la Bible* 48 (March–April) 1987, Paris, Bayard.

PRU II–VI = *Le Palais royal d'Ugarit*, Paris, Geuthner

- II: C. Virolleaud, *Textes alphabétiques des archives Est, Ouest et Centrales*, 1957
- III: J. Nougayrol, *Textes accadiens et hourrites des archives Est, Ouest et Centrales*, 1955
- IV: J. Nougayrol, *Textes accadiens des archives Sud (archives internationales)*, 1956
- V: C. Virolleaud, *Textes alphabétiques des archives Sud, Sud-ouest et du Petit-Palais*, 1965
- VI: J. Nougayrol, *Textes accadiens des archives Est, Centrales et du Petit-Palais*, 1970

Ras Shamra, 1929–1979, ed. French mission, Lyon, 1979.

RSO I–XI = *Ras Shamra-Ougarit*, Paris, ERC–ADPF

- I: O. Callot, *Une maison à Ougarit*, 1983
- II: D. Pardee, *Les textes hippiatriques*, 1986
- III: M. Yon, dir., *Le Centre de la ville, 38ᵉ–44ᵉ campagnes (1978–1984)*, 1987
- IV: D. Pardee, *Textes paramythologiques*, 1988
- V1: P. Bordreuil et al., *La trouvaille épigraphique de l'Ougarit, 1: Concordance*, 1989
- V2: J. L. Cunchillos, *La trouvaille épigraphique de l'Ougarit, 2: Bibliographie*, 1990
- VI: M. Yon, dir., *Arts et industrie de la pierre*, 1991
- VII: P. Bordreuil, dir., *Une bibliothèque au sud de la ville: Les textes de 1973*, 1991
- VIII: H. de Contenson, *Préhistoire de Ras Shamra: Les sondages stratigraphiques de 1955 à 1976*, 1992
- IX: P. Amiet, *Sceaux-cylindres en hématite et pierres diverses, Corpus des cylindres de Ras Shamra–Ougarit* II, 1992
- X: O. Callot, *La tranchée Ville sud*, 1994
- XI: M. Yon, M. Sznycer, and P. Bordreuil, dirs., *Le pays d'Ougarit autour de 1200: Actes du Colloque Paris 1993*, 1995

G. Saadé, *Ougarit: Métropole cananéenne*, Beirut, 1979.

R. Stucky, *Leukos Limen, Ras Shamra*, Paris, Geuthner, 1983.

C. F.-A. Schaeffer, *Corpus des cylindres-sceaux de Ras Shamra–Ugarit et d'Enkomi-Alasia*, Paris, ERC-ADPF, 1983.

SDB = "Ras Shamra," *Supplément au Dictionnaire de la Bible*, Paris, Letouzey & Ané, 1979, cols. 1295–1348:

J.-C. Courtois, "Archéologie"; M. Liverani, "Histoire"; D. Arnaud, "La culture suméro-accadienne"; E. Laroche, "Le milieu hurrite"; A. Caquot, "La littérature ugaritique"; M. Sznycer, "Documents

administratifs et économiques"; E. Jacob and H. Cazelles, "Ras Shamra et l'ancien testament."
Syria = Reports of the French mission of Ras Shamra, beginning in 1929, in *Syria*, Paris, IFAPO-Geuthner
Syrie, Mémoire = *Syrie: Mémoire et Civilisation*, Catalogue d'exposition, Institut du Monde Arabe, Paris, 1993
TO Mythes = A. Caquot, M. Sznycer, and A. Herdner, *Textes Ougaritiques*, I: *Mythes et légendes*, LAPO, Paris, éd. du Cerf, 1974
TO II = A. Caquot, J.-M. de Tarragon, and J.-L. Cunchillos, *Textes Ougaritiques*, II: *Textes religieux, Rituels, Correspondance*, LAPO, Paris, éd. du Cerf, 1989
Ugaritica = C. F.-A. Schaeffer, dir., *Ugaritica*, Paris, Geuthner
I, 1939; II, 1949; III, 1956; IV, 1962; V, 1968; VI, 1969; VII, 1978
J. Weulersse, *Le pays des Alaouites*, Tours, 1940.

[2005]

Bibliography after 1997

Actes du Colloque Lyon 2001, ed. Y. Calvet, Lyon, in press
A. Bounni, E. and J. Lagarce, *Ras Ibn Hani*, I: *Le Palais Nord du Bronze Récent*, BAH, Beirut, 1998.
Catalogue 2004 = *Aux origines de l'alphabet. Le royaume d'Ougarit, Catalogue Exposition Lyon 2004–2005*, ed. Y. Calvet and G. Galliano, Paris and Lyon, 2004
Handbook of Ugaritic Studies, ed. W. G. E. Watson and N. Wyatt, Leiden, 1999
D. Pardee, *Ritual and Cult at Ugarit*. Writings from the Ancient World, vol. 10. Atlanta: Society of Biblical Literature, 2002
RSO XI–XVI = *Ras Shamra-Ougarit*, Paris, ERC–ADPF
XII: D. Pardee, *Les Textes rituels*, 2000
XIII: M. Yon, V. Karageorghis, and N. Hirschfeld, *Céramiques mycéniennes*, 2000
XIV: M. Yon and D. Arnaud, eds., *Études Ougaritiques*, 1: *Travaux 1985–1995* (with P. Bordreuil, O. Callot, Y. Calvet, A. Caquot, C. Castel, A.-S. Dalix, J. Gachet, S. Lackenbacher, F. Malbran-Labat, J. Mallet, S. Marchegay, V. Matoïan, D. Pardee, M. Salvini, S. Segert), 2001
XV: J.-Y. Monchambert, *La céramique d'Ougarit, Campagnes de fouilles 1975 et 1976*, 2004
XVI: J. Gachet, *Les ivoires d'Ougarit et l'art des ivoiriers du Levant*, in press
Textes akkadiens d'Ugarit: Textes provenant des vingt-cinq premières campagnes, S. Lackenbacher, LAPO, Paris, du Cerf, 2002

Indexes

Sites and Structures

This index is a guide to the text, not a complete list of all sites and archaeological features. It contains ancient and modern geographical names of the territory of Ugarit and various terms that have been used in reports.

Note. From 1929 on, the reports and publications of the mission have used various terms, sometimes descriptive or based on proposed interpretations, to designate areas and structures excavated on the tell of Ras Shamra. We have tried to provide approximate translations of the original French names (in italics). Both the English and French terms must be considered *only conventional.*

Index of Inventory Numbers of the Mission to Ras Shamra–Ugarit Objects nos. 1–66 published on pp. 124–72

Index of Museum Inventory Numbers
Objects nos. 1–66 published on pp. 124–72

Note: Inv. = old inventory number; M. = new inventory number.

Tartus Museum

Storeroom in the dig-house of the Mission at Ibn Hani

Louvre Museum in Paris